T0185729

Essential PowerShell for Office 365

Managing and Automating Skills for Improved Productivity

Vlad Catrinescu

Apress®

Essential PowerShell for Office 365: Managing and Automating Skills for Improved Productivity

Vlad Catrinescu
Greenfield Park, Québec, Canada

ISBN-13 (pbk): 978-1-4842-3128-9   ISBN-13 (electronic): 978-1-4842-3129-6
https://doi.org/10.1007/978-1-4842-3129-6

Library of Congress Control Number: 2018936350

Managing Director, Apress Media LLC: Welmoed Spahr
Acquisitions Editor: Joan Murray
Development Editor: Laura Berendson
Coordinating Editor: Jill Balzano

Cover designed by eStudioCalamar

Cover image designed by Freepik (www.freepik.com)

Distributed to the book trade worldwide by Springer Science+Business Media New York, 233 Spring Street, 6th Floor, New York, NY 10013. Phone 1-800-SPRINGER, fax (201) 348-4505, email orders-ny@springer-sbm.com, or visit www.springeronline.com. Apress Media, LLC is a California LLC and the sole member (owner) is Springer Science + Business Media Finance Inc (SSBM Finance Inc). SSBM Finance Inc is a **Delaware** corporation.

For information on translations, please email rights@apress.com or visit http://www.apress.com/rights-permissions.

Apress titles may be purchased in bulk for academic, corporate, or promotional use. eBook versions and licenses are also available for most titles. For more information, reference our Print and eBook Bulk Sales web page at http://www.apress.com/bulk-sales.

Any source code or other supplementary material referenced by the author in this book is available to readers on GitHub via the book's product page, located at www.apress.com/9781484231289. For more detailed information, please visit http://www.apress.com/source-code.

Printed on acid-free paper

To Genviève, thank you for your love and support over the years as I followed my passions!

Table of Contents

About the Author

Vlad Catrinescu is a SharePoint and Office 365 consultant specializing in PowerShell, SharePoint, and hybrid scenarios. As an author, MVP, Microsoft Certified Trainer, and recognized international speaker, Vlad has helped hundreds of thousands of users and IT pros across the globe to get the most out of their SharePoint and Office 365 deployments. Vlad writes the popular "Absolute SharePoint Blog" and is a recipient of the "Top 25 Office 365 Influencers" award. His contributions can also be found on other sites such as CMSWire and ComputerWorld. He is author of Deploying SharePoint 2016: Best Practices for Installing, Configuring, and Maintaining SharePoint Server 2016(Apress).

About the Technical Reviewer

Jeff Collins is the owner of Coupled Technology, a SharePoint and Office 365 consulting agency. Jeff has a deep love for new technology, especially when it comes to Office 365 and SharePoint. Jeff's passion for helping businesses get the most out of the Office 365 and SharePoint services is what drives his ability to think outside of the box and implement creative solutions that maximize adoption and consumption.

CHAPTER 1

Introduction to PowerShell for Office 365

In this chapter, we will learn the tools we have available as Office 365 administrators to manage our tenant as well as why PowerShell is a critical skill for every Office 365 administrator out there. We will also review the different ways of deploying Office 365 and how each affects us when managing our tenant.

What Is Office 365?

One of the major changes in technology over the past few years has been the move to the cloud. Whether it's using an Infrastructure-As-A-Service (IaaS) provider such as Azure or Amazon Web Services (AWS) to host their virtual machines or using a Software-As-A-Service (SaaS) provider such as Office 365 for their collaboration tools, employers are moving to the cloud to provide more efficient service to their employees at a lower cost.

When Office 365 got released on June 28, 2011, it included mostly Microsoft's big three Office Servers products (Exchange, SharePoint, and Skype for Business), but in an SaaS model in the cloud. Now, Office 365 has added a dozen new products and is used by more than 100 million users every month. With the change from on-premises software to the cloud, IT professionals have less to worry about since a lot of the technology behind is managed by Microsoft, allowing IT staff to focus their time on creating productive solutions for their users. However, even if Microsoft takes care of the servers in the backend, IT professionals still have to configure Office 365 for their company as well as manage the day-to-day tasks. Let's take a look at the tools IT professionals can use to manage Office 365.

© Vlad Catrinescu 2018
V. Catrinescu, *Essential PowerShell for Office 365*, https://doi.org/10.1007/978-1-4842-3129-6_1

Office 365 Admin Tools

Microsoft offers four main tools with which to manage Office 365 that cover different scenarios and capabilities. Let's take a look at each one of them in detail.

The Office 365 Admin Center

The Office 365 Admin Center seen in Figure 1-1 is the most popular tool with which to manage Office 365 and is probably the tool you are most familiar with. The Admin Center provides a user interface where administrators can do the initial setup of Office 365, as well as an out-of-the-box solution that allows you to manage your users and licenses, as well as every product in the Office 365 suite, such as Exchange, SharePoint, Skype for Business, OneDrive, and more. While the Office 365 Admin tool is easy to use and has a lot of possibilities, not all of the properties can be seen, and a lot of common actions cannot be performed in this portal.

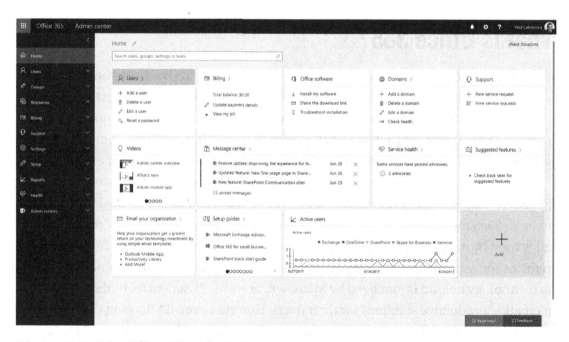

Figure 1-1. *The Office 365 Admin Center*

The Office 365 Admin App

The Office 365 Admin App seen in Figure 1-2 allows Office 365 administrators to stay connected with their Office 365 administration on the go. You can manage your users and do easy tasks, such as assigning a license, adding an alias, or resetting a password, directly from the Office 365 Admin App. You can also view the latest information about service health as well as the Office 365 Message Center and your support tickets. While the Office 365 Admin App is very useful for the admin on the go, it isn't a full management tool, and it's the tool with the fewest robust options out of the four we will look at in this chapter.

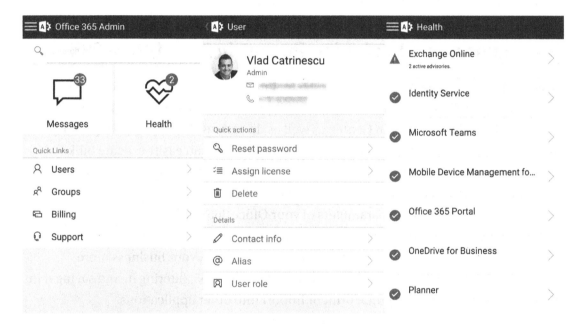

Figure 1-2. *The Office 365 Admin App*

The Office 365 Management API

The Office 365 Management API can be used by developers in your company to create applications on top of Office 365 that will make management easier as well as offer more solutions for your employees. The Office 365 Management API sits on the Microsoft Graph, and allows you to utilize data from all Office 365 products in your own application or site. Multiple independent software vendors (ISVs) have taken advantage of the API to create applications on top of Office 365.

PowerShell for Office 365

Last, but not least, is PowerShell for Office 365. PowerShell is really the most powerful tool out there to manage your Office 365 tenant without having to create a custom solution. PowerShell is a command-line environment that is designed specifically for system administration in the Microsoft ecosystem, and now extends to Linux as well. Most of the Office 365 components have their own cmdlets with which to change different settings in Office 365. PowerShell allows you to use cmdlets provided by Microsoft as well as using the client-side object model (CSOM). By using CSOM you can leverage the Microsoft API to connect and manage your Office 365 environment to accomplish tasks that Microsoft didn't release a cmdlet for.

The Importance of Learning PowerShell for Office 365

So, why is learning PowerShell for Office 365 that important when we already have the Office 365 Admin Center? Office 365 PowerShell can display properties that cannot be seen in the Office 365 Admin Center, as well as do actions that you cannot perform from the Admin Center. Furthermore, with PowerShell you can easily execute bulk operations, or operations that affect multiple Office 365 services at once. As an Office 365 administrator, you need to learn how to master PowerShell for Office 365 in order to control and manage all of the parameters of your Office 365 deployment.

PowerShell also allows you to automate stuff you do on a regular basis, therefore saving you time and enabling you to do things that will make your business more productive. PowerShell is great at getting data from Office 365, filtering it, and saving it in different formats that you can then print or import into other applications.

The Different Types of Office 365 Deployments

Office 365 is used by a wide variety of enterprises, ranging from small one-person home businesses to Fortune 100 companies with over 50,000 users. Depending on multiple factors, such as enterprise size, how new the company is, and more, an enterprise might deploy Office 365 differently. A small company that just launched and never had on-premises servers to take care of probably went 100 percent in Office 365 while a Fortune 100 company that's been around for a hundred years, had stuff hosted on-premises, and probably still has a big part of its infrastructure on-premises with some parts in the cloud. This can make a big difference in the way one manages some parts of Office 365, especially the users.

In a small company that is 100 percent in the cloud with nothing on-premises, all of the users will be what we call *cloud users*, meaning they are not synchronized from any external locations. These users have probably been created directly in Office 365, and technically they are stored in Azure Active Directory behind the scenes, as illustrated in Figure 1-3. A lot of small-business owners do not go to Azure Active Directory at all and simply manage everything from the Office 365 Admin Center.

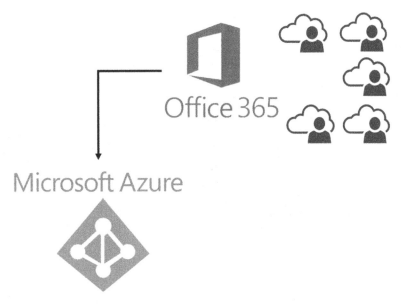

Figure 1-3. *Cloud users*

The other type of deployment, which you will find most of the time when working with enterprise customers, is one where the users are stored in Active Directory, running on-premises in the company datacenter, and are also synchronized to Azure Active Directory by using Azure AD Connect or a similar tool. This topology is illustrated in Figure 1-4. One of the main differences in this topology from a management point of view is that since users are synchronized from on-premises to Office 365, all changes to users must be done in the on-premises Active Directory, which will then update the user in Azure Active Directory and therefore in Office 365.

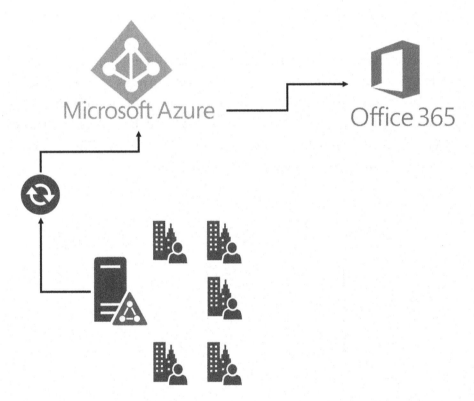

Figure 1-4. *Synchronized users*

Microsoft also offers the possibility for companies to set up a two-way sync for some properties between Azure AD and the on-premises Active Directory as seen in Figure 1-5. However, this functionality is not included in the "base" Azure Active Directory subscription, which is free, so companies must purchase the premium Azure AD Subscription, which varies between $5 and $10/user per month at the time of writing this book. As you see, for a big company with thousands of users, it can be a big price to pay if you don't need any of the other feature of Azure AD Premium, such as multi-factor authentication.

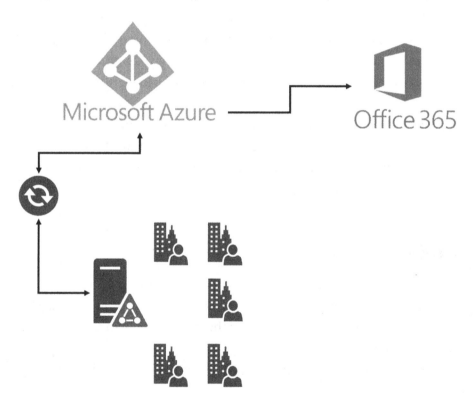

Figure 1-5. *Two-way sync*

In conclusion, knowing the type of deployment your enterprise is using is essential when managing your Office 365 tenant. If your enterprise is synchronizing users one-way from on-premises to Azure Active Directory, there is no use in modifying synchronized user properties directly in Office 365, since those will get overwritten on the next scheduled synchronization. Your first steps when starting to manage Office 365 should be to find out what the architecture looks like.

What About the Other Applications?

After figuring out how your Active Directory is designed, you need to look at how the rest of the applications are deployed. While most companies that pay for Office 365 ultimately hope to move all their workloads into the cloud, some of them simply have to stay on-premises because of customizations or regulations on data. All three main server products (Exchange, SharePoint, and Skype for Business) can be run only on-premises, purely online, or in a hybrid mode where some workloads stay on-premises and some workloads go online. While we will not go into much detail about how to implement a hybrid topology for those products, it's important to understand where everything is hosted in your organization so you know what has to be managed on-premises and what has to be managed in the cloud.

Next Steps

In this chapter, we walked through the different tools available to us to manage Office 365 and looked at why learning PowerShell for Office 365 is important. We also looked at the different topologies in which Office 365 can be implemented in the organization and how it affects us as Office 365 administrators.

Now that we know the basics, in the next chapter we will learn how to manage Office 365 users and licenses!

CHAPTER 2

Managing Users and Licenses

In this chapter, we will learn how to use PowerShell to connect to Office 365 and Azure Active Directory from a client computer. We will also learn the cmdlets available to create, modify, or delete users from Office 365. Furthermore, we will go over how to view our available licenses, how to assign a license to a user, and how to create a custom license if we don't want all the services in our subscription!

Connecting to Office 365

One of the first things we will have to do to manage our users and licenses is connect to Office 365 from PowerShell. In the past, when managing SharePoint, Exchange, Skype for Business, or Active Directory we used to simply remote desktop into the server, run the PowerShell cmdlets we had to run, and that's it. Everything was already there on the servers because when installing the server software all the PowerShell modules required to manage this server were also installed.

With Office 365 it's different because we cannot simply log on remotely to the server and do our operations, as there is no server to log onto when talking about Office 365. Therefore, the first thing we will have to do is download the required PowerShell modules on our local computer and then connect to Office 365.

For this book, we will use the Azure Active Directory V2 PowerShell Module, which is the latest version of the Azure AD PowerShell module, replacing the old Azure Active Directory (MSOnline) module. In order to be able to do all the cmdlets in this chapter, the account that you will use for the cmdlets needs to have the Office 365 Global Administrator role.

9

© Vlad Catrinescu 2018
V. Catrinescu, *Essential PowerShell for Office 365*, https://doi.org/10.1007/978-1-4842-3129-6_2

Note   We want to manage Office 365 users, so why do we need to download the Azure Active Directory Module? The answer is that Office 365 uses the cloud-based user-authentication service Azure Active Directory to store users.

The Azure Active Directory V2 PowerShell Module is hosted on the PowerShell Gallery, which is the central repository for PowerShell content from Microsoft and the community. To download modules from the PowerShell Gallery, you need to have PowerShellGet, which is included out of the box in the following releases:

- Windows 10 or newer

- Windows Server 2016 or newer

- Windows Management Framework (WMF) 5.0 or newer

- PowerShell 6

If you have an earlier version of Windows or PowerShell, you can get the PowerShellGet Module from the Microsoft Download Center. The minimum version of PowerShell supported at the time of writing this book is PowerShell 3.0.

Note   The PowerShellGet Module can be downloaded at `https://www.microsoft.com/en-us/download/details.aspx?id=51451`.

After you have installed the PowerShellGet module—or if you have one of the required releases already—you can simply open PowerShell as an administrator and run the following cmdlet to install the Azure Active Directory V2 PowerShell Module:

```
Install-Module -Name AzureAD
```

PowerShell will look in the PowerShell Gallery for the module with the name `AzureAD` and install it on your computer. You can also view the AzureAD PowerShell Module page directly on the PowerShell Gallery at `https://www.powershellgallery.com/packages/AzureAD/`. When installing the module, you might get a warning similar to that shown in Figure 2-1, which you have to accept.

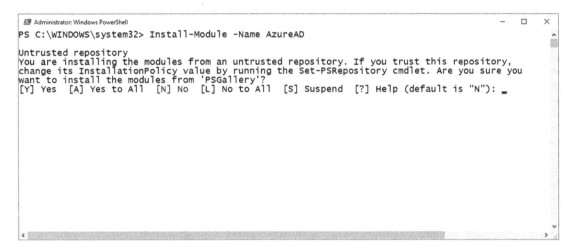

Figure 2-1. *Installing the Azure Active Directory V2 PowerShell module*

After the module finishes installing, you will be able to connect to Azure Active Directory. The first thing you will have to do is save your credentials into a variable, which you do with the Get-Credential cmdlet:

$cred = Get-Credential

The preceding command line will open a PowerShell credential request pop-up as seen in Figure 2-2, and it will save it in a variable called $cred.

Note   PowerShell will not do any validation of the credentials you enter in the pop-up window.

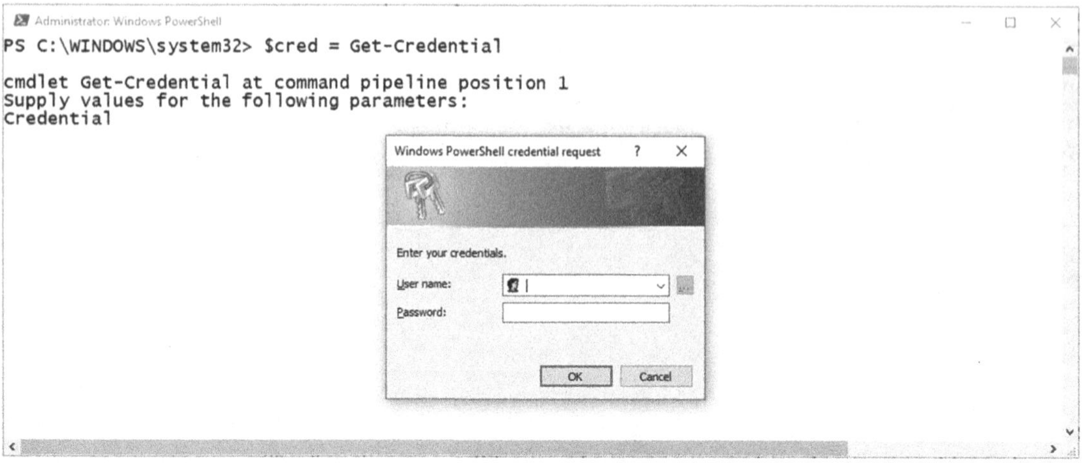

Figure 2-2. *Saving our credentials into a variable*

Afterward, run the `Connect-AzureAD` PowerShell cmdlet and specify the `-Credential` parameter with the `$cred` variable you just created. You do not need to enter a tenant name as Azure AD will automatically connect you to your tenant based on your email address, as seen in Figure 2-3.

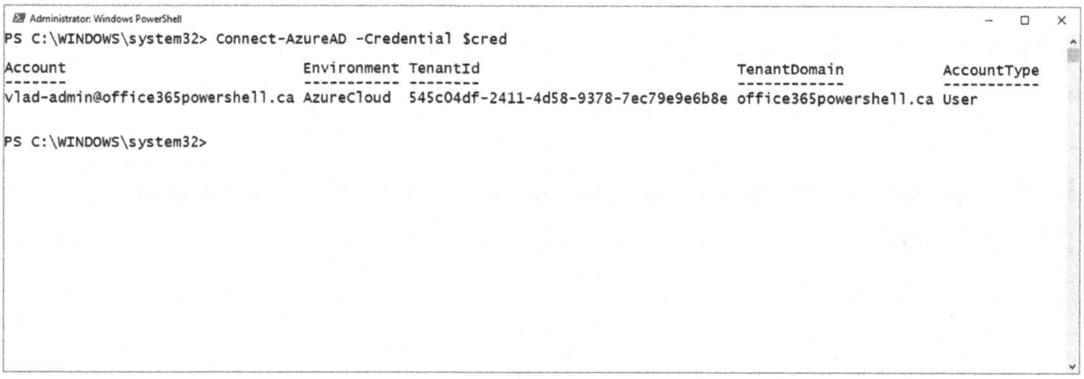

Figure 2-3. *Connecting to Azure AD*

Note   If the account you use to connect to Azure Active Directory has Multi Factor Authentication enabled, you simply need to run Connect-AzureAD without specifying the -Credential parameter.

Now that you have connected to Azure AD you can run PowerShell cmdlets against your tenant. Let's take a look at what can be done.

Managing Users with PowerShell

One of the things we can do with the Azure AD PowerShell cmdlet is manage our users as well as their properties. Let's start with viewing our users and their properties.

Viewing Users and Properties

To view all the users in your tenant you can run the Get-AzureADUser cmdlet, which will return all the users, including the external ones. You can also use PowerShell to filter on any property of that user's profile—for example, the department, as seen in Figure 2-4.

```
PS C:\WINDOWS\system32> Get-AzureADUser

ObjectId                                 DisplayName      UserPrincipalName                                   UserType
--------                                 -----------      -----------------                                   --------
1651b416-3a9c-401d-8e36-56e65a6e0ac8     Jeff Collins     Jeff@office365powershell.ca                         Member
fca50d76-9c1d-47fd-8c33-dadcdaf91008     John Smith       john@office365powershell.ca                         Member
158cd24d-8148-4c78-8168-e7a4d057afe6     Vanessa Lee      vanessa@office365powershell.ca                      Member
4fc1cc1d-bac1-4cfd-b15d-c70d565e8200     Vlad Admin       vlad-admin@office365powershell.ca                   Member
521ffed4-31df-415e-b00c-8a0149bb37da     Vlad Catrinescu  vlad_vnext.solutions#EXT#@office365powershell.ca    Guest


PS C:\WINDOWS\system32> Get-AzureADUser | Where {$_.Department -eq "Sales"}

ObjectId                                 DisplayName      UserPrincipalName            UserType
--------                                 -----------      -----------------            --------
1651b416-3a9c-401d-8e36-56e65a6e0ac8     Jeff Collins     Jeff@office365powershell.ca  Member
```

Figure 2-4. *Get-AzureADUser*

To view all the properties of a user, you can run the following cmdlet:

Get-AzureADUser -ObjectId jeff@office365powershell.ca | Format-List

Some of the properties of an Azure AD user are, however, stored elsewhere in Office 365, so a different cmdlet is needed for them, such as the manager. To get a user's manager, you need to run the Get-AzureADUserManager cmdlet and specify the User Principal Name or the Object ID of the user for which you want to know the manager, as seen in Figure 2-5.

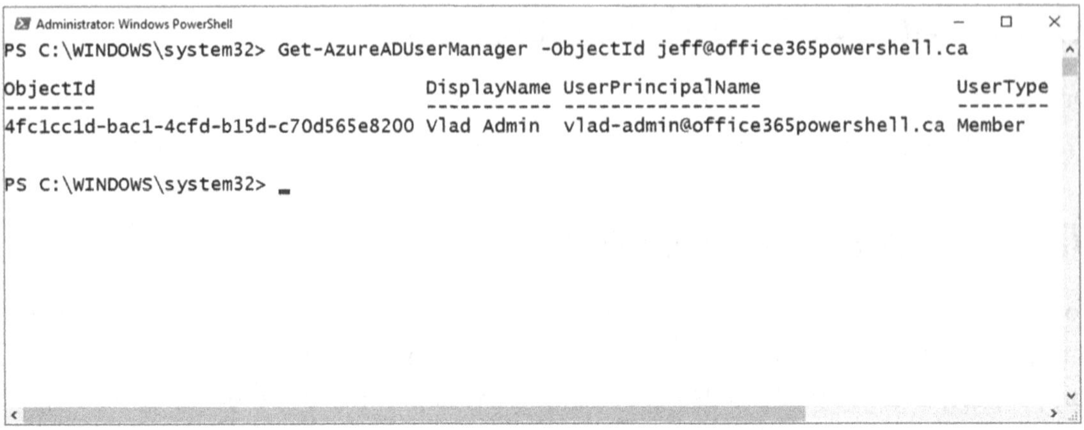

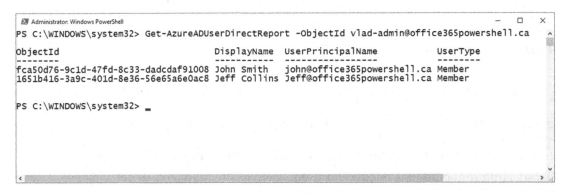

Figure 2-5. *Viewing the manager of a user*

You can also do the opposite and get the direct reports of a user by using the Get-AzureADUserDirectReport cmdlet and specifying the User Principal Name or the Object ID of the user for which you want to view the direct reports. In Figure 2-6, we see that John Smith and Jeff Collins both report to vlad-admin@office365powershell.ca.

```
Administrator: Windows PowerShell                                          —    □    ×
PS C:\WINDOWS\system32> Get-AzureADUserDirectReport -ObjectId vlad-admin@office365powershell.ca

ObjectId                            DisplayName  UserPrincipalName              UserType
--------                            -----------  ------------------              --------
fca50d76-9c1d-47fd-8c33-dadcdaf91008 John Smith   john@office365powershell.ca   Member
1651b416-3a9c-401d-8e36-56e65a6e0ac8 Jeff Collins Jeff@office365powershell.ca   Member

PS C:\WINDOWS\system32> _
```

Figure 2-6. *Viewing the direct reports of a user*

Now that we are able to view the properties, we'll learn how to modify them.

Modifying User Properties

You can also use PowerShell to change the properties of a user—for example, Department, Job Title, Phone Number, and so on—by using the Set-AzureADUser cmdlet as seen in the following example and Figure 2-7.

```
Set-AzureADUser -ObjectId jeff@office365powershell.ca -City Seattle -Country
"United States" -JobTitle "Marketing Manager" -Department "Marketing"
```

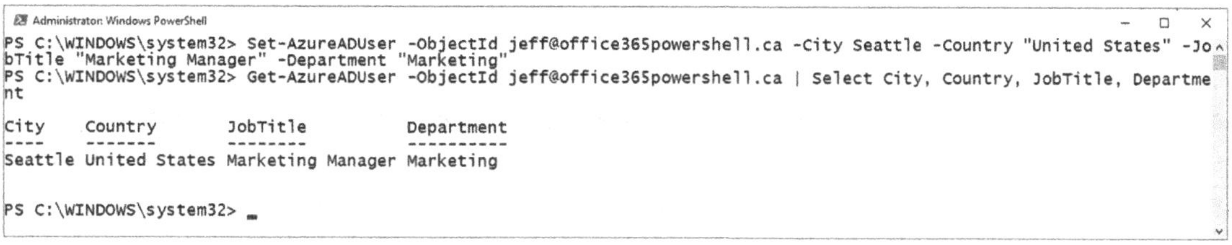

Figure 2-7. *Changing the properties of a user*

You can also change the manager by using the Set-AzureADUserManager cmdlet. For this cmdlet, you need to specify the -ObjectId parameter, which is the User Principal Name or Object ID of the user you want to change the parameter for, and the -RefObjectId parameter, which is the Object ID of the manager. For this cmdlet, you cannot specify the User Principal Name of the manager in the -RefObjectId, so you have to specify the ID of the Azure AD object to assign as manager.

You first have to get the ID of the Azure AD object of your manager, in this case vlad-admin@office365powershell.ca, by using the Get-AzureADUser cmdlet as seen in Figure 2-8. The ObjectId is in the first column.

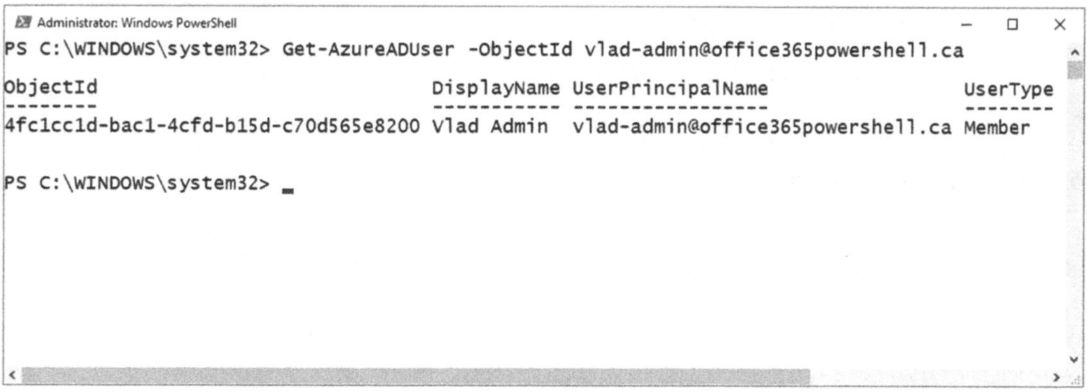

Figure 2-8. *Getting the ID of the Azure AD object*

You can then use the Set-AzureADUserManager cmdlet to specify your parameters, as follows:

```
Set-AzureADUserManager
-ObjectId vanessa@office365powershell.ca
-RefObjectId 4fc1cc1d-bac1-4cfd-b15d-c70d565e8200
```

You can then use the Get-AzureADUserManager PowerShell cmdlet to verify that it worked, as seen in Figure 2-9.

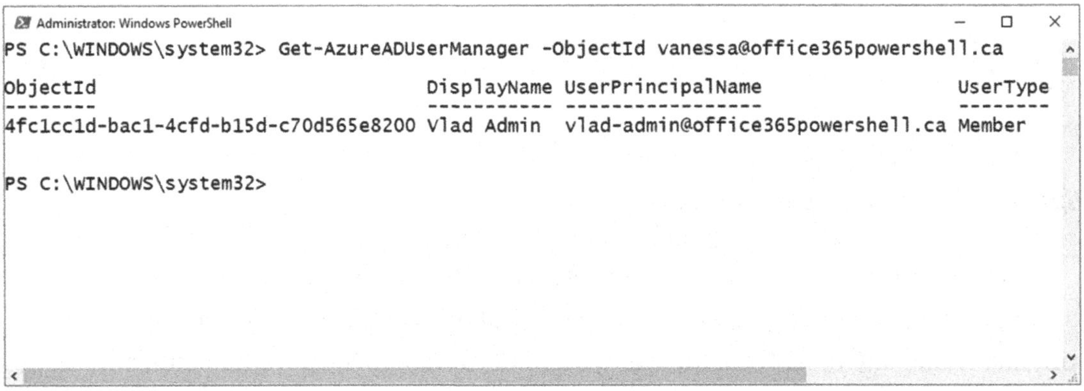

Figure 2-9. *Verifying the manager of a user*

If you are more experienced with PowerShell, you can also do the operation in a single cmdlet without having to copy and paste the ObjectId, as in the following example:

```
Set-AzureADUserManager -ObjectId vanessa@office365powershell.ca
-RefObjectId (Get-AzureADUser
    -ObjectId vlad-admin@office365powershell.ca).ObjectId
```

Now that we have successfully edited users by using PowerShell, we will look at how to create a brand-new user.

Creating Users

You can use PowerShell to create new users with the `New-AzureADUser` PowerShell cmdlet. This allows you to specify all the properties of the user on creation so you can make sure they have a complete profile from the start. One of the required parameters of the `New-AzureADUser` cmdlet is the password, which you cannot simply specify as text; you will need to first build a `Microsoft.Open.AzureAD.Model.PasswordProfile` object and pass that object as a parameter.

You will first create a variable called `$PasswordProfile` as seen in the following example:

```
$PasswordProfile = New-Object -TypeName Microsoft.Open.AzureAD.Model.
PasswordProfile
```

You will then set the `Password` property to the password that you want the user to have, as seen here:

```
$PasswordProfile.Password = "Apress2017"
```

I find it important to force the user to change their password the next time they log in to Office 365. This can be done by setting the `ForceChangePasswordNextLogin` property to `true` as seen here:

```
$PasswordProfile.ForceChangePasswordNextLogin = $true
```

To put all this together, to create the `PasswordProfile` object, you would run the following cmdlets:

```
$PasswordProfile = New-Object -TypeName Microsoft.Open.AzureAD.Model.
PasswordProfile
$PasswordProfile.Password = "Apress2017"
$PasswordProfile.ForceChangePasswordNextLogin = $true
```

You can now start creating your user with some basic properties, such as Name, Department, Job Title, and so on. In the sample cmdlet that follows, we are creating the user Jonathan King:

```
New-AzureADUser `
      -GivenName "Jonathan" `
      -Surname "King" `
      -DisplayName "Jonathan King" `
```

17

```
-UserPrincipalName "Jonathan@office365powershell.ca" `
-MailNickName "Jonathan" `
-AccountEnabled $true `
-PasswordProfile $PasswordProfile `
-JobTitle "IT Manager" `
-Department "IT" `
```

While we provided a lot of profile properties for our sample user, the minimum requirement parameters required are -UserPrincipalName, -PasswordProfile, -AccountEnabled, -DisplayName, and -MailNickName.

You can see the results in Figure 2-10 from the Office 365 Admin Center.

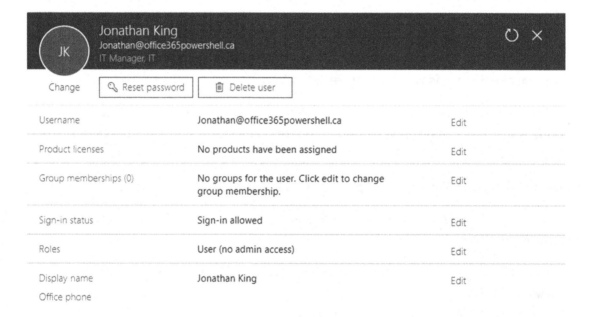

Figure 2-10. *Newly created Office 365 user*

Our user is created and can now log in, but cannot use Office 365 yet because we did not assign a license for this user. Let's take a look at how to manage licenses for Office 365 with PowerShell.

Managing Licenses with PowerShell

Another important aspect of managing users is their licenses. Unlike on-premises, where you only need to make sure you have the right amount of Client Access Licenses (CAL) and don't need to do anything manually, in Office 365 every user must be assigned a license that will specify what services they have access to. Let's learn how to view the available licenses in your tenant.

Viewing the Available Licenses

First, to view what subscriptions you have in your tenant, you need to use the Get-AzureADSubscribedSku cmdlet. As seen in Figure 2-11, this will give you the ID of your subscription as well as the internal name and that's about it. The PrepaidUnits property is displayed, but does not show us anything too useful . . . yet.

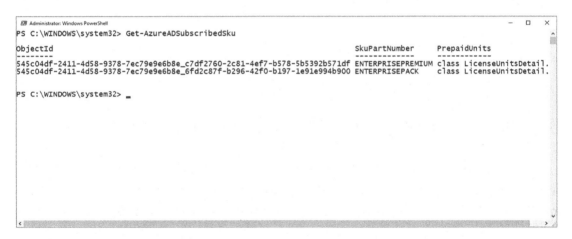

Figure 2-11. *Viewing the subscriptions of the current tenant*

However, if you expand some of the properties of the Get-AzureADSubscribedSku cmdlet, you can view more interesting things, such as the number of licenses that you have used per subscription and how many you have available. To get this information, you can run the following cmdlet:

```
Get-AzureADSubscribedSku | Select-Object  -Property ObjectId,
SkuPartNumber, ConsumedUnits -ExpandProperty PrepaidUnits
```

This will show you the Object ID, the Internal Name of the subscription, and how many licenses of that subscription you currently have assigned to users (ConsumedUnits). When expanding the PrepaidUnits property, you can view how many of them you have enabled and suspended. In Figure 2-12, you can see that in my current tenant, I have two subscriptions, an E5 (ENTERPRISEPREMIUM) and an E3 (ENTERPRISEPACK). I am currently using four licenses of the E5, but I currently pay for 25 of them. For my E3 subscription, I had 25 licenses but they are suspended (not renewed), and none of those were assigned to any users.

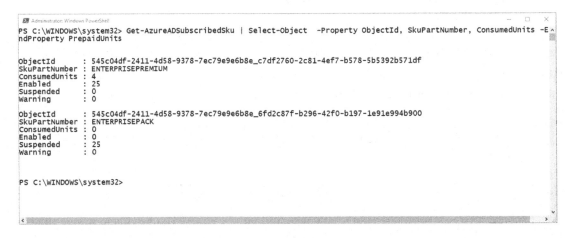

Figure 2-12. *Consumption details of the Office 365 subscription in our tenant*

You can also view the details of what services exactly are included in each subscription by expanding the ServicePlans property. In the following example, I select my E5 subscription by using its ObjectId, found earlier, and expand the ServicePlan property:

```
Get-AzureADSubscribedSku -ObjectId 545c04df-2411-4d58-9378-7ec79e9e6b8e_
c7df2760-2c81-4ef7-b578-5b5392b571df | Select-Object -ExpandProperty
ServicePlans
```

This will show me more in detail which services are applied at the user or company levels and which of them are provisioned. You can view the output in Figure 2-13.

```
Administrator: Windows PowerShell                                                    —   □   ×
PS C:\WINDOWS\system32> Get-AzureADSubscribedSku -ObjectId 545c04df-2411-4d58-9378-7ec79e9e6b8e_c7df2760-2c81-4ef7-b578-
5b5392b571df | Select-Object -ExpandProperty ServicePlans

AppliesTo ProvisioningStatus ServicePlanId                               ServicePlanName
--------- ------------------  -------------                               ---------------
User      Success             e212cbc7-0961-4c40-9825-01117710dcb1        FORMS_PLAN_E5
User      Success             6c6042f5-6f01-4d67-b8c1-eb99d36eed3e        STREAM_O365_E5
User      Success             8e0c0a52-6a6c-4d40-8370-dd62790dcd70        THREAT_INTELLIGENCE
User      Success             8c7d2df8-86f0-4902-b2ed-a0458298f3b3        Deskless
User      Success             07699545-9485-468e-95b6-2fca3738be01        FLOW_O365_P3
User      Success             9c0dab89-a30c-4117-86e7-97bda240acd2        POWERAPPS_O365_P3
User      Success             57ff2da0-773e-42df-b2af-ffb7a2317929        TEAMS1
User      Success             8c098270-9dd4-4350-9b30-ba4703f3b36b        ADALLOM_S_O365
User      Success             4de31727-a228-4ec3-a5bf-8e45b5ca48cc        EQUIVIO_ANALYTICS
User      Success             9f431833-0334-42de-a7dc-70aa40db46db        LOCKBOX_ENTERPRISE
User      Success             34c0d7a0-a70f-4668-9238-47f9fc208882        EXCHANGE_ANALYTICS
User      Success             a23b959c-7ce8-4e57-9140-b90eb88a9e97        SWAY
Company   Success             f20fedf3-f3c3-43c3-8267-2bfdd51c0939        ATP_ENTERPRISE
User      Success             4828c8ec-dc2e-4779-b502-87ac9ce28ab7        MCOEV
User      Success             3e26ee1f-8a5f-4d52-aee2-b81ce45c8f40        MCOMEETADV
User      Success             70d33638-9c74-4d01-bfd3-562de28bd4ba        BI_AZURE_P2
Company   PendingActivation   882e1d05-acd1-4ccb-8708-6ee03664b117        INTUNE_O365
User      Success             b737dad2-2f6c-4c65-90e3-ca563267e8b9        PROJECTWORKMANAGEMENT
User      Success             bea4c11e-220a-4e6d-8eb8-8ea15d019f90        RMS_S_ENTERPRISE
User      Success             7547a3fe-08ee-4ccb-b430-5077c5041653        YAMMER_ENTERPRISE
User      Success             43de0ff5-c92c-492b-9116-175376d08c38        OFFICESUBSCRIPTION
User      Success             0feaeb32-d00e-4d66-bd5a-43b5b83db82c        MCOSTANDARD
User      Success             efb87545-963c-4e0d-99df-69c6916d9eb0        EXCHANGE_S_ENTERPRISE
User      Success             5dbe027f-2339-4123-9542-606e4d348a72        SHAREPOINTENTERPRISE
User      Success             e95bec33-7c88-4a70-8e19-b10bd9d0c014        SHAREPOINTWAC
```

Figure 2-13. *Viewing the ServicePlans*

You can also use a single cmdlet to show you all the services for each different SKU by using the PowerShell formatting cmdlets, as seen in the following example:

```
Get-AzureADSubscribedSku | Select-Object -Property
SkuPartNumber  -ExpandProperty ServicePlans | Format-Table -GroupBy
SkuPartNumber
```

This will display every subscription that you have in your tenant and the plans in each one, grouped in a nice way, as seen in Figure 2-14.

```
Administrator: Windows PowerShell                                                              —  □  ×
PS C:\WINDOWS\system32> Get-AzureADSubscribedSku | Select-Object -Property SkuPartNumber   -ExpandProperty ServicePlans |
    Format-Table -GroupBy SkuPartNumber


    SkuPartNumber: ENTERPRISEPREMIUM

SkuPartNumber      AppliesTo ProvisioningStatus ServicePlanId                         ServicePlanName
-------------      --------- ------------------ -------------                         ---------------
ENTERPRISEPREMIUM  User      Success            e212cbc7-0961-4c40-9825-01117710dcb1  FORMS_PLAN_E5
ENTERPRISEPREMIUM  User      Success            6c6042f5-6f01-4d67-b8c1-eb99d36eed3e  STREAM_O365_E5
ENTERPRISEPREMIUM  User      Success            8e0c0a52-6a6c-4d40-8370-dd62790dcd70  THREAT_INTELLIGENCE
ENTERPRISEPREMIUM  User      Success            8c7d2df8-86f0-4902-b2ed-a0458298f3b3  Deskless
ENTERPRISEPREMIUM  User      Success            07699545-9485-468e-95b6-2fca3738be01  FLOW_O365_P3
ENTERPRISEPREMIUM  User      Success            9c0dab89-a30c-4117-86e7-97bda240acd2  POWERAPPS_O365_P3
ENTERPRISEPREMIUM  User      Success            57ff2da0-773e-42df-b2af-ffb7a2317929  TEAMS1
ENTERPRISEPREMIUM  User      Success            8c098270-9dd4-4350-9b30-ba4703f3b36b  ADALLOM_S_O365
ENTERPRISEPREMIUM  User      Success            4de31727-a228-4ec3-a5bf-8e45b5ca48cc  EQUIVIO_ANALYTICS
ENTERPRISEPREMIUM  User      Success            9f431833-0334-42de-a7dc-70aa40db46db  LOCKBOX_ENTERPRISE
ENTERPRISEPREMIUM  User      Success            34c0d7a0-a70f-4668-9238-47f9fc208882  EXCHANGE_ANALYTICS
ENTERPRISEPREMIUM  User      Success            a23b959c-7ce8-4e57-9140-b90eb88a9e97  SWAY
ENTERPRISEPREMIUM  Company   Success            f20fedf3-f3c3-43c3-8267-2bfdd51c0939  ATP_ENTERPRISE
ENTERPRISEPREMIUM  User      Success            4828c8ec-dc2e-4779-b502-87ac9ce28ab7  MCOEV
ENTERPRISEPREMIUM  User      Success            3e26ee1f-8a5f-4d52-aee2-b81ce45c8f40  MCOMEETADV
ENTERPRISEPREMIUM  User      Success            70d33638-9c74-4d01-bfd3-562de28bd4ba  BI_AZURE_P2
ENTERPRISEPREMIUM  Company   PendingActivation  882e1d05-acd1-4ccb-8708-6ee03664b117  INTUNE_O365
ENTERPRISEPREMIUM  User      Success            b737dad2-2f6c-4c65-90e3-ca563267e8b9  PROJECTWORKMANAGEMENT
ENTERPRISEPREMIUM  User      Success            bea4c11e-220a-4e6d-8eb8-8ea15d019f90  RMS_S_ENTERPRISE
ENTERPRISEPREMIUM  User      Success            7547a3fe-08ee-4ccb-b430-5077c5041653  YAMMER_ENTERPRISE
ENTERPRISEPREMIUM  User      Success            43de0ff5-c92c-492b-9116-175376d08c38  OFFICESUBSCRIPTION
ENTERPRISEPREMIUM  User      Success            0feaeb32-d00e-4d66-bd5a-43b5b83db82c  MCOSTANDARD
ENTERPRISEPREMIUM  User      Success            efb87545-963c-4e0d-99df-69c6916d9eb0  EXCHANGE_S_ENTERPRISE
ENTERPRISEPREMIUM  User      Success            5dbe027f-2339-4123-9542-606e4d348a72  SHAREPOINTENTERPRISE
ENTERPRISEPREMIUM  User      Success            e95bec33-7c88-4a70-8e19-b10bd9d0c014  SHAREPOINTWAC


    SkuPartNumber: ENTERPRISEPACK

SkuPartNumber   AppliesTo ProvisioningStatus ServicePlanId                         ServicePlanName
-------------   --------- ------------------ -------------                         ---------------
ENTERPRISEPACK  User      Success            2789c901-c14e-48ab-a76a-be334d9d793a  FORMS_PLAN_E3
ENTERPRISEPACK  User      Success            9e700747-8b1d-45e5-ab8d-ef187ceec156  STREAM_O365_E3
ENTERPRISEPACK  User      Success            8c7d2df8-86f0-4902-b2ed-a0458298f3b3  Deskless
ENTERPRISEPACK  User      Success            76846ad7-7776-4c40-a281-a386362dd1b9  FLOW_O365_P2
ENTERPRISEPACK  User      Success            c68f8d98-5534-41c8-bf36-22fa496fa792  POWERAPPS_O365_P2
ENTERPRISEPACK  User      Success            57ff2da0-773e-42df-b2af-ffb7a2317929  TEAMS1
ENTERPRISEPACK  User      Success            b737dad2-2f6c-4c65-90e3-ca563267e8b9  PROJECTWORKMANAGEMENT
ENTERPRISEPACK  User      Success            a23b959c-7ce8-4e57-9140-b90eb88a9e97  SWAY
```

Figure 2-14. *Showing all the services in the tenant, grouped by subscription name*

Now that we know how to view our subscriptions and services, we can look at how to view the licenses assigned to a user and how to assign them new licenses. To view the licenses assigned to a user, you can use the Get-AzureADUserLicenseDetail cmdlet. In the example that follows, I am displaying the different subscriptions assigned to Jeff Collins and showing only the Internal Name (SkuPartNumber):

Get-AzureADUserLicenseDetail -ObjectId jeff@office365powershell.ca |
Select-Object SkuPartNumber

In Figure 2-15, you can see that Jeff currently has the O365_BUSINESS_PREMIUM and the ENTERPRISEPREMIUM licenses assigned to his account.

```
Select Administrator: Windows PowerShell                                                    —  □  ×
PS C:\WINDOWS\system32> Get-AzureADUserLicenseDetail -ObjectId jeff@office365powershell.ca | Select-Object SkuPartNumber

SkuPartNumber
-------------
O365_BUSINESS_PREMIUM
ENTERPRISEPREMIUM


PS C:\WINDOWS\system32>
```

Figure 2-15. *Displaying the different subscriptions assigned to a user*

Now that we know how to view the licenses, let's take a look at how to license a new user.

Assigning a License to a User

The first thing that you will have to do is set the UsageLocation parameter for your user, as this parameter is mandatory before assigning a license. The UsageLocation parameter accepts the two-letter country code of the location from which this user will be using Office 365. To make things easier, save your user in a variable called $User so you do not have to specify the username every time:

```
$User = Get-AzureADUser -ObjectId jonathan@office365powershell.ca
Set-AzureADUser -ObjectId $User.ObjectId -UsageLocation CA
```

Now that your user is ready to be assigned a license, you first need to create two objects. The first one is the $Sku variable seen next, which is an object that represents a single subscription. The second object, which is the $Licenses variable, is the collection of licenses that will be assigned to the user. This will become useful when you want to assign multiple licenses to certain users.

```
$Sku = New-Object -TypeName Microsoft.Open.AzureAD.Model.AssignedLicense

$Licenses = New-Object -TypeName Microsoft.Open.AzureAD.Model.AssignedLicenses
```

Tip   While in most cases you will only assign a single license to a user, you might, for example, get a Power BI Pro license only for the executives of the company, while the rest of the users have a simple E3 license. The executives would have two licenses assigned, the E3 and the Power BI Pro.

Next up, you need to enter the information in the variables just created. The first step is to know the SkuID of the license that you want to assign to your user, which can be discovered with the following cmdlet:

```
Get-AzureADSubscribedSku | Select-Object -Property SkuPartNumber, SkuID
```

The result shown in Figure 2-16 shows all the possible subscription IDs.

```
Administrator: Windows PowerShell                                                    —   □   ×
PS C:\WINDOWS\system32> Get-AzureADSubscribedSku | Select-Object -Property SkuPartNumber, SkuID

SkuPartNumber            SkuId
-------------            -----
ENTERPRISEPREMIUM        c7df2760-2c81-4ef7-b578-5b5392b571df
POWER_BI_PRO             f8a1db68-be16-40ed-86d5-cb42ce701560
ENTERPRISEPACK           6fd2c87f-b296-42f0-b197-1e91e994b900
O365_BUSINESS_PREMIUM    f245ecc8-75af-4f8e-b61f-27d8114de5f3


PS C:\WINDOWS\system32> _
```

Figure 2-16. *All the subscription SkuIds in the tenant*

Next up, you need to specify the SkuId parameter of the $Sku object you just created, then tell it what license you want it to be:

```
$Sku.SkuId = "c7df2760-2c81-4ef7-b578-5b5392b571df"
```

You then need to add your $Sku object, part of the $Licenses array that you created earlier, with the following cmdlet:

```
$Licenses.AddLicenses = $Sku
```

Lastly, you need to add the licenses to your user with the Set-AzureADUserLicense cmdlet, as seen here:

```
Set-AzureADUserLicense -ObjectId $User.ObjectId -AssignedLicenses $Licenses
```

Now, to put it all together, these are the cmdlets required to add the E5 license to your user:

```
$User = Get-AzureADUser -ObjectId jonathan@office365powershell.ca
Set-AzureADUser -ObjectId $User.ObjectId -UsageLocation CA

$Sku = New-Object -TypeName Microsoft.Open.AzureAD.Model.AssignedLicense

$Licenses = New-Object -TypeName Microsoft.Open.AzureAD.Model.
AssignedLicenses
```

```
$Sku.SkuId = "c7df2760-2c81-4ef7-b578-5b5392b571df"
$Licenses.AddLicenses = $Sku

Set-AzureADUserLicense -ObjectId $User.ObjectId -AssignedLicenses $Licenses
```

You can look at the result either by using the `Get-AzureADUserLicenseDetail` cmdlet, as you saw earlier in this chapter, or from the Office 365 Admin Center. As you can see in the screenshot of the Office 365 Admin Center in Figure 2-17, you have successfully assigned the E5 license to your user.

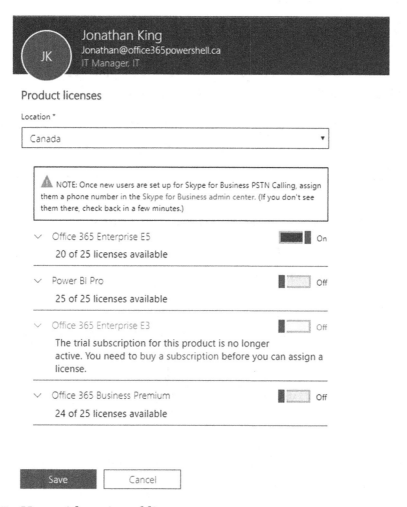

Figure 2-17. *User with assigned licenses*

Now that you have successfully assigned a license to a user, let's take a look at how you can assign multiple licenses.

Assigning Multiple Licenses

If you want to assign another license—for example, Power BI Pro—to the user that is already licensed for E3, you could simply repeat the steps from earlier, since even if the cmdlet is Set-AzureADUserLicense, and you would probably expect it to overwrite the previous setting all together, the behavior is a bit different with the Azure AD V2 Module, and you will learn how to remove or replace licenses later in this chapter. For now, let's see how to assign multiple licenses to a new user at once; for example, both Office 365 Business Premium and Power BI Pro licenses.

Start by saving your user into a variable and setting the usage location as you learned previously:

```
$User = Get-AzureADUser -ObjectId vanessa@office365powershell.ca
Set-AzureADUser -ObjectId $User.ObjectId -UsageLocation CA
```

Afterward, create two objects of type Microsoft.Open.AzureAD.Model.AssignedLicense, one for the Business Premium license and one for the Power BI Pro license:

```
$BusinessProSku = New-Object -TypeName Microsoft.Open.AzureAD.Model.
AssignedLicense
$PowerBiSku = New-Object -TypeName Microsoft.Open.AzureAD.Model.AssignedLicense
```

Next up, use the Get-AzureADSubscribedSku as seen in Figure 2-18 to get the SkuIDs of the subscriptions you want to add.

```
Administrator: Windows PowerShell                                          —  □  ×
PS C:\WINDOWS\system32> Get-AzureADSubscribedSku | Select-Object -Property SkuPartNumber, SkuID

SkuPartNumber          SkuId
-------------          -----
ENTERPRISEPREMIUM      c7df2760-2c81-4ef7-b578-5b5392b571df
POWER_BI_PRO           f8a1db68-be16-40ed-86d5-cb42ce701560
ENTERPRISEPACK         6fd2c87f-b296-42f0-b197-1e91e994b900
O365_BUSINESS_PREMIUM  f245ecc8-75af-4f8e-b61f-27d8114de5f3


PS C:\WINDOWS\system32>
```

Figure 2-18. *List of the available subscriptions*

Now that you know the SKU IDs, you can add them in the `$BusinessProSku` and `$PowerBiSku` variables that you created earlier:

```
$BusinessProSku.SkuId = "f245ecc8-75af-4f8e-b61f-27d8114de5f3"
$PowerBiSku.SkuId = "f8a1db68-be16-40ed-86d5-cb42ce701560"
```

Now, create your `$licenses` variable, which is an object of type `Microsoft.Open.AzureAD.Model.AssignedLicenses`, and add the `$BusinessProSku` and `$PowerBiSku` licenses inside:

```
$Licenses = New-Object -TypeName Microsoft.Open.AzureAD.Model.AssignedLicenses
$Licenses.AddLicenses = $BusinessProSku, $PowerBiSku
```

Lastly, run `Set-AzureADUserLicense` to assign the license to your user, as seen in the following cmdlet:

```
Set-AzureADUserLicense -ObjectId $User.ObjectId -AssignedLicenses $Licenses
```

If you look at the results of the previous cmdlet in the Office 365 Admin Center in Figure 2-19, you can see that both licenses have been successfully assigned, with all the licenses activated.

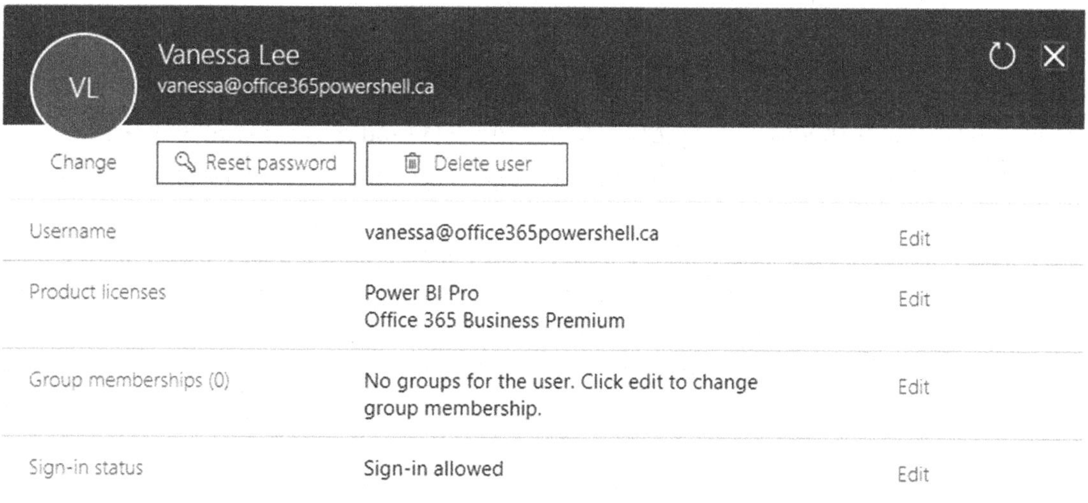

Figure 2-19. *User with multiple licenses assigned*

In the previous examples, we assigned either one license or multiple licenses at a time to a user. In some business scenarios, we might want to assign a license but not enable all the services inside.

Assigning Licenses with Some Features Disabled

In some scenarios, we might want to assign some licenses to users, but not give them access to all the services. This can happen for multiple reasons; let me give you a concrete example. I was implementing Office 365 at a customer in Canada whose data absolutely needed to stay on Canadian soil. At the time (and it might still be the case today), Yammer was only hosted out of the United States, and there was no way to have Yammer data hosted in Canada, so we had to disable it for all the existing users, as well as for the new users. Let's see how we can get this done with PowerShell.

First of all, we will save our user in a variable and set the Usage Location to Canada:

```
$User = Get-AzureADUser -ObjectId john@office365powershell.ca
Set-AzureADUser -ObjectId $User.ObjectId -UsageLocation CA
```

We will then create our Microsoft.Open.AzureAD.Model.AssignedLicense object and specify the ENTERPRISEPREMIUM SKU ID as we learned in the previous examples:

```
$Sku = New-Object -TypeName Microsoft.Open.AzureAD.Model.AssignedLicense
$Sku.SkuId = "c7df2760-2c81-4ef7-b578-5b5392b571df"
```

Next up, we need to get the ID of the Yammer Service part of the ENTERPRISEPREMIUM subscription by using the Get-AzureADSubscribedSku cmdlet, specifying the ObjectId of our ENTERPRISEPREMIUM subscription and expanding the service plans:

```
Get-AzureADSubscribedSku -ObjectId 545c04df-2411-4d58-9378-7ec79e9e6b8e_
c7df2760-2c81-4ef7-b578-5b5392b571df | Select-Object -ExpandProperty
ServicePlans
```

In the result seen in Figure 2-20, you can see the service plan ID for each service, and you can save the IDs of the one(s) you want to disable.

```
Select Administrator: Windows PowerShell                                              —  □  ×
PS C:\WINDOWS\system32> Get-AzureADSubscribedSku -ObjectId 545c04df-2411-4d58-9378-7ec79e9e6b8e_c7df2760-2c81-4ef7-b578-
5b5392b571df | Select-Object -ExpandProperty ServicePlans

AppliesTo ProvisioningStatus ServicePlanId                        ServicePlanName
--------- ------------------ -------------                        ---------------
User      Success            e212cbc7-0961-4c40-9825-01117710dcb1 FORMS_PLAN_E5
User      Success            6c6042f5-6f01-4d67-b8c1-eb99d36eed3e STREAM_O365_E5
User      Success            8e0c0a52-6a6c-4d40-8370-dd62790dcd70 THREAT_INTELLIGENCE
User      Success            8c7d2df8-86f0-4902-b2ed-a0458298f3b3 Deskless
User      Success            07699545-9485-468e-95b6-2fca3738be01 FLOW_O365_P3
User      Success            9c0dab89-a30c-4117-86e7-97bda240acd2 POWERAPPS_O365_P3
User      Success            57ff2da0-773e-42df-b2af-ffb7a2317929 TEAMS1
User      Success            8c098270-9dd4-4350-9b30-ba4703f3b36b ADALLOM_S_O365
User      Success            4de31727-a228-4ec3-a5bf-8e45b5ca48cc EQUIVIO_ANALYTICS
User      Success            9f431833-0334-42de-a7dc-70aa40db46db LOCKBOX_ENTERPRISE
User      Success            34c0d7a0-a70f-4668-9238-47f9fc208882 EXCHANGE_ANALYTICS
User      Success            a23b959c-7ce8-4e57-9140-b90eb88a9e97 SWAY
Company   Success            f20fedf3-f3c3-43c3-8267-2bfdd51c0939 ATP_ENTERPRISE
User      Success            4828c8ec-dc2e-4779-b502-87ac9ce28ab7 MCOEV
User      Success            3e26ee1f-8a5f-4d52-aee2-b81ce45c8f40 MCOMEETADV
User      Success            70d33638-9c74-4d01-bfd3-562de28bd4ba BI_AZURE_P2
Company   PendingActivation  882e1d05-acd1-4ccb-8708-6ee03664b117 INTUNE_O365
User      Success            b737dad2-2f6c-4c65-90e3-ca563267e8b9 PROJECTWORKMANAGEMENT
User      Success            bea4c11e-220a-4e6d-8eb8-8ea15d019f90 RMS_S_ENTERPRISE
User      Success            7547a3fe-08ee-4ccb-b430-5077c5041653 YAMMER_ENTERPRISE
User      Success            43de0ff5-c92c-492b-9116-175376d08c38 OFFICESUBSCRIPTION
User      Success            0feaeb32-d00e-4d66-bd5a-43b5b83db82c MCOSTANDARD
User      Success            efb87545-963c-4e0d-99df-69c6916d9eb0 EXCHANGE_S_ENTERPRISE
User      Success            5dbe027f-2339-4123-9542-606e4d348a72 SHAREPOINTENTERPRISE
User      Success            e95bec33-7c88-4a70-8e19-b10bd9d0c014 SHAREPOINTWAC
```

Figure 2-20. *Viewing the service plan IDs of the services in a subscription*

Next up, we will set the `DisabledPlans` property of the $Sku variable to the service plan ID of the `YAMMER_ENTERPRISE` service:

```
$Sku.DisabledPlans = "7547a3fe-08ee-4ccb-b430-5077c5041653"
```

If we wanted to disable multiple plans, we could create an array of plans to disable. For example, the following would disable both `YAMMER_ENTERPRISE` and `FORMS_PLAN_E5`:

```
$Sku.DisabledPlans = @("7547a3fe-08ee-4ccb-b430-5077c5041653",
"e212cbc7-0961-4c40-9825-01117710dcb1")
```

We would then create our `Microsoft.Open.AzureAD.Model.AssignedLicenses` object, add our $Sku variable as licenses to add, and apply it to our user, as seen in the following cmdlets:

```
$Licenses = New-Object -TypeName
Microsoft.Open.AzureAD.Model.AssignedLicenses
$Licenses.AddLicenses = $Sku
Set-AzureADUserLicense -ObjectId $User.ObjectId -AssignedLicenses $Licenses
```

The result as seen in Figure 2-21 is a user that is E5 licensed but has the Yammer and Forms services disabled.

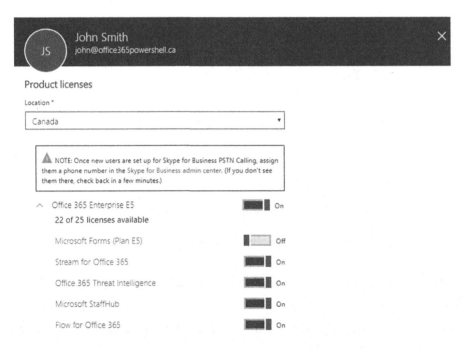

Figure 2-21. *User with E5 license and certain services disabled*

Note   In Figure 2-21, we only see the Forms service disabled due to limitations on the size of the figure that would be readable. You will have to trust me that Yammer was also disabled—or better yet, try it yourself!

We can also view the disabled plans of a user with the Get-AzureADUser cmdlet and by expanding the AssignedLicenses property as seen in the next example. In Figure 2-22, you can see the SkuId that we assigned to the user previously, as well as the IDs of the services we disabled in the DisabledPlans property:

```
Get-AzureADUser -ObjectId $User.ObjectId | Select -ExpandProperty
AssignedLicenses
```

```
Administrator: Windows PowerShell                                            –   □   ×
PS C:\WINDOWS\system32> Get-AzureADUser -ObjectId $User.ObjectId | Select -ExpandProperty AssignedLicenses

DisabledPlans                                                        SkuId
------------                                                        -----
{e212cbc7-0961-4c40-9825-01117710dcb1, 7547a3fe-08ee-4ccb-b430-5077c5041653} c7df2760-2c81-4ef7-b578-5b5392b571df

PS C:\WINDOWS\system32>
```

Figure 2-22. *Assigned licenses of a user*

We have now looked at multiple scenarios and ways to add licenses to our users. Next up, we will learn how to remove a license from a user.

Removing User Licenses

Removing a license from a user is very similar to adding a license, but instead of using the AddLicenses method of our Microsoft.Open.AzureAD.Model.AssignedLicenses object, we will use the RemoveLicenses method.

We will first save our user into a variable by using the Get-AzureADUser cmdlet as seen here:

$User = Get-AzureADUser -ObjectId john@office365powershell.ca

We will then create a Microsoft.Open.AzureAD.Model.AssignedLicenses object and save it into a variable called $Licenses as seen here:

$Licenses = New-Object -TypeName Microsoft.Open.AzureAD.Model.AssignedLicenses

Since I know the plan I want to disable is the ENTERPRISEPREMIUM cmdlet, I can run the following cmdlet to add the SKU ID of my ENTERPRISEPREMIUM plan in the RemoveLicenses property of my object. In the past, we listed the different subscriptions and manually copied their SkuId; this is just another way to do it!

$Licenses.RemoveLicenses = (Get-AzureADSubscribedSku | Where-Object -Property SkuPartNumber -Value "ENTERPRISEPREMIUM" -EQ).SkuID

Lastly, I will assign my $Licenses variable to the user by using the Set-AzureADUserLicense cmdlet:

```
Set-AzureADUserLicense -ObjectId $User.ObjectId -AssignedLicenses $Licenses
```

We can then use PowerShell for the Office 365 Admin Center to verify the result, which should be that the user does not have that license anymore. In Figure 2-23, the subscription we just removed from John Smith was the only one he had assigned, so the user is now unlicensed.

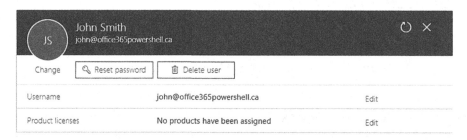

Figure 2-23. *License removed from the user*

We have now learned how to manage licenses for our users in Office 365. Next up, let's learn how to manage security groups!

Managing Security Groups with PowerShell

The last section of our "Managing Users and Licenses" chapter will deal with security groups. It's important to know that this chapter will only focus on security groups, and not on Office 365 Groups, as we will cover those in a later chapter. Let's start with creating a new security group.

Creating a New Security Group

To create a new security group, we will use the New-AzureADGroup cmdlet and specify the display name, if the group is email enabled, if the group is security enabled, and finally the mail nickname, which is mandatory, even if the group you want to create is not enabled for email. In the example that follows, we are creating a new group called IT Employees, which will only be used for security and will not be email enabled.

```
New-AzureADGroup -DisplayName "IT Employees" -MailEnabled $false
-SecurityEnabled $true -MailNickName "IT" -Description "Security Group for
employees in the IT Department"
```

We can then run the Get-AzureADGroup cmdlet to view all the groups in our Office 365 tenant, as seen in Figure 2-24.

Note   The Get-AzureADGroup cmdlet will also return Office 365 Groups, such as the "PowerShell for Office 365 Book" group.

```
Administrator: Windows PowerShell                                                         —   □   ×
PS C:\WINDOWS\system32> Get-AzureADGroup

ObjectId                               DisplayName                        Description
--------                               -----------                        -----------
370883eb-8985-4d44-8643-91dfe1fa88bd   HR Employees
39d6d22e-ce57-45c2-bcb9-a2d2cb98617b   IT Employees                       Security Group for employees in the IT Department
f0fa77fd-f0dd-4e5c-9fda-c3b73a755a2d   PowerShell for Office 365 Book     PowerShell for Office 365 Book


PS C:\WINDOWS\system32> _
```

Figure 2-24. Viewing all the AD groups in our tenant

Creating an Azure AD group is pretty easy, so now let's take a look at how we can modify the properties of an existing group.

Changing the Properties of a Security Group

To modify the properties of an Azure AD group, we will use Set-AzureADGroup, providing the object ID as well as any parameters that we would like to change. For example, in Figure 2-24, we have a group called *HR Employees* that has no description, and we want to change that.

In the example that follows, we are running the Set-AzureADGroup cmdlet, and since we need to give the ObjectId of the HR Employees group, we run Get-AzureADGroup to get it. This only works because we currently have one group with the word *HR* inside; if you have multiple, you will have to be more specific.

```
Set-AzureADGroup -ObjectId (Get-AzureADGroup -SearchString "Hr").ObjectId
-Description "Security Group for employees in the HR Department"
```

33

To verify it, we can run the Get-AzureADGroup cmdlet, and as you see in Figure 2-25, our description has been updated.

```
Administrator: Windows PowerShell                                                                    —  □  ×
PS C:\WINDOWS\system32> Get-AzureADGroup

ObjectId                             DisplayName                  Description
--------                             -----------                  -----------
370883eb-8985-4d44-8643-91dfe1fa88bd HR Employees                 Security Group for employees in the HR Department
39d6d22e-ce57-45c2-bcb9-a2d2cb98617b IT Employees                 Security Group for employees in the IT Department
f0fa77fd-f0dd-4e5c-9fda-c3b73a755a2d PowerShell for Office 365 Book PowerShell for Office 365 Book


PS C:\WINDOWS\system32> _
```

Figure 2-25. *Updated description using the Set-AzureADGroup cmdlet*

You can view some parameters that we can change in Table 2-1.

Table 2-1. *Parameters of the Set-AzureADGroup cmdlet*

Parameter	Description
-DisplayName	Specifies a display name
-MailEnabled	Indicates whether mail is enabled
-MailNickName	Specifies a nickname for the mail
-SecurityEnabled	Indicates whether security is enabled

Removing a Security Group

To remove a security group, we need to use the Remove-AzureADGroup cdmlet, specifying the object ID of the group we want to delete.

In the example that follows, we are running the Remove-AzureADGroup cmdlet, and since we need to give the ObjectId of the *IT Employees* group, we run Get-AzureADGroup to get it. This only works because we currently have one group with the word *IT* inside; if you have multiple, you will have to be more specific.

```
Remove-AzureADGroup -ObjectId (Get-AzureADGroup -SearchString "IT").ObjectId
```

We have now looked at how to create, change, remove, and view security groups. Next up, we will learn how to manage the members inside!

Managing Security Group Membership

One of the most important things, if not the most important thing, about security groups is the members inside. To view the members of a security group, we can use the Get-AzureADGroupMember cmdlet and specify the object ID of the group, as seen here:

```
Get-AzureADGroupMember -ObjectId (Get-AzureADGroup -SearchString "Hr").ObjectId
```

While the previous cmdlet returns the members of the group, we can also use the Get-AzureADGroupOwner cmdlet to view the owners of the group—and again, the only thing you have to specify is the object ID of the group.

```
Get-AzureADGroupOwner -ObjectId (Get-AzureADGroup -SearchString "Hr").ObjectId
```

You can see the result of both cmdlets in Figure 2-26.

Figure 2-26. *Results of the Get-AzureADGroupMember and Get-AzureADGroupOwner cmdlets*

To add a user, we can use the Add-AzureADGroupMember, specifying the ID of the group first, followed by the ID of the user we want to add in the -RefObjectId parameter. In the example that follows, we will first run the Get-AzureADUser and Get-AzureADGroup cmdlets to save our user and group in variables for easier access later on. Afterward, we will use the Add-AzureADGroupMember cmdlet and specify the preceding variables to add the user to the group:

```
$UserId = Get-AzureADUser -ObjectId vanessa@office365powershell.ca
$GroupId = Get-AzureADGroup -SearchString "Hr Employees"
Add-AzureADGroupMember -ObjectId $GroupId.ObjectId -RefObjectId $UserId.ObjectId
```

We can verify the result by using the `Get-AzureADGroupMember` cmdlet, and as seen in Figure 2-27, Vanessa has been added to the group!

```
Select Administrator: Windows PowerShell                                                         —    □    ×
PS C:\WINDOWS\system32> $UserId = Get-AzureADUser -ObjectId vanessa@office365powershell.ca
PS C:\WINDOWS\system32> $GroupId = Get-AzureADGroup -SearchString "Hr Employees"
PS C:\WINDOWS\system32> Add-AzureADGroupMember -ObjectId $GroupId.ObjectId -RefObjectId $UserId.ObjectId
PS C:\WINDOWS\system32> Get-AzureADGroupMember -ObjectId $GroupId.ObjectId

ObjectId                               DisplayName    UserPrincipalName              UserType
--------                               -----------    -----------------              --------
fca50d76-9c1d-47fd-8c33-dadcdaf91008   John Smith     john@office365powershell.ca    Member
158cd24d-8148-4c78-8168-e7a4d057afe6   Vanessa Lee    vanessa@office365powershell.ca Member
1651b416-3a9c-401d-8e36-56e65a6e0ac8   Jeff Collins   Jeff@office365powershell.ca    Member


PS C:\WINDOWS\system32>
```

Figure 2-27. *Adding a user to an Azure AD group*

You can also add owners of the group in the same way; you simply have to use the `Add-AzureADGroupOwner` cmdlet instead of the `Get-AzureADGroupMember` cmdlet.

Removing a user or an owner is done in a very similar way with the `Remove-AzureADGroupMember` and `Remove-AzureADGroupOwner` cmdlets. To remove a member, we will first save the member and the group in variables, as we have done previously:

```
$UserId = Get-AzureADUser -ObjectId vanessa@office365powershell.ca
$GroupId = Get-AzureADGroup -SearchString "Hr Employees"
```

We will then use `Remove-AzureADGroupMember`, specifying the `ObjectId` parameter, which is the ID of the group, and the `MemberId` of the user, which is the ID of the user we want to remove:

```
Remove-AzureADGroupMember -ObjectId $GroupId.ObjectId -MemberId $UserId.
ObjectId
```

To remove the same user from the owners of the AD group, we would use the `Remove-AzureADGroupOwner` cmdlet and specify the `-OwnerId` parameter instead, as seen here:

```
Remove-AzureADGroupOwner -ObjectId $GroupId.ObjectId -OwnerId $UserId.ObjectId
```

We can also search the groups that a member is a part of by using `Get-AzureADUserMembership` and specifying the ID of the user we want to get the information about, as seen in the following example:

```
$UserId = Get-AzureADUser -ObjectId jeff@office365powershell.ca
Get-AzureADUserMembership -ObjectId $userid.ObjectId
```

This will output all the groups that this member is a part of, as seen in Figure 2-28.

```
Administrator: Windows PowerShell                                              —  □  ×
PS C:\WINDOWS\system32> $UserId = Get-AzureADUser -ObjectId jeff@office365powershell.ca
PS C:\WINDOWS\system32> Get-AzureADUserMembership -ObjectId $userid.ObjectId

ObjectId                             DisplayName  Description
--------                             -----------  -----------
370883eb-8985-4d44-8643-91dfe1fa88bd HR Employees Security Group for employees in the HR Department

PS C:\WINDOWS\system32>
```

Figure 2-28. *Viewing the groups that a member is a part of*

We have now covered how to manage users, licenses, and Azure AD security groups using PowerShell. Now, let's take a look at how we can automate some business scenarios using what we have just learned!

Automation Scenarios

The goal of the "Automation Scenario" section of each chapter is to look at some real-life examples of how you can apply what you have learned in the chapter. These examples will be interesting and relatively simple, and in our eighth and final chapter we will look at some more-advanced scenarios that cover multiple services in Office 365!

Tip   Remember the scripts and input files demonstrated in each chapter are also downloadable from the Apress GitHub repository, which you can find at `https://github.com/apress`, or for a direct link to this book's scripts, go to the book page at `www.apress.com` and click the "Download Source Code" button.

Updating User Licenses

You have been using Office 365 as a company for the past few years with the Office 365 Business Premium licenses, and it was a perfect fit. Today, you just got news from leadership that for the next renewal cycle, they have worked with Microsoft to optimize licenses and use more Office 365 services. The new license plan can be seen in Table 2-2.

Table 2-2. *Business Requirements for New Licenses*

Department	License
Sales	Office 365 Enterprise E5
	Dynamics 365 Customer Engagement Plan Enterprise Edition
Manufacturing	Office 365 F1
Project Management	Office 365 Enterprise E5
	Project Online Professional
IT	Office 365 Enterprise E5

You are now tasked with updating the license assignment for every user by the end of the week, when your current Office 365 Business Premium licenses will expire. Let's get started!

The first thing you will do is save all the users in your tenant in a variable. You will filter on those users that are a type "Member" so you do not get external users (type "Guest"):

```
$Users = Get-AzureADUser | Where {$_.UserType -eq "Member"}
```

You will then create a new object of type `Microsoft.Open.AzureAD.Model.AssignedLicense` for each type of license that you want to assign to your users:

```
$E5Sku = New-Object -TypeName Microsoft.Open.AzureAD.Model.AssignedLicense
$DynamicsSku = New-Object -TypeName Microsoft.Open.AzureAD.Model.AssignedLicense
$F1Sku = New-Object -TypeName Microsoft.Open.AzureAD.Model.AssignedLicense
$ProjectProSku = New-Object -TypeName Microsoft.Open.AzureAD.Model.AssignedLicense
$BusinessProSku = New-Object -TypeName Microsoft.Open.AzureAD.Model.AssignedLicense
```

For each of these objects, use the `Get-AzureADSubscribedSku` that you learned earlier to get their `SkuID` and save it in the object, as seen here:

```
$E5Sku.SkuId = "c7df2760-2c81-4ef7-b578-5b5392b571df"
$DynamicsSku.SkuId = "ea126fc5-a19e-42e2-a731-da9d437bffcf"
$F1Sku.SkuId = "4b585984-651b-448a-9e53-3b10f069cf7f"
$ProjectProSku.SkuId = "53818b1b-4a27-454b-8896-0dba576410e6"
$BusinessProSku.SkuId = "f245ecc8-75af-4f8e-b61f-27d8114de5f3"
```

Next up, create your `Microsoft.Open.AzureAD.Model.AssignedLicenses` objects, which make up the collection of licenses that you will add or remove from every user. Since all the departments are different, you will need to create one for each account:

```
$SalesLicenses = New-Object -TypeName
Microsoft.Open.AzureAD.Model.AssignedLicenses
$ManufacturingLicenses = New-Object -TypeName
Microsoft.Open.AzureAD.Model.AssignedLicenses
$PMLicenses = New-Object -TypeName Microsoft.Open.AzureAD.Model.AssignedLicenses
$ITLicenses = New-Object -TypeName Microsoft.Open.AzureAD.Model.AssignedLicenses
```

With all the objects created, for each license collection you must add the different subscriptions that will be inside, as follows:

```
$SalesLicenses.AddLicenses = $E5Sku, $DynamicsSku
$ManufacturingLicenses.AddLicenses = $F1Sku
$PMLicenses.AddLicenses = $E5Sku, $ProjectProSku
$ITLicenses.AddLicenses = $E5Sku
```

Since you are removing the `BusinessPro` subscription for everyone, add the SkuID of the `BusinessPro` subscription in the `RemoveLicenses` attribute of each of your license collections:

```
$SalesLicenses.RemoveLicenses = $BusinessProSku.SkuId
$ManufacturingLicenses.RemoveLicenses = $BusinessProSku.SkuId
$PMLicenses.RemoveLicenses = $BusinessProSku.SkuId
$ITLicenses.RemoveLicenses = $BusinessProSku.SkuId
```

Now, start looping through all your users, and for each user do an `if` statement to see what department they are in; depending on the department, run the `Set-AzureADUserLicense` cmdlet and specify the appropriate license collection from earlier:

```
Foreach ($user in $users)
{
    if ($user.Department -eq "Sales")
    {
    Set-AzureADUserLicense -ObjectId $User.ObjectId -AssignedLicenses
    $SalesLicenses
    }
```

```
elseif ($user.Department -eq "Project Management")
{
Set-AzureADUserLicense -ObjectId $User.ObjectId -AssignedLicenses
$PMLicenses
}

elseif ($user.Department -eq "Manufacturing")
{
Set-AzureADUserLicense -ObjectId $User.ObjectId -AssignedLicenses
$ManufacturingLicenses
}

elseif ($user.Department -eq "IT")
{
Set-AzureADUserLicense -ObjectId $User.ObjectId -AssignedLicenses
$ITLicenses
}
}
```

That's it! After refreshing the Office 365 Admin Center, all your users will have the right licenses, as seen in Figure 2-29.

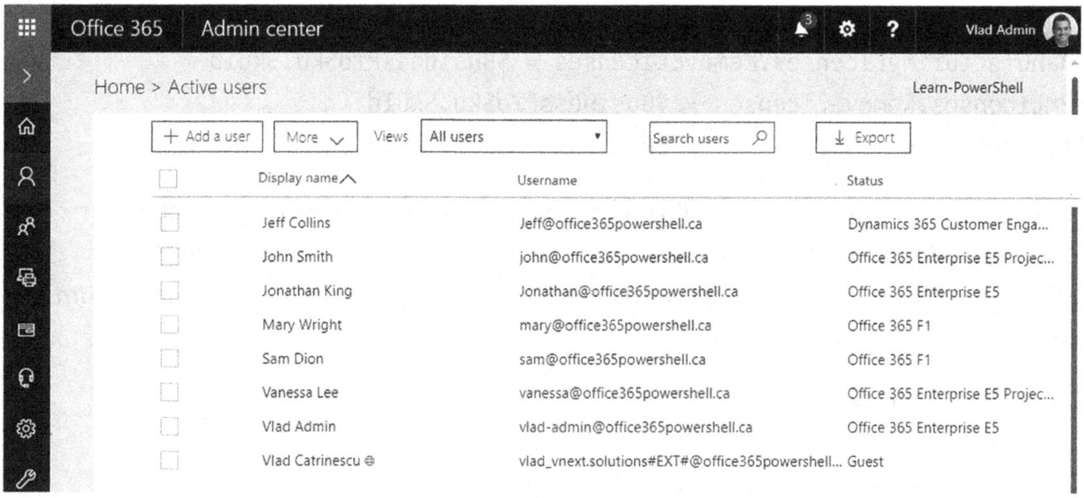

Figure 2-29. *Users and their licenses in the Office 365 Admin Center*

Creating or Updating Users from a CSV File

You are the Office 365 administrator of an 800-person company that is using Office 365 as its main collaboration suite; however, all HR-related information is stored in a third-party solution. Users have complained that data in Office 365 is not in sync with the HR system, which is always up to date, and since that system does not have any available APIs to automatically update Office 365, you can't do much other than tell users to open Helpdesk tickets.

Recently, the third-party HR solution has implemented a new feature that allows you to export changes made in the past week to a CSV file like the one seen in Figure 2-30.

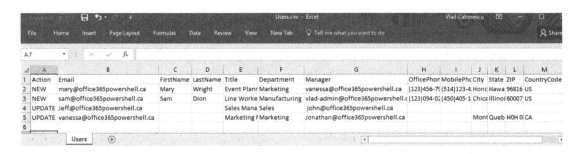

Figure 2-30. *Users input file*

Knowing that you can use CSV files as an input for your PowerShell script, you plan to use PowerShell to update the properties of each user every week based on the input file.

First things first, create your `$InputFile` variable and import the CSV file:

```
$InputFile = Import-CSV C:\PowerShell\Users.csv
```

Since you might have new users to create, you should create your Password Profile objects as well as License objects from the start, before you start looping trough the CSV file:

```
$Sku = New-Object -TypeName Microsoft.Open.AzureAD.Model.AssignedLicense
$Sku.SkuId = "c7df2760-2c81-4ef7-b578-5b5392b571df"
$Licenses = New-Object -TypeName Microsoft.Open.AzureAD.Model.AssignedLicenses
$Licenses.AddLicenses = $Sku
```

Then, start looping through each user from the input file, saving every property from the CSV file into a variable to make it easier to read later on, as follows:

```
foreach ($User in $InputFile)
{
$EMail = $User.Email
$FirstName = $User.FirstName
$LastName = $User.LastName
$Title = $User.Title
$Department = $User.Department
$Manager = Get-AzureADUser -ObjectId $User.Manager
$OfficePhone = $User.OfficePhone
$CellPhone = $User.MobilePhone
$City = $User.City
$State = $User.State
$Zip = $User.ZIP
$Country = $User.CountryCode
```

Then, create an If statement on the Action column, starting with the NEW action. Run the New-AzureADUser cmdlet to create your account, then provide all the properties that you saved in variables earlier, including the Password Profile, License, and Manager:

```
if ($user.Action -eq "NEW")
{
    $NewUser = New-AzureADUser `
        -GivenName $FirstName `
        -Surname $LastName `
        -DisplayName "$FirstName $LastName" `
        -UserPrincipalName $EMail `
        -MailNickName "FirstName.$LastName" `
        -AccountEnabled $true `
        -PasswordProfile $PasswordProfile `
        -JobTitle $Title `
        -Department $Department `
        -UsageLocation $Country `
        -PostalCode $ZIP `
        -Mobile $CellPhone `
```

```
        -TelephoneNumber $OfficePhone `
        -State $State `
        -City $City

Set-AzureADUserManager `
        -ObjectId $EMail `
        -RefObjectId $Manager.ObjectId

Set-AzureADUserLicense `
        -ObjectId $NewUser.ObjectId `
        -AssignedLicenses $Licenses

}
```

With the new users taken care of, you will need to run an elseif statement to take care of the UPDATE action. You could also do an else statement if you are 100 percent sure that there will never be another action; however, I like having a final else statement at the end that will throw an error if the action in the file is not the expected NEW or UPDATE. One of the challenges with the UPDATE action is that the HR system does not output all the columns when a user is updated, so, as you saw in Figure 2-30, some of the columns might be empty. Therefore, you should do an if statement on each of the variables that you have saved, and if the variable is not empty, you should run the Set-AzureADUser cmdlet to update the user's profile with the information from your CSV file:

```
elseif ($user.Action -eq "UPDATE")
    {
    if ($FirstName)
        {
        Set-AzureADUser `
            -ObjectId $EMail `
            -GivenName $FirstName
        }
    if ($LastName)
        {
        Set-AzureADUser `
            -ObjectId $EMail `
            -Surname $LastName
        }
```

```
if ($Title)
        {
        Set-AzureADUser `
                -ObjectId $EMail `
                -JobTitle $Title
        }
if ($Department)
        {
        Set-AzureADUser `
                -ObjectId $EMail `
                -Department $Department
        }
if ($Manager)
        {
        Set-AzureADUserManager `
                -ObjectId $EMail `
                -RefObjectId $Manager.ObjectId
        }
if ($OfficePhone)
        {
        Set-AzureADUser `
                -ObjectId $EMail `
                -TelephoneNumber $OfficePhone
        }
if ($CellPhone)
        {
        Set-AzureADUser `
                -ObjectId $EMail `
                -Mobile $CellPhone
        }
if ($City)
        {
        Set-AzureADUser `
                -ObjectId $EMail `
                -City $City
        }
```

```
if ($State)
        {
        Set-AzureADUser `
                -ObjectId $EMail `
                -State $State
        }
if ($Zip)
        {
        Set-AzureADUser `
                -ObjectId $EMail `
                -PostalCode $Zip
        }
if ($Country)
        {
        Set-AzureADUser `
                -ObjectId $EMail `
                -Country $Country `
                -UsageLocation $Country
        }

}
```

While I am sure that was not the most exciting piece of PowerShell script, it gets the job done in this business scenario!

Finally, do your else statement, in which you simply stop the PowerShell script and throw an error, then close the foreach loop that you opened earlier—and that is it!

```
else
{
Throw "Action not supported"
}}
```

The result is that all the users in the CSV file have been successfully created or updated!

Conclusion

In this chapter, we first learned how to download the AzureAD module from the PowerShell Gallery and install it on our computer. We then learned how to connect to Azure Active Directory, which is the directory of our users, even if most of the time we manage them through the Office 365 Admin Center interface.

We then learned how to view our users in order to create reports, modify their properties, or even create new users directly from our PowerShell window. We then learned how to manage our Office 365 subscriptions, from viewing what licenses and how many we have all the way to assigning licenses—with some services disabled—to users.

We also looked at how to manage Azure AD security groups, from creating them to changing their properties and adding or removing members from them. Lastly, we looked at two business scenarios that showed you how all the things you have learned in this chapter can become useful in real-life scenarios!

In the next chapter, we will look at how to manage SharePoint Online with PowerShell.

CHAPTER 3

Managing SharePoint Online

In this chapter, we will first learn how to use PowerShell to connect to SharePoint Online. We will then learn how to create and manage SharePoint sites and users using the SharePoint PowerShell cmdlets provided to us by Microsoft.

Furthermore, we will look at open source SharePoint/Office 365 Dev PnP PowerShell cmdlets that have been created by the community. We will look at what gaps those cmdlets fill in your day-to-day life and how you can use those cmdlets to make your SharePoint Online admin life easier.

Lastly, we will look at some interesting automation scenarios and examples of how you can automate with PowerShell for SharePoint Online.

Connecting to SharePoint Online

The first thing you have to do is download the SharePoint Online PowerShell module and connect to SharePoint Online. To get the PowerShell module for SharePoint Online, you need to download the SharePoint Online Management Shell from the Microsoft Download Center.

Note The SharePoint Online Management Shell can be downloaded at `https://www.microsoft.com/en-us/download/details.aspx?id=35588`.

Similar to the previous chapter, you need to be on a machine that runs Windows 7 Service Pack 1 or later or Windows Server 2008 R2 Service Pack 1 or later, as well as have an account that has the SharePoint Online Admin role assigned. You will also need to be a local administrator on your computer.

47

V. Catrinescu, *Essential PowerShell for Office 365*, https://doi.org/10.1007/978-1-4842-3129-6_3

Once you have downloaded the SharePoint Online Management Shell, you can start the installation. The first step is to accept the terms, as seen in Figure 3-1.

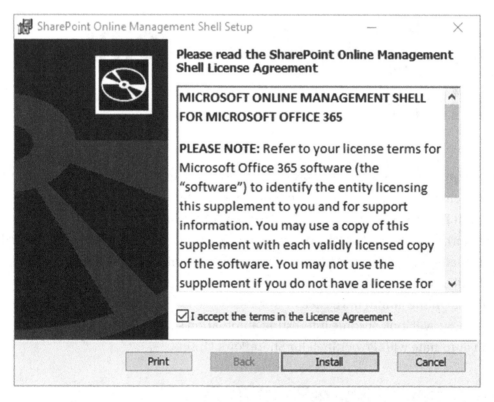

Figure 3-1. *SharePoint Online Management Shell Setup*

You then simply click on the "Install" button, and that is about it! To start managing SharePoint Online, you have to open either the SharePoint Online Management Shell or a normal PowerShell window and run the following cmdlet to import the SharePoint Online module:

```
Import-Module Microsoft.Online.SharePoint.PowerShell
```

The next parameter you will need to know is the URL of your SharePoint Online Admin Center. This URL is usually under the format of `https://<O365 Organization Name>-admin.sharepoint.com`. The easiest way to find it is by navigating to the Office 365 Admin Center, then navigating to the SharePoint Online Admin Center and copying the URL, as seen in Figure 3-2.

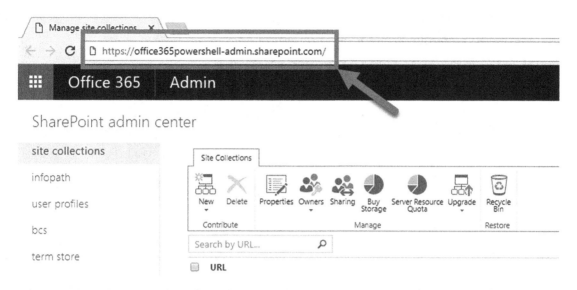

Figure 3-2. *The SharePoint Online Admin Center*

Now that you have all the information that you need, open the SharePoint
Management Shell as an administrator and run the following cmdlet to get the
credentials of the account with which you want to connect to SharePoint Online:

```
$cred = get-credential
```

The preceding command line will open up a PowerShell credential request pop-up
as seen in Figure 3-3 and will save it in a variable called $cred.

Note   PowerShell will not do any validation of the credentials you enter in the
pop-up window.

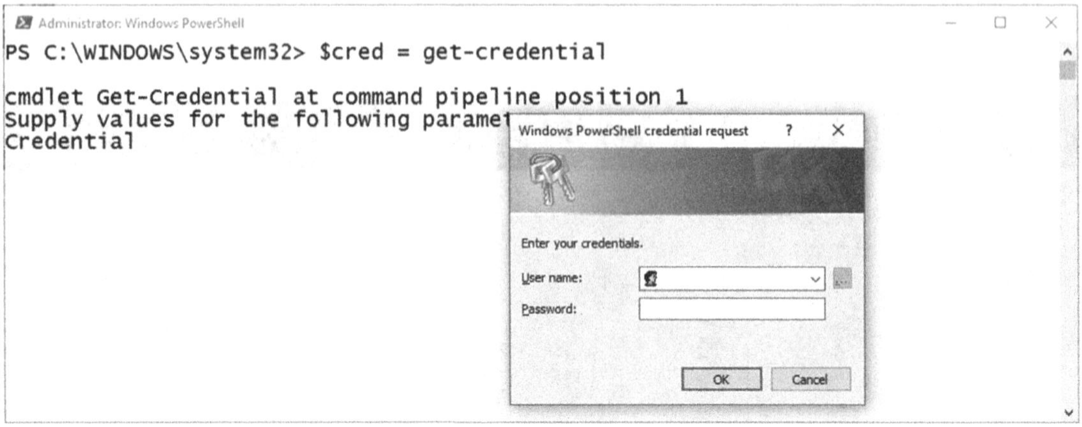

Figure 3-3. *Get-Credential*

Afterward, you will have to run the `Connect-SPOService` cmdlet and specify the URL of the SharePoint Online Admin Center you got earlier, as well as the credential you just saved. For example, to connect to the tenant you saw in Figure 3-2, you would run the following cmdlet:

```
Connect-SPOService -Url https://office365powershell-admin.sharepoint.com/
-Credential $cred
```

As seen in Figure 3-4, when connecting to SharePoint Online, no news is good news.

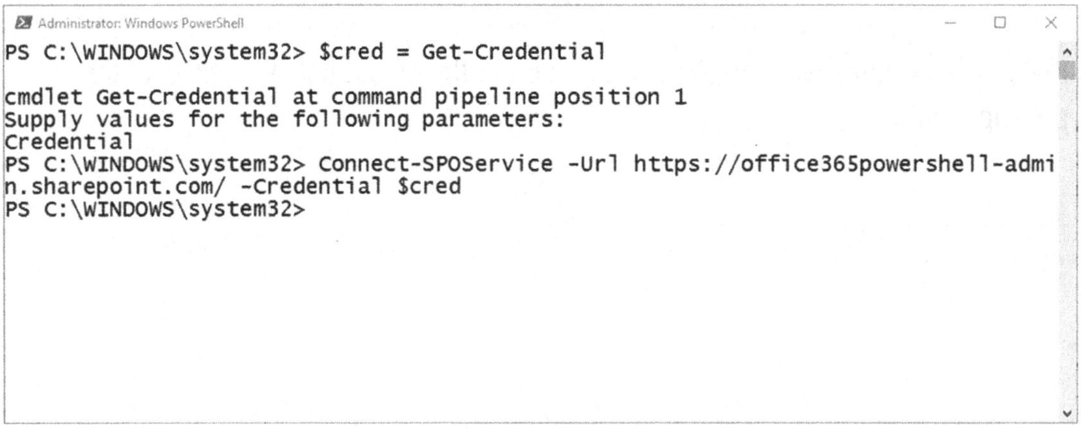

Figure 3-4. *Connecting to SharePoint Online*

Something to be aware of is that the procedure to connect to SharePoint Online is a little bit different if you have Multi-Factor Authentication (MFA) enabled. In that case, skip the previous cmdlets and simply run the `Connect-SPOService` cmdlet with the URL of your SharePoint Online Admin Center, as seen in the following command line. A pop-up will open that asks you for the credentials, as well as provides further instructions on how to provide additional authentication information, such as a verification code.

```
Connect-SPOService -Url https://office365powershell-admin.sharepoint.com/
```

You are now ready to begin executing SharePoint Online commands. Let's take a look at what we have available.

Executing PowerShell cmdlets in SharePoint Online

While the number of cmdlets in the SharePoint Online PowerShell module can change each month because of the nature of the cloud, let's take a look at some of the cmdlets that are currently available. If you want to get a list of the latest cmdlets available to you, simply run the `Get-Command` cmdlet and specify the SharePoint Online PowerShell module, as seen here:

```
Get-Command -Module Microsoft.Online.SharePoint.PowerShell
```

The Available cmdlets

Let's first look at the PowerShell cmdlets to manage Site Collections in SharePoint Online. Table 3-1 below lists the most common PowerShell cmdlets for Site Collection Management.

Table 3-1. *Site Collection cmdlets in SharePoint Online*

Cmdlet	Description
Get-SPOSite	Returns one or more site collections
New-SPOSite	Creates a new SharePoint Online site collection
Remove-SPOSite	Sends a SharePoint Online site collection to the SharePoint Online Recycle Bin
Repair-SPOSite	Checks and repairs the site collection and its contents
Set-SPOSite	Sets or updates one or more properties' values for a site collection
Test-SPOSite	Tests a SharePoint Online site collection
Upgrade-SPOSite	Starts the upgrade process on a site collection
Get-SPODeletedSite	Returns all deleted site collections from the Recycle Bin
Remove-SPODeletedSite	Removes a SharePoint Online deleted site collection from the Recycle Bin
Restore-SPODeletedSite	Restores a SharePoint Online deleted site collection from the Recycle Bin

We then have the cmdlets that allow us to manage our tenant, seen in Table 3-2. Those cmdlets allow us to view or change settings at the tenant level, such as sharing default settings and content delivery network (CDN) settings as well as more advanced ones like setting a list of allowed IP addresses that can access the tenant.

Table 3-2. *Tenant-level cmdlets in SharePoint Online*

Cmdlet	Description
Get-SPOTenant	Returns SharePoint Online organization properties
Get-SPOTenantCdnEnabled	Returns whether public content delivery network (CDN) or private CDN is enabled on the tenant level
Get-SPOTenantCdnOrigins	Lists all the configured origins under the tenancy or under a given site
Get-SPOTenantCdnPolicies	Returns the content delivery network (CDN) policies from a tenant level
Get-SPOTenantSyncClientRestriction	Returns the current OneDrive for Business Sync configuration status
Get-SPOTenantLogEntry	Retrieves SharePoint Online company logs
Set-SPOTenant	Sets properties on the SharePoint Online organization
Set-SPOTenantCdnEnabled	Enables or disables public content delivery network (CDN) or private CDN on the tenant level
Set-SPOTenantCdnPolicy	Sets the content delivery network (CDN) policies from the tenant level
Set-SPOTenantSyncClientRestriction	Controls tenant-wide options and restrictions specific to syncing files

Finally, some of the other cmdlets you will use a lot are the cmdlets that have to do with users and SharePoint groups; these can be seen in Table 3-3.

Table 3-3. *User- and SharePoint Groups–level cmdlets in SharePoint Online*

Cmdlet	Description
Get-SPOExternalUser	Returns external users in the tenant
Get-SPOSiteGroup	Gets all the groups on the specified site collection
Get-SPOUser	Returns the SharePoint Online user or security group accounts that match a given search criteria
New-SPOSiteGroup	Creates a new group in a SharePoint Online site collection
Remove-SPOSiteGroup	Removes a SharePoint Online group from a site collection
Remove-SPOUser	Removes a user or a security group from a site collection or a group
Set-SPOSiteGroup	Gets all the groups on the specified site collection
Set-SPOUser	Configures properties on an existing user

Managing Sites

Now that we have looked at some of the available cmdlets, let's start you off using them. First, simply output a list of all the site collections that exist in your tenant. To do so, you need to run the Get-SPOSite cmdlet. The SharePoint Online Management Shell will show you all the URLs, the owner, and the storage quota, as seen in Figure 3-5.

```
Administrator: Windows PowerShell                                                    —  □  ×
PS C:\WINDOWS\system32> get-sposite

Url                                                                 Owner Storage Quota
---                                                                 ----- -------------
https://office365powershell.sharepoint.com/search                         26214400
https://office365powershell.sharepoint.com/portals/hub                    26214400
https://office365powershell.sharepoint.com/sites/Project-ABC123           26214400
https://office365powershell.sharepoint.com/portals/Community              26214400
https://office365powershell.sharepoint.com/teams/HR                       26214400
https://office365powershell.sharepoint.com/sites/powershellforoffice365book 1048576
https://office365powershell-my.sharepoint.com/                            26214400
https://office365powershell.sharepoint.com/                               26214400
https://office365powershell.sharepoint.com/teams/Marketing Team Site      26214400
```

Figure 3-5. *Get-SPOSite*

Note   In some cases, PowerShell will return a warning that because there are too many site collections, they have not all been returned. To show all the site collections, add the -Limit All parameter. Your full cmdlet will be Get-SPOSite -Limit All.

You can also use PowerShell to display all the properties of the site collection directly in the window. For example, you can output the URL, title, and template for each site by running the following cmdlet:

```
Get-SPOSite | Select Url, Title, Template
```

The results can be seen in Figure 3-6.

```
Administrator: Windows PowerShell                                                            –  □  ×
PS C:\WINDOWS\system32> get-sposite | Select Url, Title, Template

Url                                                            Title                         Template
---                                                            -----                         --------
https://office365powershell.sharepoint.com/search                                            SRCHCEN#0
https://office365powershell.sharepoint.com/portals/hub         PointPublishing Hub Site      POINTPUBL...
https://office365powershell.sharepoint.com/sites/Project-ABC123 Project-ABC123               STS#0
https://office365powershell.sharepoint.com/portals/Community   Community                     POINTPUBL...
https://office365powershell.sharepoint.com/teams/HR            HR Team Site                  STS#0
https://office365powershell.sharepoint.com/sites/powershellforoffice365book PowerShell for Office 365 Book GROUP#0
https://office365powershell-my.sharepoint.com/                                               SPSMSITEH...
https://office365powershell.sharepoint.com/                    Learn-PowerShell Team Site    EHS#1
https://office365powershell.sharepoint.com/teams/Marketing Team Site Marketing Team Site     STS#0


PS C:\WINDOWS\system32>
```

Figure 3-6. *Get-SPOSite*

Tip   To view all the available properties of a cmdlet, pipe the `Get-Member` cmdlet on it. For example, to see all the available properties of the `Get-SPOSite` cmdlet, run `Get-SPOSite | Get-Member`.

Now, let's take a look at how to create a new site collection. You will use the New-SPOSite cmdlet, and you will need to provide three mandatory parameters: Url, Owner, and StorageQuota. Some of the optional parameters you might find useful are LocaleID, TimeZoneID, Title, and Template. For all the parameters and what they do, you can go to the TechNet page of the New-SPOSite cmdlet to find the latest information.

Tip   You can navigate to the TechNet page of a cmdlet without ever quitting PowerShell by using the `Get-Help` cmdlet! One of the switches of the cmdlet is `-online`, and specifying that switch will open the TechNet page of the cmdlet in your default browser. In this example, you would run the following cmdlet to navigate to the TechNet Page of the New-SPOSite cmdlet:
`Get-Help New-SPOSite -online`

Let's say you want to create a site collection with the URL https://office365powershell .sharepoint.com/teams/IT, with the title "IT Team Site," with language set to "English – United States," and with the Team Site template. Therefore, run the following cmdlet:

```
New-SPOSite `
       -Url https://office365powershell.sharepoint.com/teams/IT `
       -Owner vlad-admin@office365powershell.ca `
       -StorageQuota 1024 `
       -LocaleID 1033 -Template "STS#0" `
       -Title "IT Team Site"
```

To remove a site collection, you can run the Remove-SPOSite cmdlet, and the only mandatory parameter is the URL of the site you want to remove. You can also specify the Confirm parameter to skip the confirmation. To remove the site you just created, you would run the following cmdlet:

```
Remove-SPOSite -Identity https://office365powershell.sharepoint.com/teams/IT
```

Since you did not specify the Confirm parameter, PowerShell will ask for a confirmation of whether that's what you really want to do, as seen in Figure 3-7.

```
Administrator: Windows PowerShell                                                    –  □  ×
PS C:\WINDOWS\system32> Remove-SPOSite -Identity https://office365powershell.sharepoint.com/teams/IT

Confirm
Are you sure you want to perform this action?
Performing the operation "Remove-SPOSite" on target "https://office365powershell.sharepoint.com/teams/IT".
[Y] Yes  [A] Yes to All  [N] No  [L] No to All  [S] Suspend  [?] Help (default is "Y"):
```

Figure 3-7. *Remove-SPOSite*

To use the same cmdlet without the confirmation, you would need to include
-Confirm:$false, as seen in the following example:

```
Remove-SPOSite `
    -Identity https://office365powershell.sharepoint.com/teams/IT `
    -Confirm:$false
```

When you delete a site in SharePoint Online, it will go to a Site Collection Recycle
Bin. You can view all the sites in the SharePoint Online Site Collection Recycle Bin by
running the Get-SPODeletedSite cmdlet. PowerShell will show you the information
about the site, as well as deletion time and days remaining until the site is permanently
deleted. As you can see in Figure 3-8, the site was deleted on July 3, 2017, and still has 30
days remaining until it's permanently deleted.

Figure 3-8. *Get-SPODeletedSite*

You can restore this site by using the Restore-SPODeletedSite cmdlet. The only
parameter you have to specify is -Identity, and you must provide the URL of the site
collection you want to restore, as seen in this example:

```
Restore-SPODeletedSite -Identity https://office365powershell.sharepoint.
com/teams/IT
```

Next up, you will focus on the site collection you have created and learn how you can
change some of the properties. Because you will be modifying multiple properties on
your site, the first thing you should do is save the SPOSite in a variable so you can reuse
this variable instead of typing in the URL every time. This can be done using the
Get-SPOSite cmdlet and saving the output in a variable called $site, as seen here:

```
$site = Get-SPOSite -Identity https://office365powershell.sharepoint.com/teams/IT
```

Once you have saved your site in the $site variable, you can easily look through all its properties, as seen in Figure 3-9.

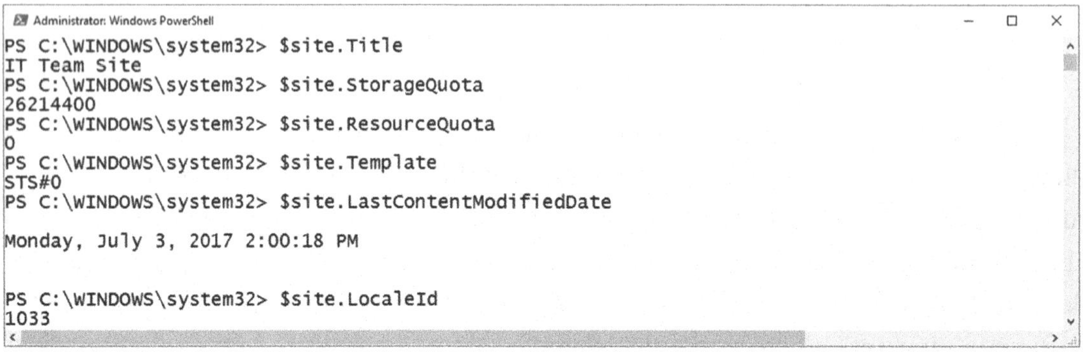

```
Administrator: Windows PowerShell                                           —  □  ×
PS C:\WINDOWS\system32> $site.Title
IT Team Site
PS C:\WINDOWS\system32> $site.StorageQuota
26214400
PS C:\WINDOWS\system32> $site.ResourceQuota
0
PS C:\WINDOWS\system32> $site.Template
STS#0
PS C:\WINDOWS\system32> $site.LastContentModifiedDate

Monday, July 3, 2017 2:00:18 PM


PS C:\WINDOWS\system32> $site.LocaleId
1033
```

Figure 3-9. *SPOSite properties*

You can also change the properties of a site. For example, you can change the title of your SharePoint Online Site Collection by running Set-SPOSite and specifying the parameter that you want to change:

```
Set-SPOSite $site `
    -Title "Information Technology Team Site"
```

You can also specify the sharing capabilities of a certain site collection. By default, when creating a new site collection in SharePoint Online, users inside that site collection can only share it with users who are a part of your organization. When looking at the Sharing screen in the user interface, there are four options, as seen in Figure 3-10.

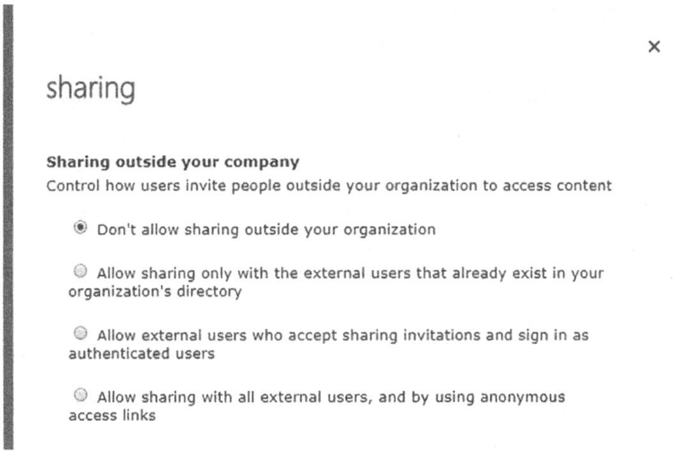

Figure 3-10. *Sharing options in the SharePoint Online Admin Center*

Of course, these settings can also be managed via PowerShell and the
SharingCapability parameter. For example, to change this site to allow external users
who accept sharing invitations and sign in as authenticated users, you would run the
following cmdlet:

```
Set-SPOSite $site -SharingCapability ExternalUserSharingOnly
```

Since there are four options in the user interface, you also have four options in
PowerShell; you can find the mapping of the PowerShell value with the UI value in
Table 3-4.

Table 3-4. *Mapping of the SharingCapability Parameter Options with the Admin Center*

PowerShell Value	User Interface Option
Disabled	Don't allow sharing outside your organization.
ExternalUserSharingOnly	Allow external users who accept sharing invitations and sign in as authenticated users.
ExternalUserAndGuestSharing	Allow sharing with all external users and by using anonymous access links.
ExistingExternalUserSharingOnly	Allow sharing only with the external users that already exist in your organization's directory.

By knowing these values, you can also query SharePoint Online via PowerShell and easily see a list of your sites and what sharing options they have, which you couldn't easily do from the user interface. For example, to see all the SharePoint Online site collections where users are allowed to share to both logged-in external users and anonymous users, you would run the following cmdlet:

```
Get-SPOSite | Where {$_.SharingCapability -eq
"ExternalUserAndGuestSharing"} | Select Url
```

As a result, you would see a list of URLs where sharing is set to external users and anonymous, as seen in Figure 3-11.

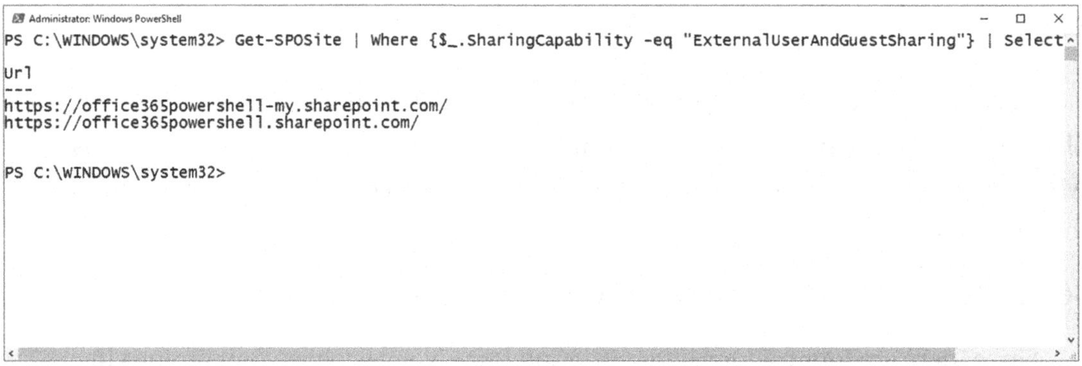

Figure 3-11. *Sites with the ExternalUserAndGuestSharing sharing option*

Something else that you might want to change is whether you want to allow non-owners to invite new users. By default in SharePoint Online, users in the "Members" group can invite other people to your site, but you might not want to allow this. Luckily, you can change this setting by using either the user interface or PowerShell. To change it via PowerShell, run the `Set-SPOSite` cmdlet, give the site URL or `SPOSite` object, and then use the `DisableSharingForNonOwners` switch. In this example, you would run the following cmdlet:

```
Set-SPOSite $site -DisableSharingForNonOwners
```

To further secure your site collection as a SharePoint Online admin, you can limit the sharing options by domain. You can either create a list of allowed domains or set a list of blocked domains. You do this using the `Set-SPOSite` cmdlet and the `SharingDomain RestrictionMode` parameter. You can find the accepted values in Table 3-5.

Table 3-5. *SharingDomainRestrictionMode Available Values*

Value	Description
None	Feature not enabled
AllowList	Allow sharing only with users from these domains.
BlockList	Don't allow sharing with users from these blocked domains.

In the same cmdlet, you will need to provide a space-delimited list of domains you want to allow, which is done using the SharingAllowedDomainList parameter, or a list of domains you want to block, which is done via the SharingBlockedDomainList. For example, to set your site collection to only allow users from the Contoso.com, vNext. solutions, and Microsoft.com domains, you would run the following cmdlet:

```
Set-SPOSite $site -SharingDomainRestrictionMode "AllowList"
-SharingAllowedDomainList "contoso.com vnext.solutions microsoft.com"
```

If you wanted to allow all domains except the domains just specified, you would run the following cmdlet:

```
Set-SPOSite $site -SharingDomainRestrictionMode "BlockList"
-SharingBlockedDomainList "contoso.com vnext.solutions microsoft.com"
```

Now that we have looked at how to create, delete, and modify site collections in SharePoint Online, let's learn how to manage users and groups.

Managing Users and Groups

Managing users' and groups' access to SharePoint is a critical part of your job as a SharePoint Online admin. By using PowerShell you are able to view the users in a site collection as well as what groups they are a part of.

The first cmdlet that you have is Get-SPOSiteGroup, which allows you to see all the groups in a certain site, as well as what permissions those groups have on a certain site collection. When running the cmdlet, you simply need to specify the -Site parameter and either give it the URL of a SharePoint Online site collection or a SPOSite object. In Figure 3-12, you can see all the groups of the IT site collection you saved in the $site variable earlier in this chapter, as well as the members in each group and the permissions those groups have on the site.

```
Administrator: Windows PowerShell                                                        —   □   ×
PS C:\WINDOWS\system32> Get-SPOSiteGroup -Site $site

LoginName       : Excel Services Viewers
Title           : Excel Services Viewers
OwnerLoginName  : SHAREPOINT\system
OwnerTitle      : System Account
Users           : {}
Roles           : {View Only}

LoginName       : IT Team Site Members
Title           : IT Team Site Members
OwnerLoginName  : IT Team Site Owners
OwnerTitle      : IT Team Site Owners
Users           : {jeff@office365powershell.ca, vanessa@office365powershell.ca}
Roles           : {Edit}

LoginName       : IT Team Site Owners
Title           : IT Team Site Owners
OwnerLoginName  : IT Team Site Owners
OwnerTitle      : IT Team Site Owners
Users           : {SHAREPOINT\system}
Roles           : {Full Control}

LoginName       : IT Team Site Visitors
Title           : IT Team Site Visitors
OwnerLoginName  : IT Team Site Owners
OwnerTitle      : IT Team Site Owners
Users           : {}
Roles           : {Read}
```

Figure 3-12. *Get-SPOSiteGroup*

If you get a bit more advanced, you can create a small PowerShell script that will loop through all the groups in a site collection and then show you the members inside. If you look at the following script, you will see that you first get all the groups in the $site site collection and save them in a variable called $Groups. You then loop through each group and simply do another Get-SPOSiteGroup, but this time you specify the group you want by using the -Group parameter and giving it the group title, and then you select the Users property.

```
$Groups = Get-SPOSiteGroup -Site $site
foreach ($Group in $Groups)
    {
        Write-Host $Group.Title -ForegroundColor "Blue"
        Get-SPOSiteGroup -Site $site -Group $Group.Title |    Select-Object
        -ExpandProperty Users
        Write-Host
    }
```

The result seen in Figure 3-13 is a list of users in each SharePoint Online group.

```
Administrator: Windows PowerShell                                                       —   □   ×
PS C:\WINDOWS\system32> $Groups = Get-SPOSiteGroup -Site $site
PS C:\WINDOWS\system32> foreach ($Group in $Groups)
>>      {
>>          Write-Host $Group.Title -ForegroundColor "Blue"
>>          Get-SPOSiteGroup -Site $site -Group $Group.Title | Select-Object -ExpandProperty Users
>>          Write-Host
>>      }
IT Team Site Members
jeff@office365powershell.ca
vanessa@office365powershell.ca

IT Team Site Owners
SHAREPOINT\system
vlad-admin@office365powershell.ca

IT Team Site Visitors
john@office365powershell.ca

PS C:\WINDOWS\system32>
```

Figure 3-13. *List of users per SharePoint Online group*

You can also query all the users in a site directly by using the Get-SPOUser cmdlet and specifying the site. This will return all the users in the site, as well as what groups they are a part of, as seen in Figure 3-14.

```
Administrator: Windows PowerShell                                                       —   □   ×
PS C:\WINDOWS\system32> Get-SPOUser -Site $site

Display Name                Login Name                                              Groups
------------                ----------                                              ------
Company Administrator       s-1-5-21-1655370125-2674026898-3842197393-1811256       {}
Everyone                    true                                                    {}
Everyone except external users spo-grid-all-users/545c04df-2411-4d58-9378-7ec79e9e6b8e {}
Jeff Collins                jeff@office365powershell.ca                             {IT Team Site Members}
John Smith                  john@office365powershell.ca                             {IT Team Site Visit...
SharePoint App              app@sharepoint                                          {}
System Account              SHAREPOINT\system                                       {IT Team Site Owners}
Vanessa Lee                 vanessa@office365powershell.ca                          {IT Team Site Members}
Vlad Admin                  vlad-admin@office365powershell.ca                       {IT Team Site Owners}
Vlad Catrinescu             vlad_vnext.solutions#ext#@office365powershell.ca        {IT Team Site Members}
YLO001\_spocrwl_818_18467   ylo001\_spocrwl_818_18467                               {}

PS C:\WINDOWS\system32>
```

Figure 3-14. *Users in the IT site collection*

Another cmdlet that will be useful is the Get-SPOExternalUser cmdlet, which allows you to view all the users outside the company that have permission on at least one site in your tenant.

The Get-SPOExternalUser cmdlet accepts the cmdlets seen in Table 3-6.

Table 3-6. *Get-SPOExternalUser Properties*

Parameter	Description
Filter	Limits the results to only those users whose first name, last name, or email address begins with the text in the string, using a case-insensitive comparison
PageSize	Specifies the maximum number of users to be returned in the collection. The value must be less than or equal to 50.
Position	Used to specify the zero-based index of the position in the sorted collection of the first result to be returned
SiteUrl	Specifies the site to retrieve external users for. If no site is specified, the external users for all sites are returned.
SortOrder	Specifies the sort results in ascending or descending.

In Figure 3-15, I am running the Get-SPOExternalUser cmdlet and selecting the first 50 external users in my tenant. As you can see, I currently only have one external user in my organization.

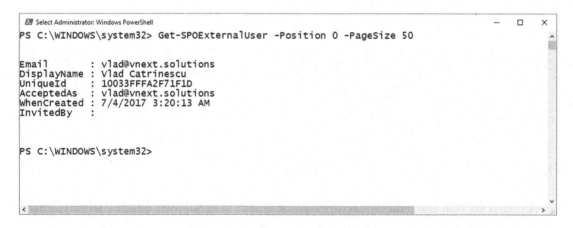

Figure 3-15. *The first 50 external users from my tenant*

Furthermore, if you specify the site collection, as seen in Figure 3-16, you also have access to the information on who invited this user to the site collection, which can be very valuable if you need more information about this external user.

```
Administrator: Windows PowerShell                                    —    □    ×
PS C:\WINDOWS\system32> Get-SPOExternalUser -Position 0 -PageSize 50 -SiteUrl $site.url


Email       : vlad@vnext.solutions
DisplayName : Vlad Catrinescu
UniqueId    : 10033FFFA2F71F1D
AcceptedAs  : vlad@vnext.solutions
WhenCreated : 7/4/2017 3:20:13 AM
InvitedBy   : vlad-admin@office365powershell.ca


PS C:\WINDOWS\system32> _
```

Figure 3-16. *External users in a certain site collection*

The previous examples only showed the first 50 External Users from your tenant, or from the Site Collection you have specified. In order to return more than 50, you will have to create a loop that will get 50 users at a time, while changing the Position parameter. The following script will return all the external users from the tenant

```
try {
    for ($i=0;;$i+=50) {
        $ExternalUsers += Get-SPOExternalUser -PageSize 50 -Position
        $i -ea Stop
    }
}
catch {
}
$ExternalUsers
```

PowerShell can also be used to add users to certain groups. For example, if I wanted to add John Smith to the IT Team Site Members group, I would run the following cmdlet:

```
Add-SPOUser -Site $site -LoginName john@office365powershell.ca -Group "IT
Team Site Members"
```

You can also remove users from a group by using the `Remove-SPOUser` cmdlet and the same parameters. If you do not specify the `-Group` parameter, the user will be removed from all the groups:

```
Remove-SPOUser -Site $site -LoginName john@office365powershell.ca -Group
"IT Team Site Members"
```

If you want to create a new group, you can do so with the New-SPOSiteGroup cmdlet. You will need to specify the site where you want to create the new group, the group name, and what permission level you want the group to have. In the following example, I create a new SharePoint Online Group named IT Managers that has full control on my site:

```
New-SPOSiteGroup -Site $site -Group "IT Managers" -PermissionLevels "Full Control"
```

Now that we have reviewed what we can do with PowerShell to manage our users and groups, let's take a look at what settings we can configure at the tenant level.

Managing Tenant-level Settings

When you make changes at the tenant level, you affect all the site collections and the users in your organization, so it is important to understand what a certain cmdlet does before running it as it may change the way users in your organization get things done. First of all, you can use the Get-SPOTenant cmdlet to view all the settings of your tenant. This will not only give you all the current properties of your tenant, but will also show you a list of the properties that you can change. In Table 3-7, you can see some of the most popular ones.

Table 3-7. *Set-SPOTenant Properties*

Parameter	Description
BccExternalSharingInvitations	Enables the BCC for External Sharing feature. When the feature is enabled, all external sharing invitations will blind copy the email messages listed in the BccExternalSharingsInvitationList. Accepts a value of true (enabled) or false (disabled). By default, this feature is set to false.
BccExternalSharingInvitationsList	Specifies a list of email addresses to be BCC'd when the BCC for External Sharing feature is enabled. Multiple addresses can be specified by creating a comma-separated list with no spaces.

(continued)

Table 3-7. (*continued*)

Parameter	Description
DefaultSharingLinkType	Lets administrators choose what type of link is selected in the "Get a Link" sharing dialog box in OneDrive for Business and SharePoint Online. The values are: • None • Direct • Internal • AnonymousAccess
DisplayStartASiteOption	Determines whether tenant users see the "Start a Site" menu option
StartASiteFormUrl	Specifies URL of the form to load in the "Start a Site" dialog
OneDriveStorageQuota	Sets a default OneDrive for Business storage quota for the tenant. It will be used for new OneDrive for Business sites created.
OrphanedPersonalSites RetentionPeriod	Specifies the number of days after a user's Active Directory account is deleted that their OneDrive for Business content will be deleted. The value range is in days, between 30 and 3650. The default value is 30.
RequireAcceptingAccountMatch InvitedAccount	Ensures that an external user can only accept an external sharing invitation with an account matching the invited email address. The parameter accepts two values: True or False. True—User must accept this invitation with bob@contoso.com. False—When a document is shared with an external user, bob@contoso.com, it can be accepted by any user with access to the invitation link in the original email.

(*continued*)

Table 3-7. (*continued*)

Parameter	Description
RequireAnonymousLinksExpireInDays	Specifies that all anonymous links that have been created (or will be created) will expire after the set number of days
SharingDomainRestrictionMode	Specifies the external sharing mode for domains. The allowed values are: • None • AllowList • BlockList
SharingAllowedDomainList	Specifies a list of email domains that are allowed for sharing with external collaborators. Use the space character as the delimiter for entering multiple values.
SharingBlockedDomainList	Specifies a list of email domains that are blocked or prohibited for sharing with external collaborators. Use space character as the delimiter for entering multiple values.
SharingCapability	Determines what level of sharing is available for the site. The possible values are: Disabled—external user sharing (share by email) and guest link sharing are both disabled; ExternalUserSharingOnly—external user sharing (share by email) is enabled, but guest link sharing is disabled; or ExternalUserAndGuestSharing—external user sharing (share by email) and guest link sharing are both enabled.

You can change all these properties with the Set-SPOTenant PowerShell cmdlet. For example, let's say you want to make the following changes to your tenant to adhere to business regulations and security requirements:

- BCC yourself and admin@office365powershell.ca on all external invites

- Set the default sharing link type to Internal

- Hide the "New Site" button in the SharePoint home

- Keep the MySites of users who have been deleted from the Active Directory for ten years

- Require external users to log in with the same account that the invite was sent to

- Only allow your users to share with external users that log in, and do not allow them to create anonymous links

To meet those requirements, you would run the following cmdlet:

```
Set-SPOTenant `
    -BccExternalSharingInvitations $true `
    -BccExternalSharingInvitationsList "vlad-admin@office365powershell.
     ca,admin@office365powershell.ca" `
    -DefaultSharingLinkType Internal `
    -DisplayStartASiteOption $false `
    -OrphanedPersonalSitesRetentionPeriod 3650 `
    -RequireAcceptingAccountMatchInvitedAccount $true `
    -SharingCapability ExternalUserSharingOnly
```

Some other settings not included in the Get/Set-SPOTenant cmdlets are the settings for OneDrive for Business. Office 365 allows you to configure OneDrive for Business to only allow users to sync files on a domain-joined machine, as well as to block certain extensions. This can be done by using the Set-SPOTenantSyncClientRestriction cmdlet. In Table 3-8 you can find some the parameters of this cmdlet.

Table 3-8. *Set-SPOTenantSyncClientRestriction Parameters*

Parameter	Description
BlockMacSync	Block Mac sync clients—the Beta version and the new sync client (OneDrive.exe) The values for this parameter are True and False. The default value is False.
DomainGuids	Sets the domain GUID to add to the safe recipient list. Requires a minimum of one domain GUID. The maximum number of domain GUIDs allowed is 125.
Enable	Enables the feature to block sync originating from domains that are not present in the safe recipients list
ExcludedFile Extensions	Blocks certain file types from syncing with the new sync client (OneDrive.exe).

> **Tip**   To find out your domain GUID for the -DomainGuids parameter, follow this guide on TechNet: https://technet.microsoft.com/en-us/library/dn938435.aspx.

For example, let's say you have the following business requirements:

- Users can only sync OneDrive for Business to computers joined to the office365powershell.ca domain.

- Users on a MAC cannot use OneDrive for Business to sync files.

- Users cannot sync JavaScript files with OneDrive for Business.

Before running the Set-SPOTenantSyncClientRestriction cmdlet, it's important to note that this cmdlet uses parameter sets; therefore, you might not be able to specify all the parameters that you want in a single cmdlet. You can view the parameter sets by using the Get-Help cmdlet, as seen in Figure 3-17. Because of the parameter sets, you cannot, for example, specify the -Enable, -DomainGuids, and -ExcludeFileExtensions parameters in the same cmdlet.

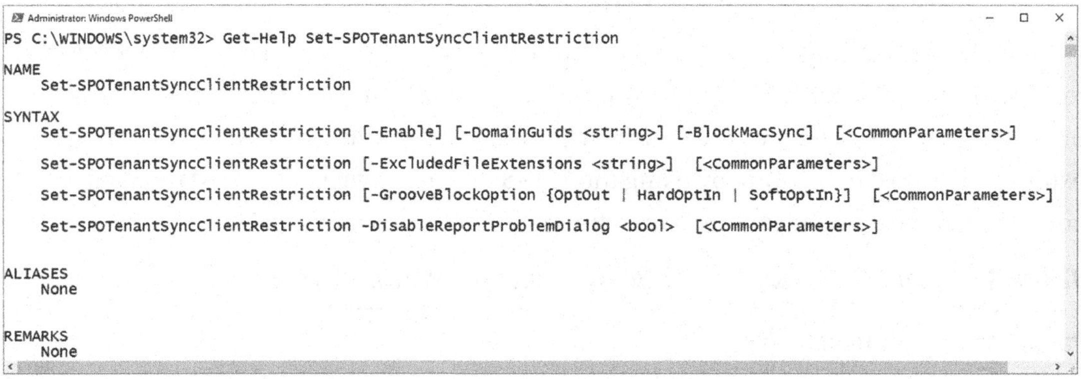

Figure 3-17.   Set-SPOTenantSyncClientRestriction parameter sets

In going back to the example, you will find that the PowerShell cmdlets to follow the business requirements discussed are as follows:

```
Set-SPOTenantSyncClientRestriction -Enable -DomainGuids "508C857F-B879-
4413-AB1E-AC33FA7D4477" -BlockMacSync:$true
Set-SPOTenantSyncClientRestriction -ExcludedFileExtensions "js"
```

Note   It may take up to 24 hours for the sync restriction to take effect.

That completes the tour around the PowerShell cmdlets available for your tenant, and thus, when you include the previous sections, we have looked at all the available cmdlets for SharePoint Online. You might think that you are very limited in what you can do versus, for example, SharePoint On-Premises, and that is not untrue. There are no PowerShell cmdlets to create SharePoint subsites, or lists/libraries in the SharePoint Online PowerShell module provided by Microsoft, so, out of the box, you are limited in what you can do. Luckily, the huge community behind SharePoint and Office 365 has built some extensions for PowerShell that allow us to get more cmdlets.

Community Extensions

Even if the SharePoint Online PowerShell module has a limited number of cmdlets, Office 365 administrators with development skills are able to do more by using the client-side object model (CSOM) and SharePoint Online APIs directly from PowerShell. However, since most Office 365 administrators are IT professionals that do not write code on a daily basis, this is not the easiest option.

While there are a few community-created extensions for SharePoint Online PowerShell out there, this book will focus on the OfficeDev Patterns and Practices (PnP) PowerShell cmdlets. If you are new to the SharePoint PnP program, here is a definition from their site at `https://dev.office.com/patterns-and-practices`:

> *"SharePoint Patterns and Practices (PnP) is an open source initiative coordinated by SharePoint engineering. It's a channel for the SharePoint engineering to share documentation, guidance, samples and reusable component for the community. PnP initiative coordinates all SharePoint developer documentation and guidance across on-premises and online. Day to day work is coordinated by the PnP Core team, which consists of Microsoft internal people and external MVPs."*

While most of what the PnP program publishes is code samples, there is also a PowerShell extension for Office 365 that contains over 200 cmdlets for SharePoint Online and Office 365. Let's first look at how to get the module installed on your computer.

Getting the Office 365 Dev PnP PowerShell Cmdlets

The Office 365 Dev PnP PowerShell Cmdlets is an open source project that is hosted on GitHub and can be found at https://github.com/SharePoint/PnP-PowerShell. You will find all the latest releases as well as the documentation for each cmdlet in the extension.

There are two options to install the module. The first—and recommended—option is to install them from the PowerShell gallery. If you are running Windows 10, you can use the PowerShell gallery without installing any extra software. If you are running an older version of Windows, you will need to install Windows Management Framework (WMF) 5.0 or download the PowerShellGet module from the Microsoft Download Center.

Note   Download links for the latest PowerShellGet module can be found on the PowerShell gallery home page at https://www.powershellgallery.com/.

Once these prerequisites have been met, you simply need to run the following cmdlet to install the latest version of the SharePoint Patterns and Practices PowerShell Cmdlets for SharePoint Online on your computer:

```
Install-Module -Name SharePointPnPPowerShellOnline
```

The second option is to download a setup package from the "Releases" section of the PnP PowerShell GitHub repository, which you can find at https://github.com/SharePoint/PnP-PowerShell/releases.

If you already have a version of the PnP PowerShell Cmdlets installed, you can either download the latest setup package or, if you got the cmdlets from the PowerShell gallery, run the following cmdlet:

```
Update-Module SharePointPnPPowerShell*
```

Now that we have the latest version of the cmdlets installed, let's learn how to use them to connect to SharePoint Online.

Connecting to SharePoint

Connecting to SharePoint Online using this module is a bit different than connecting with the Microsoft official module since with the PnP PowerShell module you connect to a particular site collection instead of connecting to the whole tenant. You will first need to get the credential by using the Get-Credential cmdlet and saving it to a variable as seen here:

```
$cred = Get-Credential
```

You then need to connect to a site collection by using the Connect-PnPOnline cmdlet, specifying the URL and the credential as seen here:

```
Connect-PnPOnline -Url https://office365powershell.sharepoint.com
-Credentials $cred
```

You are now connected to this site collection and can execute PowerShell cmdlets on it. Let's take a look at those cmdlets.

Sample cmdlets

The PnP SharePoint PowerShell module has over 200 cmdlets that can allow you to do anything from creating new site collections to creating new subsites, lists/libraries, and content types and even adding documents. Let's take a look at a few of the cmdlets we have available.

Tip   Similar to Office 365, the PnP SharePoint PowerShell library is always changing. You can find the latest version of the cmdlets included in this module as well as the help for each cmdlet on the GitHub repository at https://github. com/SharePoint/PnP-PowerShell/blob/master/Documentation/ readme.md.

For this section, we will concentrate on a few sample cmdlets that allow you to do stuff you cannot do with the module provided by Microsoft. For example, by using the New-PnPWeb cmdlet you can create a subsite in the current site collection. You will now create a subsite of the site collection you connected to earlier, being sure to satisfy the business requirements from Table 3-9.

Table 3-9. *Business Requirements for a New Subsite*

Item	Value
Title	Managers Only Site
URL	https://office365powershell.sharepoint.com/Managers
Template	Team Site
Security	Broken inheritance from the top-level site
Locale	English – United States
Description	Use this subsite to communicate about sensitive information between managers.

The PowerShell cmdlet to build this subsite would be as follows:

```
New-PnPWeb -Url Managers `
    -Title "Managers Only Site" `
    -Template "STS#0" `
    -BreakInheritance `
    -Locale 1033 `
    -Description "Use this subsite to communicate about sensitive
      information between managers."
```

You can also create lists or libraries. For example, to create a new list titled "Team Announcements" with the Announcements template, you would run the following cmdlet:

```
New-PnPList -Title "Team Announcements" -Template Announcements
```

Something else the PnP PowerShell module allows you to do is view the recycle bin of your sites as well as restore their content. For example, you can use the Get-PnPRecycleBinItem cmdlet to view all the items in the site collection recycle bin, as seen in Figure 3-18. You could then use the Restore-PnpRecycleBinItem cmdlet to restore an item back to the library.

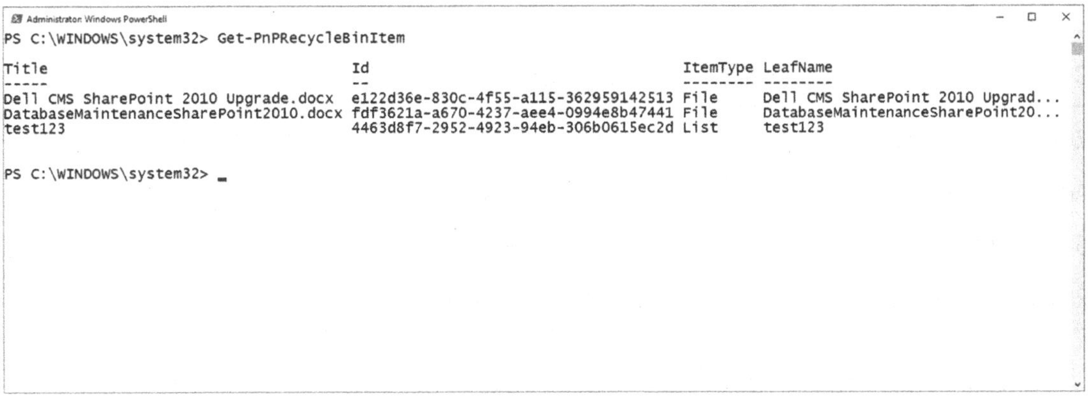

```
Administrator: Windows PowerShell                                                           —   □   ×
PS C:\WINDOWS\system32> Get-PnPRecycleBinItem

Title                               Id                                    ItemType LeafName
-----                               --                                    -------- --------
Dell CMS SharePoint 2010 Upgrade.docx  e122d36e-830c-4f55-a115-362959142513  File     Dell CMS SharePoint 2010 Upgrad...
DatabaseMaintenanceSharePoint2010.docx fdf3621a-a670-4237-aee4-0994e8b47441  File     DatabaseMaintenanceSharePoint20...
test123                             4463d8f7-2952-4923-94eb-306b0615ec2d  List     test123


PS C:\WINDOWS\system32> _
```

Figure 3-18. *Get-PnPRecycleBinItem*

There are also cmdlets for the lists and libraries. In Table 3-10, you can see some of the cmdlets that are available for handling lists and list items.

Table 3-10. *PnP PowerShell cmdlets for Lists*

Cmdlet	Description
Get-PnPDefaultColumnValues	Gets the default column values for all folders in document library
Set-PnPDefaultColumnValues	Sets default column values for a document library
Get-PnPList	Returns a List object
New-PnPList	Creates a new list
Remove-PnPList	Deletes a list
Set-PnPList	Updates list settings
Add-PnPListItem	Adds an item to a list
Get-PnPListItem	Retrieves list items
Remove-PnPListItem	Deletes an item from a list
Set-PnPListItem	Updates a list item
Set-PnPListItemPermission	Sets list item's permissions
Move-PnPListItemToRecycleBin	Moves an item from a list to the recycle bin
Set-PnPListPermission	Sets list's permissions

(*continued*)

Table 3-10. (*continued*)

Cmdlet	Description
Request-PnPReIndexList	Marks the list for full indexing during the next incremental crawl
Add-PnPView	Adds a view to a list
Get-PnPView	Returns one or all views from a list
Remove-PnPView	Deletes a view from a list

In Table 3-11, you can see some of the cmdlets used to manage files and folders within document libraries.

Table 3-11. *PnP PowerShell cmdlet for Files and Folders*

Cmdlet	Description
Add-PnPFile	Uploads a file to Web
Copy-PnPFile	Copies a file or folder to a different location
Find-PnPFile	Finds a file in the virtual file system of the Web
Get-PnPFile	Downloads a file
Move-PnPFile	Moves a file to a different location
Remove-PnPFile	Removes a file
Rename-PnPFile	Renames a file in its current location
Set-PnPFileCheckedIn	Checks in a file
Set-PnPFileCheckedOut	Checks out a file
Add-PnPFolder	Creates a folder within a parent folder
Ensure-PnPFolder	Returns a folder from a given site-relative path and will create it if it does not already exist
Get-PnPFolder	Returns a folder object
Move-PnPFolder	Moves a folder to another location in the current Web
Remove-PnPFolder	Deletes a folder within a parent folder
Rename-PnPFolder	Renames a folder
Get-PnPFolderItem	Lists content in folder

These are only a few examples of what you can do with the PnP SharePoint PowerShell module. As you can see from the cmdlets we have talked about, the PnP SharePoint PowerShell module offers a lot more cmdlets to Office 365 administrators, allowing them to manage site collections, subsites, lists, libraries, and even items. Since there are over 200 cmdlets in the module and they constantly get updated or change, it's recommended you always look at the most up-to-date list of cmdlets on the GitHub repository at `https://github.com/SharePoint/PnP-PowerShell`.

Now that we have looked at both the SharePoint Online module provided by Microsoft and the PnP SharePoint PowerShell module, let's find out how we can implement some interesting automation scenarios in SharePoint Online.

Automation Scenarios

One of the big benefits of using PowerShell is being able to automate tasks that you have to do often and that can be boring to complete. Let's look at two examples of things that you can automate with PowerShell for SharePoint Online.

Create Sites from a CSV File

In this first example, you will focus on a specific business case at a fictional company called Learn Office 365 PowerShell. Whenever a fiscal year begins, the Project Management Office gets approvals for a lot of projects for the whole year, and each project needs a new site collection.

The first step in automating this business case is to create an Excel file that you can send to the Project Management Office in which they can supply information about the sites they will need created. In Figure 3-19, you can see a sample Excel file that includes three columns: Site Name, Site URL, and Owner. Since all these sites will use the Team Site template, this column is not included; however, you can customize the columns according to your business requirements.

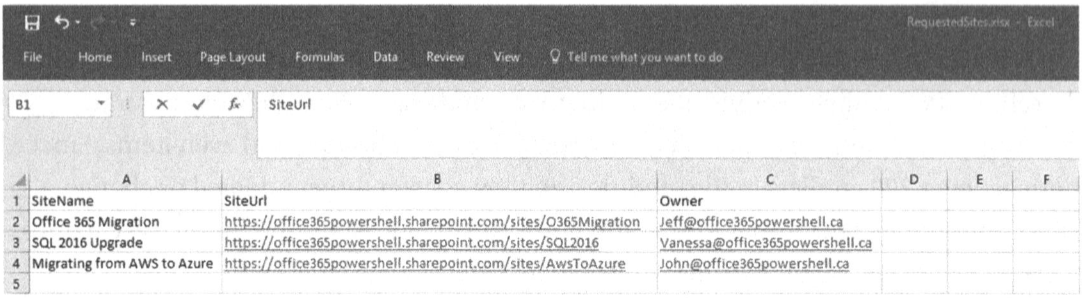

Figure 3-19. *Sample Excel file to request sites*

After receiving the file, save it in the Comma Separated Values (CSV) file format, since that makes it a lot easier to handle in PowerShell. The first thing you should do in your PowerShell script is import the CSV file by using the `Import-CSV` cmdlet and then save it into a variable as seen here:

```
$SiteCollections = Import-CSV C:\Apress\Ch03\RequestedSites.csv
```

Then, do a `for` each loop and loop through every line in the CSV file, saving each line object in a variable called `$Site`:

```
foreach ($Site in $SiteCollections){
}
```

Next, save each property of the site in a variable:

```
$Title = $Site.SiteName
$Url = $Site.SiteUrl
$Owner = $Site.Owner
```

Lastly, write a message to the PowerShell window to let the administrator know what site is currently being created, then run the `New-SPOSite` cmdlet to create your new site collection by specifying the variables you saved earlier:

```
Write-Host "Creating the $Title Site Collection at $Url with Site Owner $Owner"
New-SPOSite -Url $Url -Title $Title -Owner $Owner -Template STS#0 -
StorageQuota 512
```

This is what it looks like if we put it all together:

```
$SiteCollections = Import-CSV C:\Apress\Ch03\RequestedSites.csv
foreach ($Site in $SiteCollections)
 {
 $Title = $Site.SiteName
 $Url = $Site.SiteUrl
 $Owner = $Site.Owner
 Write-Host "Creating the $Title Site Collection at $Url with
 Site Owner $Owner"
 New-SPOSite -Url $Url -Title $Title -Owner $Owner -Template STS#0 -
 StorageQuota 512
 }
```

With only nine lines of PowerShell we are able to automate the creation of site collections from an Excel file! Let's take a look at our second automation scenario.

Copy User Permissions

One of the challenges that companies are facing is assigning permissions to new employees when they join the company and making sure they have access to all the sites and team sites they are supposed to have access to. Since a lot of new employees replace an employee who just left, or is leaving soon, HR often sends the Office 365 administrator a request asking them to assign the new employee the same rights that the old employee had. While this may seem like an easy task, it can take quite a while to do so manually. Let's see how you can automate this by using PowerShell.

You will first create an input file of type CSV with two columns, UserName and TemplateUserName, as seen in Figure 3-20. The UserName column is for the username of the new user, and the TemplateUserName is the one you want to copy permission wise.

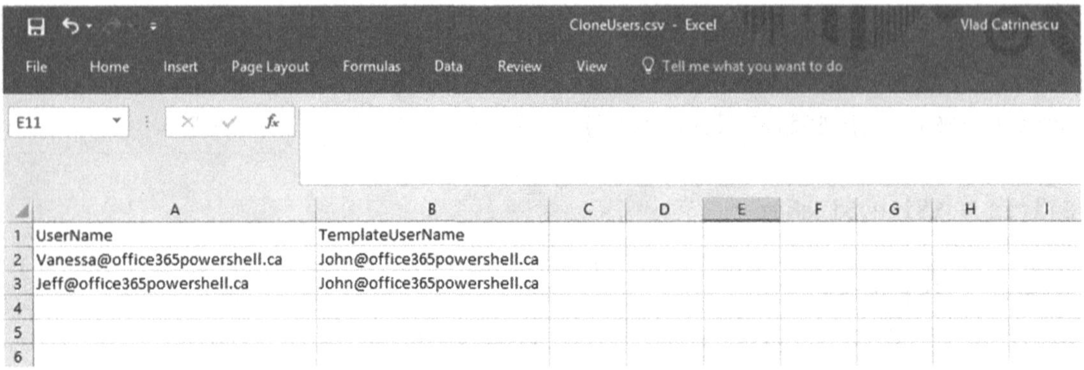

Figure 3-20. *Copy user permissions input file*

The first step in your script will be to save the site collection that you want to run this script on in a variable, as well as all the groups in that site collection. Lastly, import the CSV file into your script and save it in a variable as seen here:

```
$Site = Get-SPOSite https://office365powershell.sharepoint.com
$Groups = Get-SPOSiteGroup -Site $Site
$Users = import-csv 'C:\Apress\Ch03\CloneUsers.csv'
```

> **Note** In this sample script, the user permission cloning will only be done on a site collection. You can modify this script to make it apply to all of your site collections by adding an extra `for each` loop at the site-collection level.

Then, start a `for` each user in the input file loop and save each of the properties of the user in a variable:

```
foreach ($User in $Users){
$NewUser = $User.UserName
$TemplateUser = $User.TemplateUserName
```

You then need to start looping through the content. Loop through every group in the site collection, and then loop again through every user of that group. Compare every

user with your template user, and if the username is the same, it means you have to add
the new user to that group as well as write a message to the host, as seen here:

```
foreach ($Group in $Groups)
 {
 foreach ($SPOUser in $Group.Users)
  {
  if ($SPOUser -eq $TemplateUser)
   {
    $GroupName = $Group.LoginName
    Write-Host "Adding $NewUser to $GroupName"
    Add-SPOUser -Site $Site -LoginName $NewUser -Group $GroupName | out-null
 }}}
```

If you put everything together, the script looks like this:

```
$Site = Get-SPOSite https://office365powershell.sharepoint.com
$Groups = Get-SPOSiteGroup -Site $Site
$Users = import-csv 'C:\Apress\Ch03\CloneUsers.csv'
foreach ($User in $Users){

 $NewUser = $User.UserName
 $TemplateUser = $User.TemplateUserName

 foreach ($Group in $Groups)
 {
  foreach ($SPOUser in $Group.Users)
  {
   if ($SPOUser -eq $TemplateUser)
    {
    $GroupName = $Group.LoginName
    Write-Host "Adding $NewUser to $GroupName"
    Add-SPOUser -Site $Site -LoginName $NewUser -Group $GroupName | out-null
    }
  }
 }
}
```

When running the script, you will see which users have been added to which group, as seen in Figure 3-21.

```
Administrator: Windows PowerShell                                                               —  □  ×
PS C:\WINDOWS\system32> $Site = Get-SPOSite https://office365powershell.sharepoint.com
PS C:\WINDOWS\system32> $Groups = Get-SPOSiteGroup -Site $Site
PS C:\WINDOWS\system32> $Users = import-csv 'C:\Apress\Ch03\CloneUsers.csv'
PS C:\WINDOWS\system32> foreach ($User in $Users){
>>
>> $NewUser = $User.UserName
>> $TemplateUser = $User.TemplateUserName
>>
>> foreach ($Group in $Groups)
>> {
>> foreach ($SPOUser in $Group.Users)
>> {
>> if ($SPOUser -eq $TemplateUser)
>> {
>> $GroupName = $Group.LoginName
>> Write-Host  "Adding  $NewUser   to  $GroupName"
>> Add-SPOUser -Site $Site -LoginName $NewUser -Group $GroupName | out-null
>> }
>> }
>> }
>> }
Adding  Vanessa@office365powershell.ca  to  Team Site Members
Adding  Vanessa@office365powershell.ca  to  Team Site Visitors
Adding  Jeff@office365powershell.ca  to  Team Site Members
Adding  Jeff@office365powershell.ca  to  Team Site Visitors
```

Figure 3-21. *Copying user permissions with PowerShell*

Conclusion

In this chapter, we have looked at how to manage SharePoint Online using PowerShell. We first looked at how to get the SharePoint Online module from Microsoft and how to connect to SharePoint Online, as well as how to manage our site collections, our users and groups, and our tenant.

We then looked at the most popular and complete community-driven PowerShell module, which is the Office 365 Dev PnP PowerShell module for SharePoint. We learned what it is and where to find it, as well as how to get it installed on our computer. We also looked at a few sample cmdlets that exist in the PnP PowerShell module that you cannot find an equivalent of in the SharePoint Online PowerShell module provided by Microsoft.

Lastly, we looked at two automation scenarios in which you took what you learned in this chapter and applied it to real business cases.

In the next chapter, we will look at how to manage Exchange Online with PowerShell.

CHAPTER 4

Managing Exchange Online

In this chapter, we will first learn the prerequisites, as well as how to use PowerShell to connect to Exchange Online. We will then learn how to manage the different aspects of Exchange Online, such as mailboxes, distribution lists, contacts, permissions, and more!

We will also look at a few real-life scenarios where PowerShell with Exchange Online would help you automate boring tasks and save you time.

Connecting to Exchange Online

Connecting to Exchange Online with PowerShell is done by creating a remote PowerShell session from your local computer to Exchange Online. Unless you use multi-factor authentication (MFA), you do not need to download any modules before connecting, as a temporary module will be downloaded every time you connect. We will cover how to authenticate using MFA a bit later in this chapter. You first get your credentials by running the Get-Credential cmdlet and saving it in a variable called $cred:

```
$cred = Get-Credential
```

Then, use the following cmdlet to connect to create a new remote PowerShell session:

```
$Session = New-PSSession -ConfigurationName Microsoft.Exchange `
-ConnectionUri https://outlook.office365.com/powershell-liveid/ `
-Credential $cred `
-Authentication Basic `
-AllowRedirection
```

© Vlad Catrinescu 2018

V. Catrinescu, *Essential PowerShell for Office 365*, https://doi.org/10.1007/978-1-4842-3129-6_4

The ConnectionUri used in this example will be the same for all tenants except in two situations:

1. If your tenant is in the Office 365 Germany tenant, use the following ConnectionUri: https://outlook.office.de/powershell-liveid/.

2. If your Office 365 tenant is operated by 21Vianet, use the following ConnectionUri: https://partner.outlook.cn/PowerShell.

Lastly, import the PowerShell Session by using the Import-PSSession cmdlet as seen here:

```
Import-PSSession $Session
```

If everything goes well, PowerShell will download a temporary module, and you will now be connected to Exchange Online with PowerShell. Some of the Exchange Online PowerShell cmdlets use verbs that are not in the PowerShell-approved list, so when connecting, you will get a warning, as seen in Figure 4-1.

Figure 4-1. *Connecting to Exchange Online using PowerShell*

You have now connected to Exchange Online using PowerShell. In a lot of organizations, accounts that have admin access to Office 365 have multi-factor authentication enabled, which makes the procedure a bit different. Let's take a look at how to connect to Exchange Online when MFA is enabled!

Connecting with Multi-Factor Authentication

If multi-factor authentication is enabled on your account, you will first need to install the Exchange Online Remote PowerShell module on your computer. To get the module, you open the Office 365 Admin Center and navigate to the Exchange Online Admin Center, then to the Hybrid section. On that page, you will see the option to configure the Exchange Online PowerShell module, as seen in Figure 4-2.

Note   This step must be done using Internet Explorer. If you are using any other browser, you will get an error, which will be shown later in this chapter.

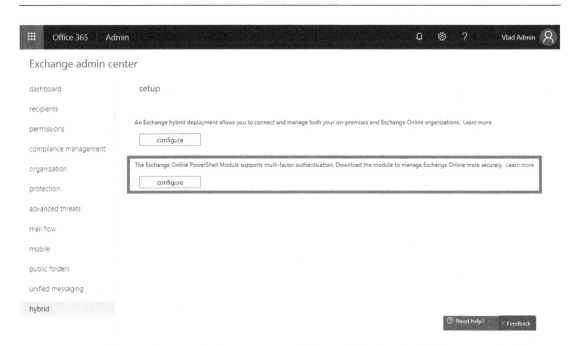

Figure 4-2.   *The Exchange Online PowerShell module in the Office 365 Admin Center*

After you click on the Configure button, an application will be downloaded which you will have to double click to start. You will first get prompted if you want to Install the application as seen in Figure 4-3.

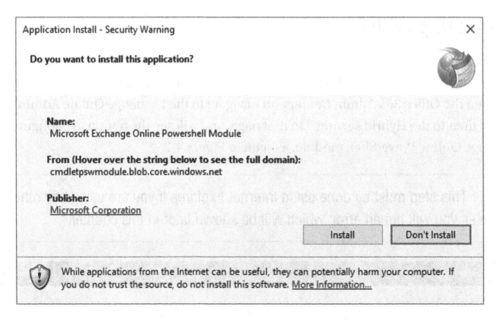

Figure 4-3. *Exchange Online PowerShell module install prompt*

If you have used a browser other than Internet Explorer, you will get an error similar to that in Figure 4-4 when you try to run the application.

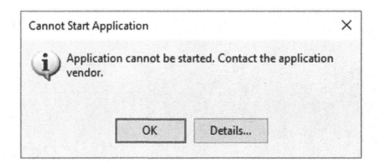

Figure 4-4. *Application error when using a browser other than Internet Explorer*

After the application has been installed, you can find it under Microsoft Exchange Online PowerShell module in your applications, as seen in Figure 4-5.

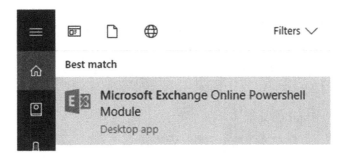

Figure 4-5. *The Exchange Online PowerShell module*

To connect to most Office 365 tenants, you would run the following cmdlet using your Office 365 username:

```
Connect-EXOPSSession -UserPrincipalName Jeff@office365powershell.ca
```

A pop-up will prompt you to enter your password, as seen in Figure 4-6.

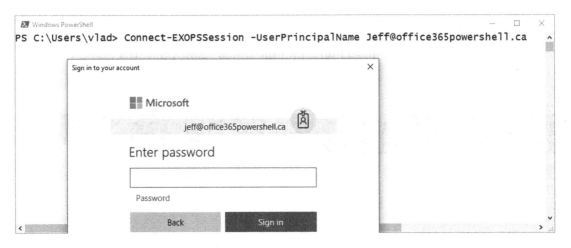

Figure 4-6. *Exchange Online PowerShell module password prompt*

Next up, depending on your MFA authentication method, you will be prompted to enter your second layer of authentication, as seen in Figure 4-7.

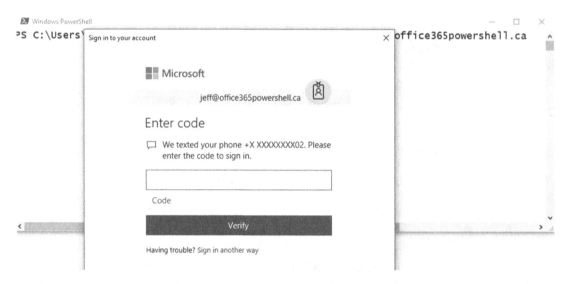

Figure 4-7. *Exchange Online PowerShell module second layer of*
authentication

Once logged in, you will see a warning similar to the one in Figure 4-8 explaining that
some commands in the Exchange Online module use unapproved verbs.

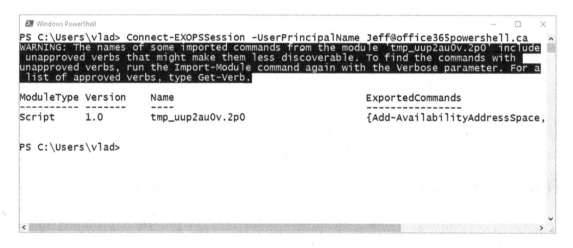

Figure 4-8. *Successfully connected to Exchange Online with multi-factor*
authentication

If your tenant is in the Office 365 Germany region, you would need to provide
two more parameters when connecting to Exchange Online PowerShell using MFA,
specifically the `ConnectionUri` and `AzureADAuthorizationEndPointUri` parameters.

If you wanted to log in to Office 365 Germany with the `Jeff@office365powershell.ca` account, you would use the following cmdlet:

```
Connect-EXOPSSession `
-UserPrincipalName Jeff@office365powershell.ca `
-ConnectionUri https://outlook.office.de/PowerShell-LiveID `
-AzureADAuthorizationEndPointUri https://login.microsoftonline.de/common
```

You have now learned how to connect to Exchange Online by using both multi-factor authentication and normal authentication. Next up, let's learn the different cmdlets you can use to manage Exchange Online using PowerShell!

Managing Users and Mailboxes

Let's start by having you learn how to manage probably the most important part of it all: the users and mailboxes inside your Office 365 tenant. In this section, you will learn how to change user properties, assign user permissions on other mailboxes, send emails via PowerShell, and also manage users' calendars!

Users

You previously learned how to manage users with the Azure Active Directory PowerShell module (Chapter 2), but you can also use the Exchange Online PowerShell module to view most user properties. If you want to see all the users in your Exchange Online tenant, you can run the `Get-User` cmdlet as seen in Figure 4-9.

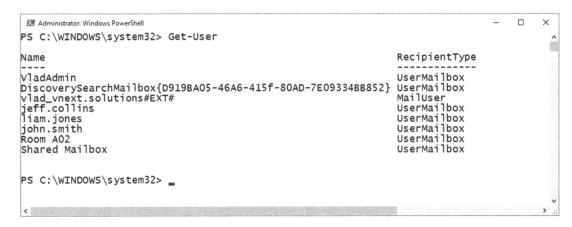

Figure 4-9. *Running the Get-User cmdlet*

You can also select properties that make it easier for you to see the different types of mailboxes that you have in your tenant. The following example cmdlet, also seen in Figure 4-10, allows you to see the full email address, the recipient type, and the details. In this example, you can easily see if it's a user mailbox, a shared mailbox, a room mailbox, or a guest user.

```
Get-User | Select UserPrincipalName, RecipientType, RecipientTypeDetails |
Format-Table -Wrap
```

```
Administrator: Windows PowerShell                                                                        —  □  ×
PS C:\WINDOWS\system32> Get-User | Select UserPrincipalName,  RecipientType, RecipientTypeDetails  | Format-Table -Wrap

UserPrincipalName                                                                       RecipientType RecipientTypeDeta
                                                                                                      ls
-----------------                                                                       ------------- -----------------
vlad-admin@office365powershell.ca                                                       UserMailbox   UserMailbox
DiscoverySearchMailbox{D919BA05-46A6-415f-80AD-7E09334BB852}@Office365PowerShell.onmicrosoft.com UserMailbox DiscoveryMailbox
vlad_vnext.solutions#EXT#@office365powershell.ca                                        MailUser      GuestMailUser
jeff.collins@office365powershell.ca                                                     UserMailbox   UserMailbox
liam.jones@office365powershell.ca                                                       UserMailbox   UserMailbox
john.smith@office365powershell.ca                                                       UserMailbox   UserMailbox
roomA02@office365powershell.ca                                                          UserMailbox   RoomMailbox
shared@office365powershell.ca                                                           UserMailbox   SharedMailbox
```

Figure 4-10. *Selecting different properties with the Get-User cmdlet*

You can also change user properties via the Set-User cmdlet, which will update it throughout Office 365. In the example that follows, I am changing the display name of a user with username jeff.collins@office365Powershell.ca to Jeff Collins.

```
Set-User jeff.collins@office365Powershell.ca -DisplayName "Jeff Collins"
```

In Figure 4-11, you can see that I first used the Azure AD PowerShell cmdlets to verify the display name, which was Collins, Jeff, and after the display name was changed with the Exchange Online PowerShell cmdlets, it also got changed in Azure Active Directory.

```
Administrator: Windows PowerShell                                          —    □    ×
PS C:\WINDOWS\system32> Get-AzureADUser -ObjectId jeff.collins@office365Powershell.ca

ObjectId                          DisplayName   UserPrincipalName                   UserType
--------                          -----------   -----------------                   --------
dd797881-b469-40bc-8c4f-ae9e4e311ce5 Collins, Jeff jeff.collins@office365powershell.ca Member

PS C:\WINDOWS\system32> Set-User jeff.collins@office365Powershell.ca -DisplayName "Jeff Collins"
PS C:\WINDOWS\system32> Get-AzureADUser -ObjectId jeff.collins@office365Powershell.ca

ObjectId                          DisplayName   UserPrincipalName                   UserType
--------                          -----------   -----------------                   --------
dd797881-b469-40bc-8c4f-ae9e4e311ce5 Jeff Collins jeff.collins@office365powershell.ca Member

PS C:\WINDOWS\system32> _
```

Figure 4-11. *Updating global Office 365 properties by using the Exchange Online PowerShell module*

Let's now look at how to manage contacts in Exchange Online!

Contacts

Contacts in Exchange Online allow you to publish external emails into your Global Address List in order to make them easier to find for your users. For example, organizations often have external employee-assistance programs or external financial organizations managing their 401K plan. Even if those email addresses are external, by using Exchange Online Contacts you can easily add those to each employee's Global Address List.

To create a new mail contact, you use the New-MailContact cmdlet, specifying the name of the contact as well as their email address:

```
New-MailContact -Name "401K Questions" -ExternalEmailAddress companyname@
financialcompany.com

New-MailContact -Name "Employee Assistance Program" -ExternalEmailAddress
companyname@eapprovider.com
```

When employees start typing part of the word, Outlook will automatically propose one of the contacts that you have saved previously, as seen in Figure 4-12.

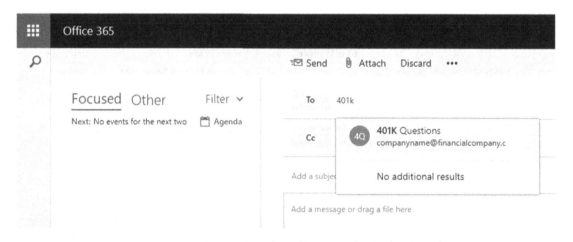

Figure 4-12. *Mail contacts suggested in Outlook on the Web*

You can also change a mail contact by using the Set-MailContact PowerShell cmdlet. For example, you can use the following cmdlet to change the email address of the 401k contact:

```
Set-MailContact -Identity "401K Questions" -ExternalEmailAddress questions@
newfinancialcompany.com
```

You can also use PowerShell to update multiple contacts at once. For example, let's assume your company has a new policy where all the external email addresses in the Global Address List must have the word "[External]" in their display name in order for users to know right away that they are sending an email outside the organization. In PowerShell, you could run the following script to automatically update all the contacts in the organization to add the required words in the display name:

```
$Contacts = Get-MailContact
foreach ($contact in $contacts){
Set-MailContact -Identity $contact.Name -DisplayName "$contact [External]"
}
```

The result, seen in Figure 4-13, shows how the contacts are displayed after the previous script.

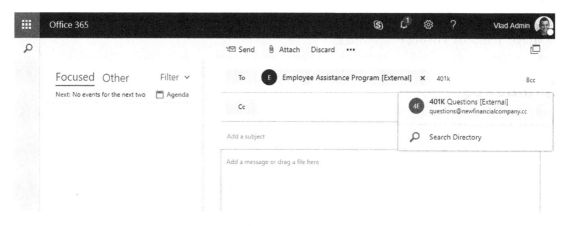

Figure 4-13. *Office 365 mail contacts shown with the [External] warning*

You can also assign MailTips to each mail contact. For example, if you wanted to remind employees not to send confidential information by email to a contact, you could run the following cmdlet:

```
Set-MailContact -Identity "401K Questions" -MailTip "Do not send
confidential information to this mailbox!"
```

The MailTip will appear at the top of the email as seen in Figure 4-14.

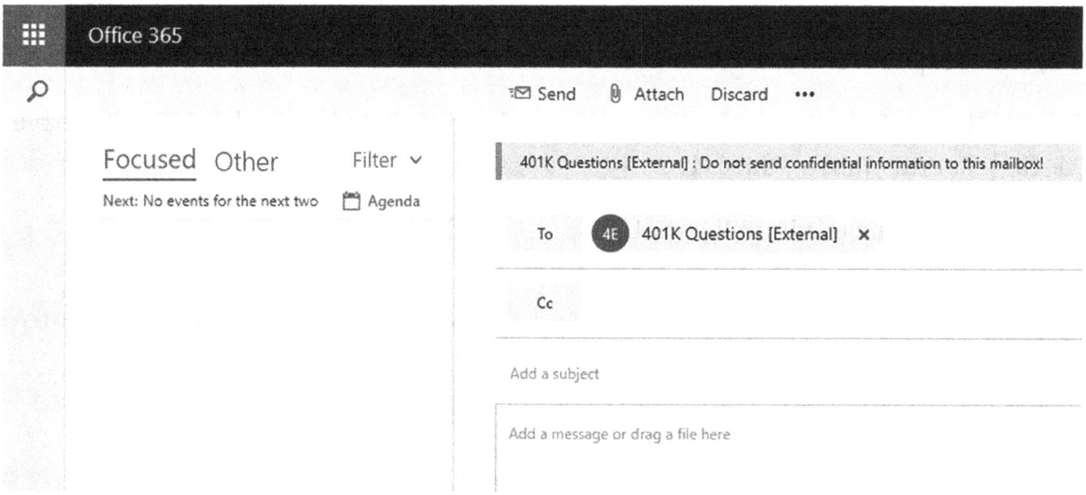

Figure 4-14. *MailTips in Outlook Online*

Now that you have learned how to work with mail contacts, it's time to look at how to manage mailboxes using PowerShell!

Mailboxes

To see all the mailboxes inside your Office 365 tenant, you can run the `Get-Mailbox` PowerShell cmdlet, which will return basic information, as seen in Figure 4-15.

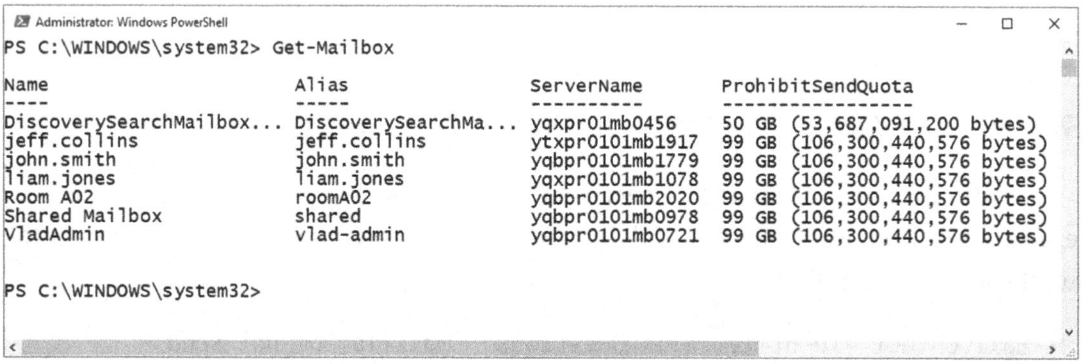

```
Administrator: Windows PowerShell
PS C:\WINDOWS\system32> Get-Mailbox

Name                      Alias                 ServerName        ProhibitSendQuota
----                      -----                 ----------        -----------------
DiscoverySearchMailbox... DiscoverySearchMa...  yqxpr01mb0456     50 GB (53,687,091,200 bytes)
jeff.collins              jeff.collins          ytxpr0101mb1917   99 GB (106,300,440,576 bytes)
john.smith                john.smith            yqbpr0101mb1779   99 GB (106,300,440,576 bytes)
liam.jones                liam.jones            yqxpr0101mb1078   99 GB (106,300,440,576 bytes)
Room A02                  roomA02               yqbpr0101mb2020   99 GB (106,300,440,576 bytes)
Shared Mailbox            shared                yqbpr0101mb0978   99 GB (106,300,440,576 bytes)
VladAdmin                 vlad-admin            yqbpr0101mb0721   99 GB (106,300,440,576 bytes)

PS C:\WINDOWS\system32>
```

Figure 4-15. *All mailboxes inside the organization*

You can also filter by any of the properties of the mailbox; for example, with the following cmdlet you also get information about the display name, what type of mailbox it is, and the quota for the mailbox:

```
Get-Mailbox | Select DisplayName,  RecipientTypeDetails,ProhibitSendReceive
Quota | Format-Table -autosize
```

You can see the results in Figure 4-16.

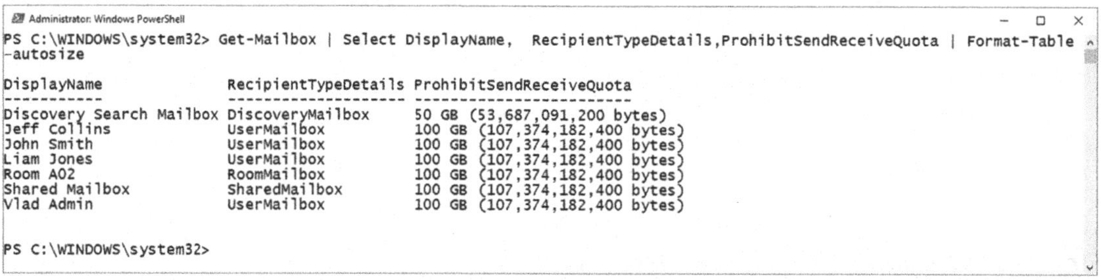

```
Administrator: Windows PowerShell
PS C:\WINDOWS\system32> Get-Mailbox | Select DisplayName,  RecipientTypeDetails,ProhibitSendReceiveQuota | Format-Table
-autosize

DisplayName            RecipientTypeDetails ProhibitSendReceiveQuota
-----------            -------------------- ------------------------
Discovery Search Mailbox DiscoveryMailbox   50 GB (53,687,091,200 bytes)
Jeff Collins           UserMailbox          100 GB (107,374,182,400 bytes)
John Smith             UserMailbox          100 GB (107,374,182,400 bytes)
Liam Jones             UserMailbox          100 GB (107,374,182,400 bytes)
Room A02               RoomMailbox          100 GB (107,374,182,400 bytes)
Shared Mailbox         SharedMailbox        100 GB (107,374,182,400 bytes)
Vlad Admin             UserMailbox          100 GB (107,374,182,400 bytes)

PS C:\WINDOWS\system32>
```

Figure 4-16. *Selecting certain properties of the mailbox*

If you want to modify a certain mailbox, you can use the `Set-Mailbox` PowerShell cmdlet. For example, if you wanted to hide the "Shared Mailbox" (seen in earlier figures) from the Global Address List, you would run the `Set-Mailbox` cmdlet, specifying the alias—which is "shared"—and the `HiddenFromAddressListsEnabled` property, as seen here:

```
Set-Mailbox -Identity Shared -HiddenFromAddressListsEnabled $true
```

The result, seen in Figure 4-17, is that this mailbox will not be suggested or appear in search results when users search for an e-mail address in the Global Address List.

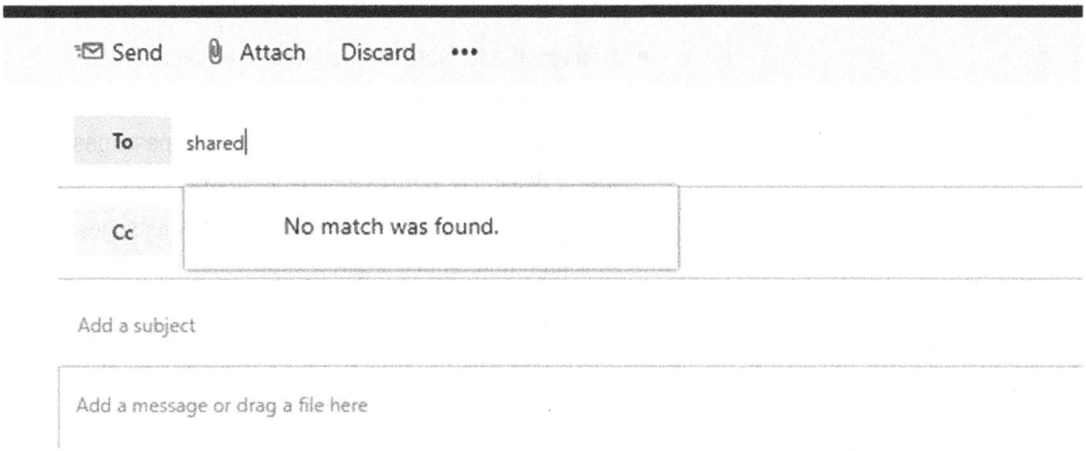

Figure 4-17. *Shared mailbox not displayed in search results*

Note   It might take some time for the `HiddenFromAddressListEnabled` parameter to take effect, but usually it will work in less than an hour.

Another popular change that administrators often apply to mailboxes is a permanent forward when an employee leaves the company. To adjust this property, you need to configure the properties shown in Table 4-1.

Table 4-1. *Set-Mailbox Permissions*

Property	Description
DeliverToMailboxAndForward	This parameter specifies the message-delivery behavior when a forwarding address is specified by the ForwardingAddress or ForwardingSmtpAddress parameters. Valid values are: • **$true** Messages are delivered to this mailbox and forwarded to the specified recipient or email address. • **$false** If a forwarding recipient or email address is configured, messages are delivered only to the specified recipient or email address, and messages aren't delivered to this mailbox. If no forwarding recipient or email address is configured, messages are delivered only to this mailbox. The default value is $false. The value of this parameter is meaningful only if you configure a forwarding recipient or email address.
ForwardingAddress	This parameter specifies a forwarding address for messages that are sent to this mailbox. A valid value for this parameter is *a recipient in your organization*.
ForwardingSmtpAddress	This parameter specifies a forwarding SMTP address for messages that are sent to this mailbox. Typically, you use this parameter to specify *external email addresses* that aren't validated. If you configure values for both the ForwardingAddress and ForwardingSmtpAddress parameters, the value of ForwardingSmtpAddress is ignored.

If John Smith is leaving the company, you would probably want to forward John's email to his manager, who is Jeff Collins. In this scenario, the company policy dictates that email must be only forwarded to Jeff, but new mails must not be kept in John's mailbox. Furthermore, we will hide John from the Global Address List so new employees do not find him by accident.

```
Set-Mailbox -Identity john.smith `
-HiddenFromAddressListsEnabled $true `
-DeliverToMailboxAndForward $false `
-ForwardingAddress jeff.collins@office365powershell.ca
```

Another setting that you can change for your user's experience is the Focused Inbox. With the Focused Inbox feature, Microsoft uses its machine-learning algorithms to decide which emails are important for you and which are less important. Your inbox is separated into two tabs—Focused and Other. Your most important emails are on the Focused tab while the rest remain accessible on the Other tab. Figure 4-18 showcases the Focused Inbox in Outlook Online, but the same functionality also exists in Outlook client. As you can see in the figure, I currently have no emails in my Focused inbox; however, I have 40 unread emails in my inbox, and I need to switch over to the Other tab in order to see them.

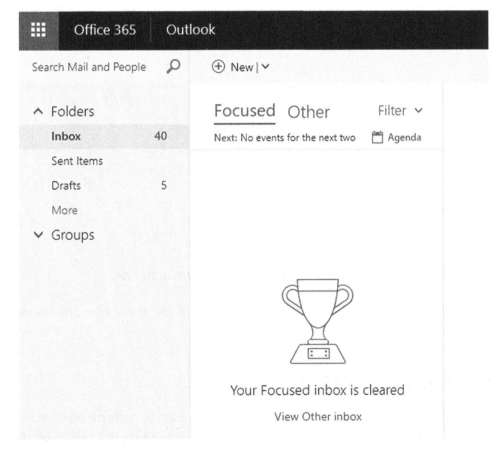

Figure 4-18. *Focused Inbox versus Other tab*

While most users and organizations like the features, some prefer not to have two different tabs in their inbox. You can turn Focused Inbox on/off either at the mailbox level or at the tenant level. We will look at the tenant-level permissions a bit later in this chapter. To turn the Focused Inbox feature on/off you would use the Set-FocusedInbox cmdlet, specifying the identity of the mailbox and the FocusedInboxOn parameter. In the example that follows, I am turning off the Focused Inbox feature for a single mailbox:

```
Set-FocusedInbox -Identity vlad-admin@office365powershell.ca
-FocusedInboxOn $False
```

The result, seen in Figure 4-19, is that this user will have normal inbox functionality without the Focused and Other tabs.

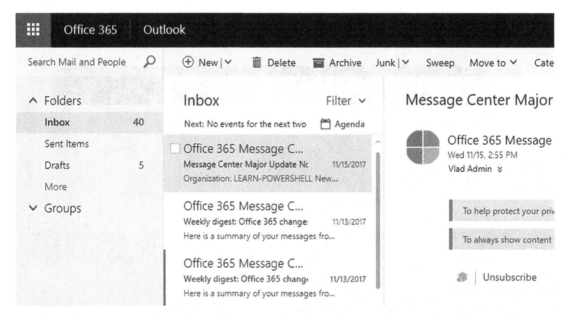

Figure 4-19. *Inbox without the Focused Inbox feature activated*

Now that you have learned how to manage mailboxes, let's look at how to manage calendars with PowerShell!

Calendar and Out of Office

There are multiple administrative operations you might want to perform on a user's calendar. One common event is that when a user leaves the company, sometimes they forget to cancel recurring meetings, and you probably want to cancel them since you do not want a nonexistent user to be the organizer of those meetings. Some companies also use Exchange to manage conference room reservations, and having those meetings still exist will keep the room busy even if the user is no longer working for the company. The Remove-CalendarEvents cmdlet allows you to cancel all upcoming meetings where the mailbox is the meeting organizer and the meeting has one or more attendees or resources. To delete all the upcoming meetings organized by John Smith, I would run the following cmdlet:

```
Remove-CalendarEvents `
-Identity john.smith@office365powershell.ca `
-CancelOrganizedMeetings
```

In other cases, maybe the employee has only taken a maternity/paternity leave or a leave of absence, and you do not want to cancel all their future meetings. By using the QueryStartDate and QueryWindowInDays parameters, you can specify a starting date and date range for which events should be canceled. In the example that follows, I am canceling events by Jeff Collins starting on January 1, 2018, for 30 days. The date format is defined by the Regional Options on the computer that is running the command.

```
Remove-CalendarEvents `
-Identity jeff.collins@office365powershell.ca `
-CancelOrganizedMeetings `
-QueryStartDate 1/1/2018 `
-QueryWindowInDays 30
```

In both these scenarios, another setting you might want to change is the Automatic Reply for that mailbox to let other people know that the user is no longer working for the company or is on an extended leave for a certain period of time. Let's assume that the account Vlad Admin has left the organization. You can first run the Get-MailboxAutoReplyConfiguration cmdlet to see the current settings. As you can see in Figure 4-20, the user has set an External Message linking to his LinkedIn account, but did not specify who to contact in your organization, and that is not what the company wants.

```
Administrator: Windows PowerShell                                                        —  □  ×
PS C:\WINDOWS\system32> Get-MailboxAutoReplyConfiguration -Identity vlad-admin@office365powershell.ca

RunspaceId                        : 24ab0241-ce40-40b4-9175-51494a6dae1b
AutoDeclineFutureRequestsWhenOOF  : False
AutoReplyState                    : Enabled
CreateOOFEvent                    : False
DeclineAllEventsForScheduledOOF   : False
DeclineEventsForScheduledOOF      : False
EventsToDeleteIDs                 :
EndTime                           : 12/20/2017 8:00:00 PM
ExternalAudience                  : All
ExternalMessage                   : <html>
                                    <head>
                                    <style type="text/css" style="display:none">
                                    <!--
                                    p
                                         {margin-top:0;
                                         margin-bottom:0}
                                    -->
                                    </style>
                                    </head>
                                    <body dir="ltr">
                                    <div id="divtagdefaultwrapper" dir="ltr" style="font-size:12pt; color:#000000;
                                    font-family:Calibri,Helvetica,sans-serif">
                                    <p style="margin-top:0; margin-bottom:0">Please Note that I am no longer working
                                    for this organizations, please connect with me on LinkedIn: <a
                                    href="https://www.linkedin.com/in/vladcatrinescu/"
                                    class="OWAAutoLink">https://www.linkedin.com/in/vladcatrinescu/</a></p>
                                    </div>
                                    </body>
                                    </html>
InternalMessage                   : <html>
```

Figure 4-20. *Running the Get-MailboxAutoReplyConfiguration cmdlet*

As an administrator, you could create an Out of Office message and even use HTML and CSS to make it match the content and style you want. You should first create a here-string with the HTML code of the message that you want to use:

```
$Body = @"
"Hello </br> </br>
Please Note I am not currently working for Office 365 PowerShell anymore.
</br> </br>
Please contact Jeff Collins <a href="mailto:jeff.collins@
office365powershell.ca">jeff.collins@office365powershell.ca</a> for any
questions. </br> </br>
Thanks!"
"@
```

You would then assign this message to the mailbox by using the Set-MailboxAutoReplyConfiguration cmdlet as seen in the following example:

```
Set-MailboxAutoReplyConfiguration `
-Identity vlad-admin@office365powershell.ca `
-ExternalMessage $body `
-InternalMessage $body
```

The result, as seen in Figure 4-21, is the Out of Office message that users will receive with the preceding cmdlets.

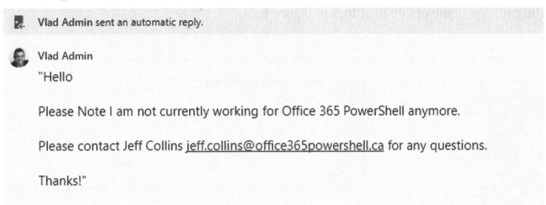

Figure 4-21. *Out of Office message result*

If the Out of Office message were not yet enabled, and you wanted to enable it, you would need to add the AutoReplyState parameter. To enable it without a schedule, you would run the following cmdlet:

```
Set-MailboxAutoReplyConfiguration `
-Identity vlad-admin@office365powershell.ca `
-ExternalMessage $body `
-InternalMessage $body `
-AutoReplyState Enabled
```

If you only wanted to enable this message for a certain period of time, you would need to set the AutoReplyState parameter to Scheduled and specify the start and end times, as seen in the following example:

```
Set-MailboxAutoReplyConfiguration `
-Identity vlad-admin@office365powershell.ca `
-ExternalMessage $body `
-InternalMessage $body `
-AutoReplyState Scheduled `
-StartTime 1/1/2018 `
-EndTime 1/30/2018
```

This would enable the Out of Office message only between January 1 and January 30, 2018.

You can also view all the calendar settings, such as work days, work hours, default reminder times, and more by using the Get-MailboxCalendarConfiguration cmdlet. You can view some of those settings in Figure 4-22.

```
Administrator: Windows PowerShell                                                                    —   □   ×
PS C:\WINDOWS\system32> Get-MailboxCalendarConfiguration -Identity vlad-admin@office365powershell.ca | Format-List

RunspaceId                        : 24ab0241-ce40-40b4-9175-51494a6dae1b
WorkDays                          : Weekdays
WorkingHoursStartTime             : 08:00:00
WorkingHoursEndTime               : 17:00:00
WorkingHoursTimeZone              : Eastern Standard Time
WeekStartDay                      : Sunday
ShowWeekNumbers                   : False
FirstWeekOfYear                   : FirstDay
TimeIncrement                     : ThirtyMinutes
RemindersEnabled                  : True
ReminderSoundEnabled              : True
DefaultReminderTime               : 00:15:00
WeatherEnabled                    : FirstRun
WeatherUnit                       : Default
WeatherLocations                  : {LocationId:105808079;Name:Redmond, WA;Latitude:47.67399;Longitude:-122.12151
WeatherLocationBookmark           : 0
DefaultMeetingDuration            : 30
AgendaMailEnabled                 : False
SkipAgendaMailOnFreeDays          : True
DailyAgendaMailSchedule           : Default
AgendaMailIntroductionEnabled     : True
EventsFromEmailEnabled            : True
EventsFromEmailDelegateChecked    : False
EventsFromEmailShadowMailboxChecked : False
ReportEventsCreatedFromEmailEnabled : True
CreateEventsFromEmailAsPrivate    : True
FlightEventsFromEmailEnabled      : True
DiningEventsFromEmailEnabled      : True
```

Figure 4-22. *All calendar configuration events*

You can change any of these settings by using the Set-MailboxCalendarConfiguration PowerShell cmdlet and specifying the name of the parameter you want to change.

Now that you have learned how to manage the calendar and Out of Office events, let's look at how to manage different mailbox permissions in Exchange Online with PowerShell.

SendAs and Mailbox Permissions

As an Exchange administrator, you have probably already been tasked with granting "SendAs" permission to a user's mailbox. This is done with the Add-RecipientPermission cmdlet. If I wanted to allow the account Vlad Admin to send emails that appear to come directly from Jeff Collins, I would run the following cmdlet:

Add-RecipientPermission jeff.collins -AccessRights SendAs -Trustee vlad-admin@office365powershell.ca

To view permissions on a certain mailbox, you can run the `Get-RecipientPermission` cmdlet, specifying the `-Identity` parameter. In Figure 4-23, you can see that Jeff Collins himself, as well as Vlad Catrinescu, have SendAs permissions on the `jeff.collins` mailbox.

```
Administrator: Windows PowerShell                                              —    □    ×
PS C:\WINDOWS\system32> Get-RecipientPermission -Identity jeff.collins

Identity        Trustee                              AccessControlType AccessRights Inherited
--------        -------                              ----------------- ------------ ---------
jeff.collins    NT AUTHORITY\SELF                    Allow             {SendAs}     False
jeff.collins    vlad-admin@office365powershell.ca Allow                {SendAs}     False


PS C:\WINDOWS\system32> _
```

Figure 4-23. *Get-RecipientPermission for a mailbox*

You can also use the `-Trustee` parameter to find out what mailboxes a certain user (trustee) can send emails as. In Figure 4-24, you can see that `vlad-admin@office365powershell.ca` can send emails as three other identities.

```
Administrator: Windows PowerShell                                              —    □    ×
PS C:\WINDOWS\system32> Get-RecipientPermission -Trustee vlad-admin@office365powershell.ca

Identity        Trustee                              AccessControlType AccessRights Inherited
--------        -------                              ----------------- ------------ ---------
jeff.collins    vlad-admin@office365powershell.ca Allow                {SendAs}     False
john.smith      vlad-admin@office365powershell.ca Allow                {SendAs}     False
Shared Mailbox  vlad-admin@office365powershell.ca Allow                {SendAs}     False


PS C:\WINDOWS\system32>
```

Figure 4-24. *Get-RecipientPermission for a trustee*

Note   It can take a few hours for new permissions to be visible for the user in Outlook client or Outlook Online.

If you want to assign other permissions, such as full control of the mailbox, you need to use the `Add-MailboxPermission` PowerShell cmdlet. Table 4-2 showcases some of the most important parameters of the cmdlet

Table 4-2. *Parameters of the Add-MailboxPermission cmdlet*

Parameter	Description
Identity	The Identity parameter specifies the identity of the mailbox that's getting permissions added.
AccessRights	The AccessRights parameter specifies the rights needed to perform the operation. Valid values include: • FullAccess • ExternalAccount • DeleteItem • ReadPermission • ChangePermission • ChangeOwner
Owner	The Owner parameter specifies the owner of the mailbox object.
User	The User parameter specifies the user mailbox that the permissions are being granted to on the other mailbox.
AutoMapping	The AutoMapping parameter specifies whether to ignore the auto-mapping feature in Microsoft Outlook. This parameter accepts $true or $false values.
InheritanceType	The InheritanceType parameter specifies whether permissions are inherited by folders within the mailbox.

In the following cmdlet, I am granting Vlad Admin full control of Jeff Collins' mailbox:

```
Add-MailboxPermission -Identity jeff.collins `
-User vlad-admin@office365powershell.ca `
-AccessRights FullAccess `
-InheritanceType All
```

Since I let the AutoMapping parameter to its default value of True, Jeff Collins' mailbox is automatically added to my Outlook client when I add the vlad-admin account, as seen in Figure 4-25.

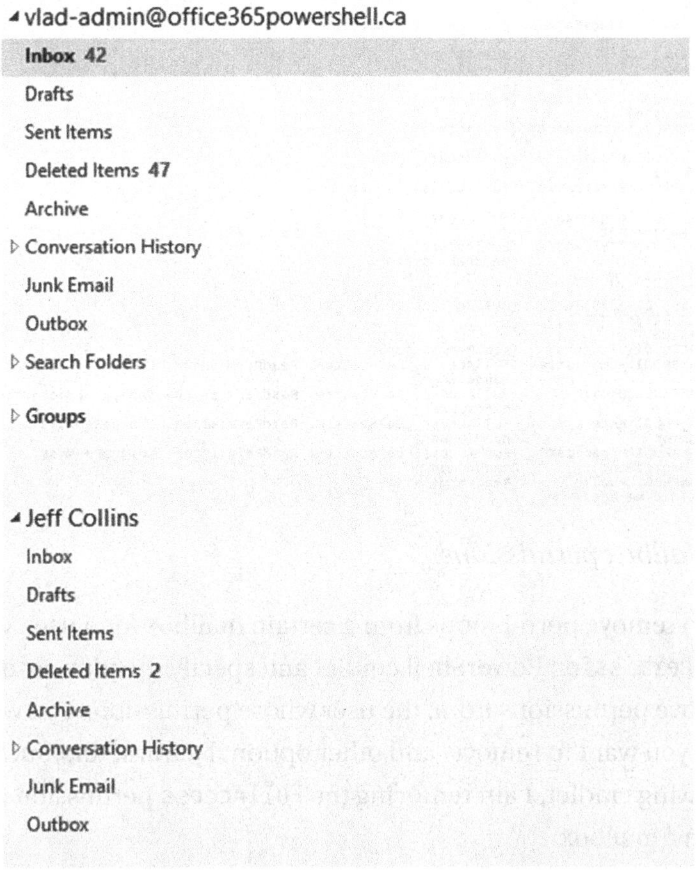

⊿ vlad-admin@office365powershell.ca

Inbox 42

Drafts

Sent Items

Deleted Items 47

Archive

▷ Conversation History

Junk Email

Outbox

▷ Search Folders

▷ Groups

⊿ Jeff Collins

Inbox

Drafts

Sent Items

Deleted Items 2

Archive

▷ Conversation History

Junk Email

Outbox

Figure 4-25. *Account automatically added with AutoMapping feature*

If you want to see the permissions for a certain mailbox, you can run the
`Get-MailboxPermission` permission cmdlet, specifying the identity of the mailbox that
you want to get the permissions for. As you can see in Figure 4-26, this will output all
permissions, including the ones you have manually assigned and some Microsoft service
accounts.

```
Administrator: Windows PowerShell                                                    —  □  ×
PS C:\WINDOWS\system32> Get-MailboxPermission -Identity jeff.collins | Format-Table -Wrap

Identity         User                    AccessRights                                              IsInherited Deny
--------         ----                    ------------                                              ----------- ----
jeff.collins     NT AUTHORITY\SELF       {FullAccess, ReadPermission}                              False       False
jeff.collins     vlad-admin@office365    {FullAccess}                                              False       False
                 powershell.ca
jeff.collins     CANPRD01\Administrat    {FullAccess}                                              True        True
                 or
jeff.collins     CANPRD01\Domain         {FullAccess}                                              True        True
                 Admins
jeff.collins     CANPRD01\Enterprise     {FullAccess}                                              True        True
                 Admins
jeff.collins     CANPRD01\Organizatio    {FullAccess}                                              True        True
                 n Management
jeff.collins     NT AUTHORITY\SYSTEM     {FullAccess}                                              True        False
jeff.collins     NT                      {ReadPermission}                                          True        False
                 AUTHORITY\NETWORK
                 SERVICE
jeff.collins     S-1-5-21-1589316702-    {ReadPermission}                                          True        False
                 2032257147-380728827
                 6-5106
jeff.collins     PRDTSB01\JitUsers       {ReadPermission}                                          True        False
jeff.collins     CANPRD01\Administrat    {FullAccess, DeleteItem, ReadPermission, ChangePermission, True       False
                 or                      ChangeOwner}
jeff.collins     CANPRD01\Domain         {FullAccess, DeleteItem, ReadPermission, ChangePermission, True       False
                 Admins                  ChangeOwner}
jeff.collins     CANPRD01\Enterprise     {FullAccess, DeleteItem, ReadPermission, ChangePermission, True       False
                 Admins                  ChangeOwner}
jeff.collins     CANPRD01\Organizatio    {FullAccess, DeleteItem, ReadPermission, ChangePermission, True       False
                 n Management            ChangeOwner}
jeff.collins     CANPRD01\Public         {ReadPermission}                                          True        False
                 Folder Management
```

Figure 4-26. *Mailbox permissions*

If you want to remove permissions from a certain mailbox for a user, you can use the Remove-MailboxPermission PowerShell cmdlet and specify the identity of the mailbox you want to remove permissions from, the user whose permissions you want to remove, the access rights you want to remove, and other optional parameters, such as inheritance type. In the following cmdlet, I am removing the FullAccess permission that Vlad-Admin had on Jeff Collins' mailbox:

```
Remove-MailboxPermission -Identity jeff.collins `
-User vlad-admin@office365powershell.ca `
-AccessRights FullAccess `
-InheritanceType All
```

Office 365 also gives you the ability to restore a mailbox to its default permissions by using the ResetDefault parameter. This will remove mailbox permissions such as Full Access, but will retain recipient permissions such as SendAs and SendOnBehalf. To restore Jeff Collins' mailbox to default permissions, I would run the following cmdlet:

```
Remove-MailboxPermission -Identity jeff.collins -ResetDefault
```

We have now covered how to manage SendAs and Mailbox permissions with PowerShell. Next up, let's learn how to manage organization settings!

CHAPTER 4   MANAGING EXCHANGE ONLINE

Managing Organization Settings

Exchange Online offers the ability to apply settings at the mailbox level, as you saw earlier, but you can also enable or disable features at the tenant level. If you want to see the configuration data for the Exchange organization, you can run the `Get-OrganizationConfig` cmdlet. This cmdlet will return a lot of information, but you can export it to a file if needed, to make reading easier, with this example cmdlet:

```
Get-OrganizationConfig | Out-File c:\Users\Vlad\Desktop\OrgConfig.txt
```

To change the organization settings, you need to use the `Set-OrganizationConfig` PowerShell cmdlet. Table 4-3 displays the most common parameters of the cmdlet, which will also allow you to better understand the values from the `Get-OrganizationConfig` cmdlet.

> **Note**   Some parameters control features that are not available in all license plans, such as Microsoft Bookings or Customer Lockbox. Make sure you have the required licenses before changing those settings.

Table 4-3. *Set-OrganizationConfig cmdlet Parameters*

Parameter	Description
AppsForOfficeEnabled	This parameter specifies whether to enable apps for Outlook features. By default, the parameter is set to $true. If the flag is set to $false, no new apps can be activated for any user in the organization.
BookingsEnabled	This parameter specifies whether to enable Microsoft Bookings in an Exchange Online organization.
CustomerLockboxEnabled	CustomerLockboxEnabled specifies whether Customer Lockbox requests are enabled or disabled for the organization.
DirectReportsGroupAuto CreationEnabled	This parameter specifies whether to enable or disable the automatic creation of direct-report Office 365 Groups.

(continued)

Table 4-3. (*continued*)

Parameter	Description
DistributionGroupName BlockedWordsList	This parameter specifies words that can't be included in the names of distribution groups. Separate multiple values with commas.
DistributionGroup NamingPolicy	The DistributionGroupNamingPolicy parameter specifies the template applied to the name of distribution groups that are created in the organization.
FocusedInboxOn	The FocusedInboxOn parameter enables or disables Focused Inbox for the organization.
LinkPreviewEnabled	The LinkPreviewEnabled parameter specifies whether a link preview of URLs in email messages is allowed for the organization.

Tip   To view all the parameters of the Set-OrganizationConfig cmdlet, you can run Get-Help Set-OrganizationConfig -Online, which will automatically open the TechNet page of the cmdlet in your default browser.

If, for example, you wanted to disable Focused Inbox, Link Previews, and Microsoft Bookings, you would run the following cmdlet:

```
Set-OrganizationConfig `
-FocusedInboxOn $false `
-LinkPreviewEnabled $false `
-BookingsEnabled $false
```

Some of the parameters specified in Table 4-3 also talk about the governance of distribution lists and allowing you to set a naming convention, as well as blocked words. Let's look at those in detail. If you wanted to block the words *Apress*, *Contoso*, and *CEO* from any distribution list name, you would run the following cmdlet:

```
Set-OrganizationConfig -DistributionGroupNameBlockedWordsList
Apress,Contoso,CEO
```

If you tried to create a distribution list using those words, you would be shown an error similar to that in Figure 4-27.

```
Administrator: Windows PowerShell                                                    —  □  ×
PS C:\WINDOWS\system32> New-DistributionGroup -Name "Apress Clients"
The group name contains the word "Apress", which isn't allowed in group names in your organization. Please rename your
group.
    + CategoryInfo          : NotSpecified: (:) [New-DistributionGroup], DataValidationException
    + FullyQualifiedErrorId : [Server=YQBPR0101MB0721,RequestId=939faf33-1d64-4b65-bbca-10f488cb3e62,TimeStamp=12/20/2
    017 3:29:51 PM] [FailureCategory=Cmdlet-DataValidationException] EBEDFDDF,Microsoft.Exchange.Management.RecipientT
asks.NewDistributionGroup
    + PSComputerName        : outlook.office365.com

PS C:\WINDOWS\system32> _
```

Figure 4-27. *Blocked words in distribution lists*

The next option is the Distribution Group Naming Policy, which allows you to set a naming policy for each distribution list; the policy can also be dynamic depending on who creates it. Exchange Online allows you to add a prefix and a suffix to each distribution list. For example, if you wanted every distribution group to start with the word *DL*, have the requested group name, and finish with the country of the user who created it, you would run the following cmdlet:

```
Set-OrganizationConfig -DistributionGroupNamingPolicy  "DL_<GroupName>_
<CountryOrRegion>"
```

After applying the policy, if you wanted to create a group with the name "PowerShell Book Review," the final name would be *DL_PowerShell Book Review_Canada* as seen in Figure 4-28.

```
Administrator: Windows PowerShell                                                    —  □  ×
PS C:\WINDOWS\system32> New-DistributionGroup -Name "PowerShell Book Review"
New! Office 365 Groups are the next generation of distribution lists.
Groups give teams shared tools for collaborating using email, files, a calendar, and more.
You can start right away using the New-UnifiedGroup cmdlet.

Name                            DisplayName                        GroupType PrimarySmtpAddress
----                            -----------                        --------- ------------------
DL_PowerShell Book Review_Canada DL_PowerShell Book Review_Canada Universal DL_PowerShellBookReview_Canada@Office365

PS C:\WINDOWS\system32>
```

Figure 4-28. *Distribution created with new naming convention*

We have now viewed how to manage organization changes for Exchange Online, including the distribution list governance policies. Next up, let's continue looking at how to manage distribution groups using PowerShell!

Managing Distribution Groups

Distribution groups have been around for quite some time, and a lot of organizations use them every day. While Microsoft recommends upgrading distribution groups to Office 365 Groups due to the additional features Office 365 Groups offer, those additional features are not always needed. You will start by learning how to see the distribution groups in your tenant!

To view all the distribution groups in your environment, you need to use the `Get-DistributionGroup` PowerShell cmdlet. In Figure 4-29, we are getting the alias, display name, and primary email address of every distribution group.

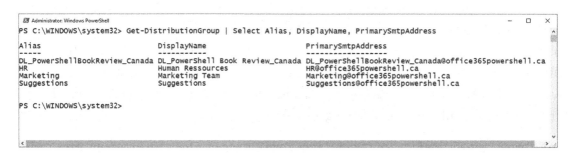

Figure 4-29. *Get-DistributionGroup Cmdlet*

To create a new distribution group, you must use `New-DistributionGroup` and specify the name of the distribution group, as well as any parameters you might want to configure. Some of the most common parameters are listed in Table 4-4.

Table 4-4. *New-DistributionGroup Parameters*

Parameter	Description
Name	This parameter specifies the unique name of the group. The maximum length is 64 characters.
Alias	This parameter specifies the Exchange alias (also known as the mail nickname) for the recipient.
DisplayName	The DisplayName parameter specifies the display name of the group.

(continued)

Table 4-4. (*continued*)

Parameter	Description
IgnoreNamingPolicy	The IgnoreNamingPolicy switch specifies whether to prevent this group from being affected by your organization's distribution group naming policy.
ManagedBy	The ManagedBy parameter specifies an owner for the group. A group must have at least one owner. If you don't use this parameter to specify the owner when you create the group, the user account that created the group is the owner.
Members	The Members parameter specifies the recipients (mail-enabled objects) that are members of the group.
PrimarySmtpAddress	The PrimarySmtpAddress parameter specifies the primary return email address that's used for the recipient.
RequireSender AuthenticationEnabled	The RequireSenderAuthenticationEnabled parameter specifies whether to accept messages only from authenticated (internal) senders.

If you wanted to create a new distribution group with the following requirements:

- Name: Contoso News

- Owners: John Smith

- Members: Jeff Collins, Vlad Admin

- Can only receive emails from internal employees

- Email Address: cnews@office365PowerShell.ca

you would run the following cmdlet:

```
New-DistributionGroup `
-Name "Contoso News" `
-Members jeff.collins,VladAdmin `
-ManagedBy john.smith `
-IgnoreNamingPolicy `
-RequireSenderAuthenticationEnabled $true `
-PrimarySmtpAddress cnews@office365PowerShell.ca
```

111

To modify the properties of a distribution group, you need to use the
Set-DistributionGroup PowerShell cmdlet. You can change all the parameters that
you saw in Table 4-4, as well as configure some new ones. Table 4-5 showcases some of
the most common parameters that you can change using the Set-DistributionGroup
cmdlet.

Table 4-5. *Parameters of the Set-DistributionGroup cmdlet*

Parameter	Description
AcceptMessagesOnlyFrom	The AcceptMessagesOnlyFrom parameter specifies who is allowed to send messages to this recipient. Messages from other senders are rejected.
HiddenFromAddressListsEnabled	The HiddenFromAddressListsEnabled parameter specifies whether this recipient is visible in address lists.
MailTip	The MailTip parameter specifies the custom MailTip text for this recipient. The MailTip is shown to senders when they start drafting an email message to this recipient.

If you wanted to modify a distribution group you previously created to have a
MailTip, as well as to hide the Distribution Group from the Global Address List, you
would run the following cmdlet:

```
Set-DistributionGroup cnews@office365PowerShell.ca `
-MailTip "Please Note this e-mail adress is reserved for Management Only" `
-HiddenFromAddressListsEnabled $true
```

Finally, to remove a distribution group, you can run the Remove-DistributionGroup
cmdlet, specifying which group you want to remove, as in the following example:

```
Remove-DistributionGroup cnews@office365PowerShell.ca
```

Now that we know how to manage distribution groups, let's learn how to manage the
members inside them.

Manage Distribution Group Membership

To view the members of a distribution group, you simply have to run the Get-DistributionGroupMember cmdlet and specify for which group you want to see the membership, as seen in Figure 4-30.

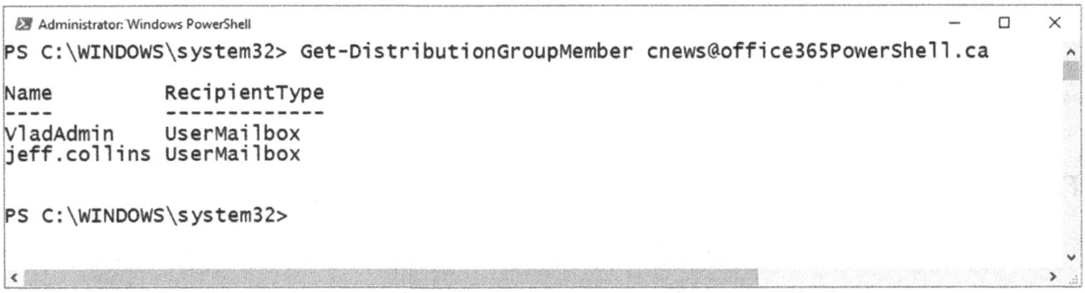

```
Administrator: Windows PowerShell                                    —    □    ×
PS C:\WINDOWS\system32> Get-DistributionGroupMember cnews@office365PowerShell.ca

Name           RecipientType
----           -------------
VladAdmin      UserMailbox
jeff.collins   UserMailbox


PS C:\WINDOWS\system32>
```

Figure 4-30.   *Viewing the members of a distribution group*

To add a member to a distribution group, you need to use Add-DistributionGroupMember, specifying the group that you want to add the member to and the user that you wish to add, as seen in the following example:

```
Add-DistributionGroupMember `
-Identity cnews@office365PowerShell.ca `
-Member john.smith
```

You can also completely replace the members of a group by using the Update-DistributionGroupMember cmdlet. This will remove all previous members and add the ones you specify inside. If you run the following cmdlet, it will replace all members inside with only Jeff Collins and Liam Jones, as you can see in Figure 4-31.

```
Update-DistributionGroupMember `
-Identity cnews@office365PowerShell.ca `
-Member liam.jones, jeff.collins `
-Confirm:$False
```

```
Administrator: Windows PowerShell                                                      −   □   ×
PS C:\WINDOWS\system32> Get-DistributionGroupMember cnews@office365PowerShell.ca

Name            RecipientType
----            -------------
VladAdmin       UserMailbox
jeff.collins    UserMailbox
liam.jones      UserMailbox
john.smith      UserMailbox


PS C:\WINDOWS\system32> Update-DistributionGroupMember -Identity cnews@office365PowerShell.ca -Member liam.jones, jeff.c
ollins -Confirm:$False
PS C:\WINDOWS\system32> Get-DistributionGroupMember cnews@office365PowerShell.ca

Name            RecipientType
----            -------------
jeff.collins    UserMailbox
liam.jones      UserMailbox


PS C:\WINDOWS\system32> _
```

Figure 4-31. *Updating the members of a distribution group*

Lastly, to remove a member from a distribution group, you can run the Remove-DistributionGroupMember cmdlet, specifying the identity of the distribution group and the member to remove. In the example that follows, Jeff Collins is being removed from the distribution group:

```
Remove-DistributionGroupMember `
-Identity cnews@office365PowerShell.ca `
-Member jeff.collins
```

That's it for distribution group membership management with PowerShell! Next up, let's look at what reports we can have on our Exchange mailboxes.

Mailbox Reporting

Exchange Online provides us with cmdlets that allow us as administrators to get information about how users are using their mailboxes. One of the first cmdlets we will look at is the Get-MailboxStatistics cmdlet, which allows you to view the usage on mailboxes. Simply running the cmdlet and specifying the identity of the mailbox will show you the display name, how many items are in that mailbox, and the last logon time, as you can see in Figure 4-32.

Figure 4-32. *Viewing mailbox statistics for a user*

You can also view multiple other properties; for example, running the following cmdlet will show you the information on size and deleted items you see in Figure 4-33.

```
Get-MailboxStatistics -Identity vlad-admin@office365powershell.ca | Select
DisplayName, DeletedItemCount, ItemCount, TotalItemSize, LastLogonTime
```

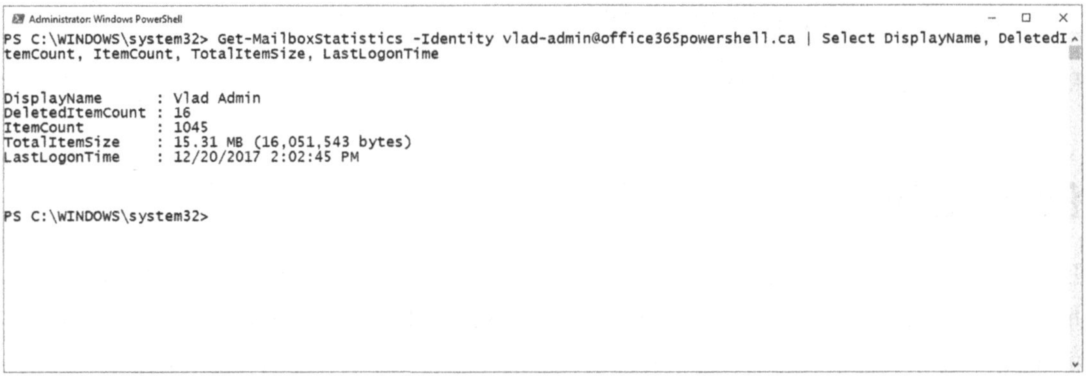

Figure 4-33. *Filtered mailbox properties*

You can also run the cmdlet across all mailboxes. For example, the following cmdlet will return the display name of every user who hasn't logged on since December 15, 2017:

```
Get-Mailbox | Get-MailboxStatistics | Where-Object {$_.LastLogonTime -lt
"12/15/2017"} | Select DisplayName
```

Another useful feature would be to return all the mailboxes that have more than 20,000 emails in their mailbox, which is done with the following cmdlet:

```
Get-Mailbox | Get-MailboxStatistics | Where-Object {$_.ItemCount -gt 20000}
```

As you can see, Get-MailboxStatistics allows you to see how users are using Exchange Online and gives you information you couldn't normally see.

Before finishing this chapter, it is important you learn how to disconnect your remote PowerShell Session from Exchange Online.

Disconnecting from Exchange Online

When you are done with the tasks you wanted to do with PowerShell, make sure to disconnect the remote PowerShell session. There is a limit to how many sessions you can connect to Exchange Online, and if you simply close the PowerShell window without disconnecting the session you might use all of the available sessions, forcing you to wait until they expire before being able to reconnect. To disconnect the remote PowerShell session, you can run the following cmdlet:

```
Remove-PSSession $Session
```

Conclusion

In this chapter, we learned how to manage Exchange Online using PowerShell. We first looked at how to connect to Exchange Online, whether you are using simple authentication or multi-factor authentication. We then learned how to manage users and mailboxes, as well as a few common tasks such as managing Out of Office replies and permissions on other mailboxes.

We then looked at how to manage organizational settings that apply to the whole tenant as well as how to manage distribution groups. Lastly, we learned how to view reports on our Exchange Online mailboxes and how to disconnect from Exchange Online.

In the next chapter, we will learn how to manage Skype for Business Online with PowerShell.

CHAPTER 5

Managing Skype for Business Online

In this chapter, we will first learn how to get the Skype for Business PowerShell module and connect to Skype for Business Online. We will then learn how to manage both the tenant and the per-user Skype for Business policies using PowerShell.

Finally, we will look at how to run PowerShell cmdlets for Skype for Business when you are working in a hybrid scenario where you have part of your topology running a Skype for Business server on-premises and part using Skype for Business Online, part of Office 365.

Connecting to Skype for Business Online

Similar to SharePoint and Azure Active Directory, the first thing that you have to do to connect to Skype for Business Online is download a module from the Microsoft Download Center. This PowerShell module contains all the PowerShell cmdlets that allow us to connect to Skype for Business Online.

Note   The Skype for Business Online Windows PowerShell Module can be downloaded at `https://www.microsoft.com/en-us/download/details.aspx?id=39366`.

Similar to the previous chapters, you need to be on a 64-bit machine that runs Windows 7 Service Pack 1 or later, or Windows Server 2008 R2 Service Pack 1 or later, as well as have an account that has the Skype for Business Admin Role assigned. You will also need to be a local administrator on your computer in order to be able to install the module.

117

© Vlad Catrinescu 2018
V. Catrinescu, *Essential PowerShell for Office 365*, https://doi.org/10.1007/978-1-4842-3129-6_5

After you download the Skype for Business Online Windows PowerShell Module from the preceding link, you can start the installation. The first step is to agree to the terms, as seen in Figure 5-1.

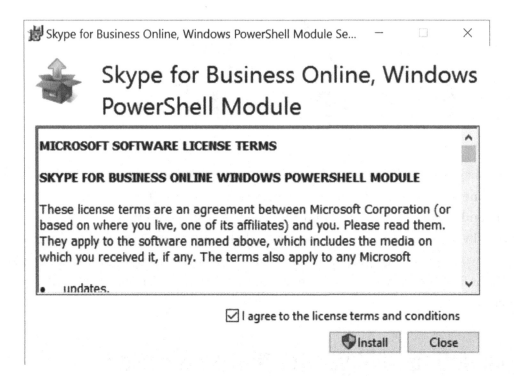

Figure 5-1. *Skype for Business Online PowerShell Module Setup*

You then have to click on Install and wait a few seconds for the module to be installed on your computer. This module only contains the cmdlets to connect to Skype for Business Online, and not all the cmdlets that you can use in Skype for Business. Similar to Exchange Online, a temporary module is downloaded every time you connect to Skype for Business Online.

Once the module is installed, to connect to Skype for Business you will first have to save the credentials with which you wish to connect in a variable. In the following example, we are saving those credentials in a variable called $cred:

```
$cred=Get-Credential
```

We then need to connect to Skype for Business Online by using New-CsOnlineSession and saving the information in a variable; for example, $session:

```
$session = New-CsOnlineSession -Credential $cred
```

Optionally, you can add the -Verbose parameter if you want a more transparent view of what PowerShell is doing in the background to connect to Skype for Business, as seen in Figure 5-2:

```
$session = New-CsOnlineSession -Credential $cred -Verbose
```

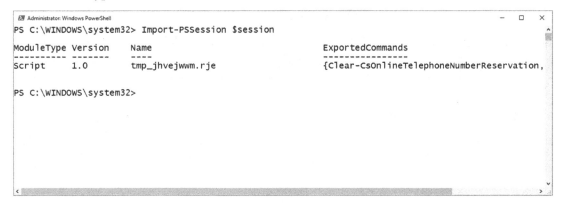

Figure 5-2. *New-CSOnlineSession*

Next, we have to import the session into our current PowerShell session to be able to manage Skype for Business; we do this by using Import-PSSession:

```
Import-PSSession $session
```

This will import a temporary PowerShell module into our PowerShell session that contains all the latest Skype for Business Online cmdlets. The module name can be seen in the Name field, as seen in Figure 5-3. This name will be different every time you connect to Skype for Business Online.

```
Administrator: Windows PowerShell                                          —    □    ×
PS C:\WINDOWS\system32> Import-PSSession $session

ModuleType Version    Name                          ExportedCommands
---------- -------    ----                          ----------------
Script     1.0        tmp_jhvejwwm.rje              {Clear-CsOnlineTelephoneNumberReservation,

PS C:\WINDOWS\system32>
```

Figure 5-3. *Import-PSSession*

You are now connected to Skype for Business Online. Since you know the module name, you can always run `Get-Command -Module <Module Name>` to see the most up-to-date list of available cmdlets. Let's take a look at some of the ones you will probably use the most.

Available cmdlets

The PowerShell module for Skype for Business Online allows you to configure policies for certain users or for the whole tenant, as well as use more advanced cmdlets to configure Conferencing, PTSN, and IP telephone.

In Table 5-1, you can see some of the cmdlets available to help you manage users in Skype for Business Online.

Table 5-1. *User cmdlets for Skype for Business Online*

Cmdlet	Description
Get-CsOnlineUser	Use this cmdlet to return information about users who have accounts homed on Skype for Business Online.
Set-CsUser	Use this cmdlet to modify Skype for Business Online properties for an existing user account.
Get-CsUserPstnSettings	Use the Get-CsUserPstnSettings cmdlet to retrieve a voice-enabled user's public switched telephone network (PSTN) settings.
Set-CsUserPstnSettings	Use the Set-CsUserPstnSettings cmdlet to modify an existing voice-enabled user's public switched telephone network (PSTN) settings.
Get-CsUserSession	Use the Get-CsUserSession cmdlet to retrieve user session information within a specified date range.

We also have cmdlets that allow us to manage policies for the client, conferencing, external access, presence, and more! In Table 5-2 you can see some of those.

Table 5-2. *Policy cmdlets in Skype for Business Online*

Cmdlet	Description
Get-CsClientPolicy	This cmdlet returns information about the client policies configured for use in your organization. Among other things, client policies help determine the features that are available to Skype for Business Online users; for example, you might give some users the right to transfer files while denying this right to other users.
Grant-CsClientPolicy	This cmdlet assigns a client policy to a user or a group of users.
Get-CsConferencing Policy	This cmdlet returns information about the conferencing policies that have been configured for use in your organization. Conferencing policies determine the features and capabilities that can be used in a conference; this includes everything from whether or not the conference can include IP audio and video to the maximum number of people who can attend a meeting.
New-CsConferencing Policy	This cmdlet creates a new conferencing policy for use in your Skype for Business Online organization.
Get-CsMobilityPolicy	This cmdlet retrieves information about the mobility policies currently in use in an organization. Mobility policies determine whether or not a user can use the Skype for Business app. These policies also manage a user's ability to employ Call via Work, a feature that enables users to make and receive phone calls on their mobile phone by using their work phone number instead of their mobile phone number. Mobility policies can also be used to require Wi-Fi connections when making or receiving calls.
Remove-CsMobilityPolicy	This cmdlet removes an existing mobility policy.
Get-CsOnline VoicemailPolicy	Use the Get-CsOnlineVoicemailPolicy cmdlet to get a list of all pre-configured policy instances of the Voicemail service.
Get-CsExternalAccess Policy	This cmdlet returns information about the external access policies that have been configured for use in your organization. External access policies determine whether or not your users can 1) communicate with users who have Session Initiation Protocol (SIP) accounts with a federated organization; 2) communicate with users who have SIP accounts with a public instant messaging (IM) provider such as Windows Live; and 3) access Skype for Business Server 2015 over the Internet without having to log on to your internal network.

Another category of cmdlets that you might use often are the ones for Skype Broadcast. Skype Meeting Broadcast is a feature of Skype for Business Online that allows you to broadcast meetings to an audience of up to 10,000 attendees. This is very useful when you want to invite the whole company to an announcement and so on. In comparison, at the time of writing this book the limit for a normal Skype for Business Online meeting was 250 participants. You can see the available cmdlets in Table 5-3.

Table 5-3. *Skype for Business Online Broadcast cmdlets*

Cmdlet	Description
Get-CsBroadcastMeeting Configuration	Use the Get-CsBroadcastMeetingConfiguration cmdlet to retrieve the global (and only) broadcast meeting configuration for your organization.
Set-CsBroadcastMeeting Configuration	Use the Set-CsBroadcastMeetingConfiguration cmdlet to modify the settings of your global (and only) broadcast meeting configuration.
Get-CsBroadcastMeeting Policy	Use the Get-CsBroadcastMeetingPolicy cmdlet to retrieve the predefined broadcast meeting policies and their settings.
Grant-CsBroadcastMeeting Policy	Use the Grant-CsBroadcastMeetingPolicy cmdlet to assign a broadcast meeting policy to a user.

Now that we have looked at a few of the available cmdlets, let's learn how to use them.

Executing PowerShell cmdlets for Skype for Business Online

Now that we are connected to Skype for Business Online, we can manage our users as well as our policies via PowerShell. Let's start with the users.

Managing Users and Policies

To see all the users—as well as all their properties—we need to use the Get-CsOnlineUser cmdlet. This cmdlet returns a lot of properties for each user, but you can filter the results that you want to show or output by using pipelines. In Figure 5-4, we opted to only show the usernames and the SIP address of all our Skype for Business users.

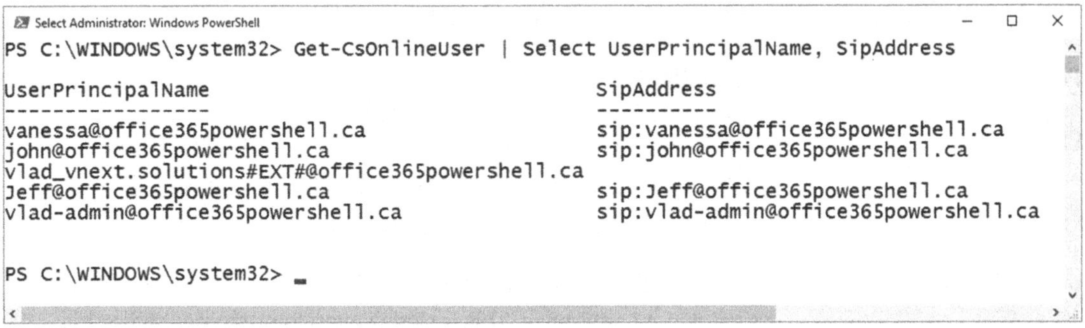

Figure 5-4. *Get-CSOnlineUser*

To modify a user's properties, you could use the Set-CsUser PowerShell cmdlet. For example, if you would like to block the user vanessa@office365powershell.ca from using audio and video, you would use the following cmdlet:

```
Set-CsUser -Identity vanessa@office365powershell.ca -AudioVideoDisabled
$true
```

While this can easily also be done via the user interface, PowerShell becomes very useful if you want to apply this setting to a whole department. For example, if you wanted to apply the same block to the whole Research department you could run the following cmdlet:

```
Get-CsOnlineUser -LdapFilter "Department=Research" | Set-CsUser
-AudioVideoDisabled $true
```

Another thing that you can do only with PowerShell in Skype for Business Online is apply different policies to users. Let's take a look at what those are!

Managing Policies

Policies help determine the Skype for Business Online features and capabilities that are available to certain users and/or to the whole organization. In Table 5-4, you can see the available policy categories that are available.

Table 5-4. *Skype for Business Online Policy Categories*

Policy	Description
Client Policy	Client policies are used to determine the Lync client features that are available to users. For example, you might give the capability to transfer files to some users but not to others.
Conferencing Policy	Conferencing policies determine the features and capabilities that can be used in a conference. This includes everything from whether the conference can include IP audio and video to the maximum number of people who can attend a meeting.
External Access Policy	External access policies are used to determine whether your users are allowed to communicate with users from federated domains, and/or whether your users are allowed to communicate with users who have accounts on public IM providers, such as Windows Live or AOL.
Voice Policy	Voice policies are used to manage Enterprise Voice features, such as simultaneous ringing (the ability to have a second phone ring each time someone calls your office phone) and call forwarding.

In Skype for Business Online, you cannot create a custom policy as you could in the on-premises version of Lync or Skype for Business Server. Instead, you need to use one of the policies that has been pre-created by Microsoft specifically for Office 365. At the time of writing this book, the following policies were available in Skype for Business Online:

- 4 different client policies

- 224 different conferencing policies

- 5 different dial plans

- 5 different external access policies

- 1 hosted voicemail policy

- 4 different voice policies

Each type of policy has different parameters and can be assigned to individual users or to the whole organization. There are two ways to find the name of the policy that you are looking to assign to a certain user.

The first option is to export all the policies of a certain type to a CSV file so you can analyze them. For example, you can export the external access policies to a CSV file by using the following cmdlet:

```
Get-CsExternalAccessPolicy | Select Identity,
EnableFederationAccess, EnableXmppAccess, EnablePublicCloudAccess,
EnablePublicCloudAudioVideoAccess, EnableOutsideAccess |  Export-csv
C:\Apress\Ch05\Policies\externalacess.csv -NoTypeInformation
```

The result will be a CSV file as seen in Figure 5-5; it will show the identity, parameters, and values for each available policy.

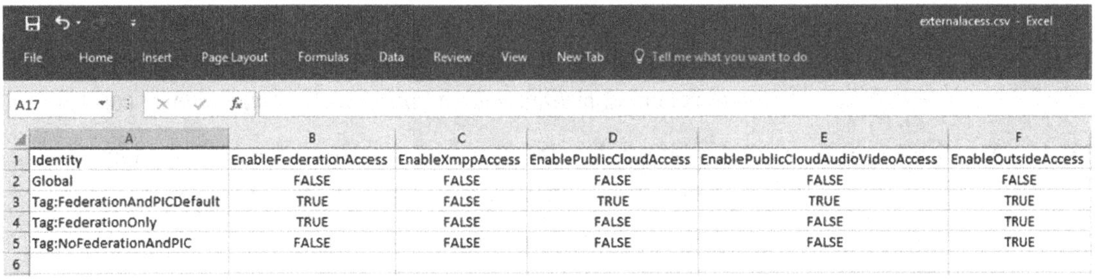

	A	B	C	D	E	F
1	Identity	EnableFederationAccess	EnableXmppAccess	EnablePublicCloudAccess	EnablePublicCloudAudioVideoAccess	EnableOutsideAccess
2	Global	FALSE	FALSE	FALSE	FALSE	FALSE
3	Tag:FederationAndPICDefault	TRUE	FALSE	TRUE	TRUE	TRUE
4	Tag:FederationOnly	TRUE	FALSE	FALSE	FALSE	TRUE
5	Tag:NoFederationAndPIC	FALSE	FALSE	FALSE	FALSE	TRUE
6						

Figure 5-5. *External access policies in Skype for Business Online*

The next step will be to understand what each parameter does. In Table 5-5, you can see the definition and implication for each parameter.

Table 5-5. *External Access Policy Parameters in Skype for Business Online*

Parameter	Description
EnableFederation Access	Indicates whether the user is allowed to communicate with people who have SIP accounts with a federated organization
EnableXmppAccess	Indicates whether the user is allowed to communicate with users who have SIP accounts with a federated XMPP (Extensible Messaging and Presence Protocol) partner; the default value is False
EnablePublicCloud Access	Indicates whether the user is allowed to communicate with people who have SIP accounts with a public Internet connectivity provider such as MSN
EnablePublicCloudAudio VideoAccess	Indicates whether the user is allowed to conduct audio/video conversations with people who have SIP accounts with a public Internet connectivity provider such as MSN. When set to False, audio and video options in Skype for Business will be disabled any time a user is communicating with a public Internet connectivity contact.
EnableOutsideAccess	Indicates whether the user is allowed to connect to Skype for Business Server 2015 over the Internet without logging on to the organization's internal network

Now that we know what each parameter means, if we want to allow Vanessa to communicate with Federated Users, but not with Windows Live Users, we would need to find a policy where EnableFederationAccess is true and EnablePublicCloudAccess is false. By looking at the CSV file in Figure 5-5, we can see that the only available policy with this criteria is Tag:FederationOnly.

The second way to find a policy that fits our needs is to query PowerShell directly. This of course requires us to know exactly what parameters we want and with what values. Since I know I want a policy where EnableFederationAccess is true and EnablePublicCloudAccess is false, I could run the following cmdlet:

```
Get-CsExternalAccessPolicy | Where-Object {$_.EnableFederationAccess -eq
$True -and $_.EnablePublicCloudAccess -eq $False}
```

The result seen in Figure 5-6 is the same policy as with the other method.

```
PS C:\WINDOWS\system32> Get-CsExternalAccessPolicy | Where-Object {$_.EnableFederationAccess -eq $True -and $_.EnablePub
licCloudAccess -eq $False}

Identity                         : Tag:FederationOnly
Description                      :
EnableFederationAccess           : True
EnableXmppAccess                 : False
EnablePublicCloudAccess          : False
EnablePublicCloudAudioVideoAccess : False
EnableOutsideAccess              : True
```

Figure 5-6. *Get-CsExternalAccessPolicy*

After we know the policy we want to assign, we can use the Grant-
CsExternalAccessPolicy cmdlet to assign this policy to Vanessa, as seen in the
following example.

Note   While the identity of certain policy names includes the word Tag:, you
must not include it when granting a policy to a user.

```
Grant-CsExternalAccessPolicy -Identity "vanessa@office365powershell.ca"
-PolicyName "FederationOnly"
```

Now that we have reviewed the external access policies, what about the others? In
Table 5-6 you can see the cmdlet to get the properties for each of the available policy
types.

Table 5-6. *Skype for Business Online Policy Cmdlets*

Policy	Cmdlets
Client Policy	Get-CsClientPolicy
Conferencing Policy	Get-CsConferencingPolicy
External Access Policy	Get-CsExternalAccessPolicy
Voice Policy	Get-CsVoicePolicy

You can use the Export-CSV cmdlet to export all the properties available into a CSV
file; then, you will be able to filter and find the policies that you want.

External Communications

Skype for Business Online allows you to configure multiple settings for how your users can communicate outside the company. Most of the settings at the organizational level can be done via the `Set-CsTenantFederationConfiguration` cmdlet.

To turn off external communications completely, you can set `-AllowFederatedUsers` to false as seen here:

```
Set-CsTenantFederationConfiguration -AllowFederatedUsers $false
```

If you keep it on (default) you can set either an allowed list or a blocked list of domains. If you set an allowed list, your employees will only be allowed to add and talk to external users from that domain. If you set a blocked list, your users will be able to add users from every domain except the ones specified in the blocked list. You can be in either "allowed list" or "blocked list" mode, but not both at the same time.

As an example, let's enable external communication for our users, but only for the `Microsoft.com` and `Apress.com` domains. We first need to create a new domains object by using the `New-CsEdgeDomainPattern` cmdlet:

```
$domain = New-CsEdgeDomainPattern -Domain "Microsoft.com"
$domain2 = New-CsEdgeDomainPattern -Domain "Apress.com"
```

We then need to create a new allowed list by using the `New-CSEdgeAllowList` cmdlet:

```
$AllowedList = New-CSEdgeAllowList –AllowedDomain $domain,$domain2
```

Lastly, we have to apply this list to our tenant by using the `Set-CsTenantFederation Configuration` cmdlet:

```
Set-CsTenantFederationConfiguration -AllowedDomains $AllowedList
```

It may take up to 24 hours for this to be applied, so wait a day before testing it out; however, the change can be seen in the Skype for Business Online Admin Center right away. The result of the preceding cmdlets can be seen in Figure 5-7.

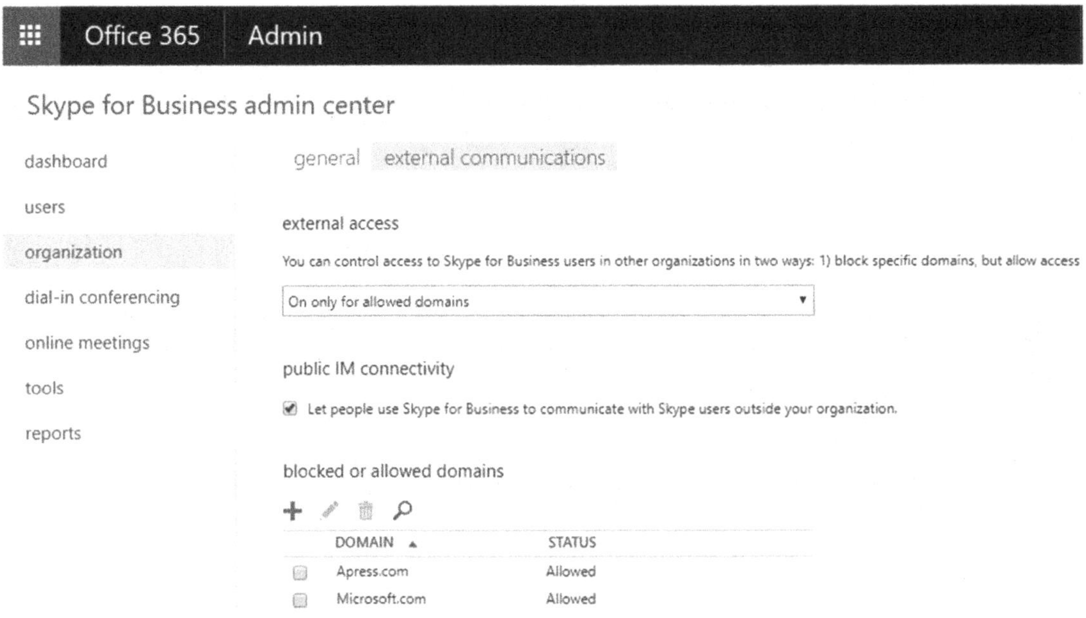

Figure 5-7. *External communications in the Skype for Business Admin Center*

We have just looked at how to control external communications in our Skype for Business tenant; now, let's take a look at Skype for Business Broadcast.

Skype for Business Broadcast

Skype for Business Broadcast is disabled by default in your Office 365 tenant because this feature may not respect all the latest rules of the European Union. Here is the note, as described by Microsoft on the `support.office.com` website.

Warning   Skype Meeting Broadcast is turned off by default because distribution of the media content of a broadcast meeting uses Microsoft Azure's Content Delivery Network (CDN) to achieve very high scale to support thousands of people watching a broadcast. The chunked media content passing through the CDN is encrypted, and the CDN cache has a limited lifetime. Also, the Azure CDN component may not yet meet all elements of the EU Model Clauses stemming from the EU Data Protection Directive. By enabling this feature you acknowledge this notice.

To view the current settings of Skype for Business Broadcast in your tenant, you need to run the Get-CsBroadcastMeetingConfiguration cmdlet. To view if Skype for Business Broadcast is enabled or not, you can look at the EnableBroadcastMeeting cmdlet as highlighted in Figure 5-8.

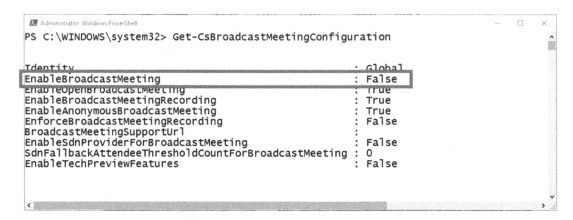

Figure 5-8. *Get-CsBroadcastMeetingConfiguration*

To change the configuration of Skype for Business Broadcast, you must use the Set-CsBroadcastMeetingConfiguration cmdlet and specify the parameters you want to change. You can view some of those parameters in Table 5-7.

Table 5-7. *Skype for Business Broadcast Parameters*

Parameter	Description
BroadcastMeeting SupportUrl	Specifies a URL where broadcast meeting attendees can find support information or FAQs specific to that meeting. The URL will be displayed during the broadcast meeting.
EnableAnonymous BroadcastMeeting	Specifies whether non-authenticated attendees are allowed to join and view the web-based portion of the meeting. Valid input for this parameter is $true or $false. The default value is $true.
EnableBroadcast Meeting	Specifies whether broadcast meetings are enabled. Valid input for this parameter is $true or $false. The default value is $false.
EnableBroadcastMeeting Recording	Specifies whether broadcast meetings can be recorded at the server level. Valid input for this parameter is $true or $false. The default value is $true.
EnableOpenBroadcast Meeting	Specifies if the organizer is allowed to create broadcast meetings that allow anyone in the organizer's organization to attend. The default and only setting is $true.
EnableTechPreview Features	Set to $true to enable use of features available in a technical preview program. Set to $false to disable the technical-preview features.
EnforceBroadcastMeeting Recording	Specifies whether all meetings will be recorded. Valid input for this parameter is $true or $false. The default value is $false.

For example, a company might have the following business requirements:

- Skype for Business Broadcast must be enabled.

- Only authenticated members can join any Skype for Business Broadcast.

- All Skype for Business Broadcast meetings must be recorded.

In order to respect these business requirements, here is the PowerShell cmdlet we must run:

```
Set-CsBroadcastMeetingConfiguration
    -EnableBroadcastMeeting $true
    -EnableAnonymousBroadcastMeeting $false
    -EnforceBroadcastMeetingRecording $true
```

You can also assign a different configuration per user by assigning them a Skype for Business Broadcast meeting policy. You can get all the policy options by using the Get-CsBroadcastMeetingPolicy cmdlet. As discussed earlier in this chapter, I have used the following cmdlet to export the available policies and their parameters to a CSV file, which you can see in Figure 5-9.

```
Get-CsBroadcastMeetingPolicy | Select Identity, AllowBroadcastMeeting,
AllowOpenBroadcastMeeting, AllowAnonymousBroadcastMeeting,
BroadcastMeetingRecordingEnforced | Export-CSV C:\Apress\Ch05\Policies\
Broadcast.csv -NoTypeInformation
```

Identity	AllowBroadcastMeeting	AllowOpenBroadcastMeeting	AllowAnonymousBroadcastMeeting	BroadcastMeetingRecordingEnforced
Global	TRUE	TRUE	TRUE	FALSE
Tag:BroadcastMeetingPolicyDefault	TRUE	TRUE	TRUE	FALSE
Tag:BroadcastMeetingPolicyDisabled	FALSE	FALSE	FALSE	FALSE
Tag:BroadcastMeetingPolicyAllEnabled	TRUE	TRUE	TRUE	FALSE
Tag:BroadcastMeetingPolicyAnonymousDisabled	TRUE	TRUE	FALSE	FALSE
Tag:BroadcastMeetingPolicyRecordingDisabled	TRUE	TRUE	TRUE	FALSE
Tag:BroadcastMeetingPolicyAnonymousDisabledAndRecordingNotEnforced	TRUE	TRUE	FALSE	FALSE
Tag:BroadcastMeetingPolicyAnonymousDisabledAndRecordingEnforced	TRUE	TRUE	FALSE	TRUE
Tag:BroadcastMeetingPolicyAnonymousAndRecordingDisabled	TRUE	TRUE	FALSE	FALSE

Figure 5-9. *Skype for Business Online Broadcast policies*

That's about it for the Skype for Business Online PowerShell cmdlets that we can run in our tenant. While a lot of companies are running Skype for Business in either cloud-only mode or on-premises only, some organizations are running Skype for Business in hybrid mode. Let's take a look at how to run PowerShell cmdlets in a hybrid deployment.

Running cmdlets in a Hybrid Environment

A hybrid deployment is when we have Skype for Business Server or Lync Server running on-premises for some of our users, while some are using Skype for Business Online. If you are someone who has been a Lync or Skype for Business admin for a while, you might have already realized that most Skype for Business Online cmdlets are the same as the PowerShell cmdlets used in Lync Server 2013 or Skype for Business Server 2015. Since you probably have all the tools to manage Skype for Business on your on-premises server, you will likely want to connect to Skype for Business Online from there as well. When you connect to Skype for Business Online from your Skype for Business on-premises server, you will still have to download the required PowerShell module, save your Office 365 credential, and start a New-CSOnlineSession as seen here:

```
$cred = Get-Credential
$Session= New-CsOnlineSession -Credential $cred
```

What is different is that when you run the Import-PSSession cmdlet, you must specify the -AllowClobber switch, as seen here:

```
Import-PSSession $Session -AllowClobber
```

After you have successfully connected to Skype for Business Online, you will need to find out what your tenant ID is by running the following cmdlet:

```
Get-CsTenant | Select TenantId
```

When running a cmdlet that is meant for Skype for Business Online, you will need to specify the -Tenant parameter and specify the tenant ID. For example, the first cmdlet that follows will get the external access policy for Skype for Business Online:

```
Get-CsExternalAccessPolicy
-Identity "global"
-Tenant "bf19b7db-6960-41e5-a139-2aa373474354"
```

This next one will get the same information, but from Skype for Business Server or Lync Server on-premises:

```
Get-CsExternalAccessPolicy
-Identity "global"
```

Specifying the tenant ID is only required when running cmdlets aimed at Skype for Business Online on a Lync server or Skype for Business server.

Conclusion

In this module, we have learned how to manage Skype for Business Online by using PowerShell. We have learned that we first need to download the Skype for Business PowerShell module, which only includes the cmdlets required to connect to Office 365. We have also learned how to create a remote PSSession and import it into our current session in order to be able to run cmdlets for Skype for Business Online from our machine.

We have looked at how to manage our Skype for Business user's properties and how to assign policies to a user, to a department, or to the whole organization using PowerShell. Since Skype for Business Online does not allow us to create our custom policies, we have learned how to view the available ones and how to export them to CSV files to make them easier to consume.

We have also learned how to manage external communications as well as Skype for Business Broadcast settings using PowerShell, and also how to run cmdlets in a Skype for Business hybrid environment.

In the next chapter, we will learn how to manage the Office 365 Compliance Center using PowerShell.

CHAPTER 6

Managing the Office 365 Security & Compliance Center

The Office 365 Security & Compliance Center allows companies to create compliance searches, put in place data-loss prevention (DLP) policies, create retention policies, and more. In this chapter, we will first learn how to use PowerShell to connect to the Compliance Center in Office 365. We will then look at the available cmdlets and learn how to use them to manage the Compliance Center.

Connecting to the Office 365 Security & Compliance Center

The Office 365 Security & Compliance Center does not have a module you need to install before connecting to it; you simply need to have a computer running Windows 7 Service Pack 1/Windows Server 2008 R2 Service Pack 1 or later as well as have Microsoft .Net Framework 4.5 and Windows Management Framework 4.0 installed.

After validating these requirements, open PowerShell as an administrator; the first thing you will have to do is save the credentials with which you wish to connect to the Office 365 Compliance Center in a variable.

In the following example, we are saving those credentials in a variable called $cred:

```
$cred=Get-Credential
```

© Vlad Catrinescu 2018
V. Catrinescu, *Essential PowerShell for Office 365*, https://doi.org/10.1007/978-1-4842-3129-6_6

We then need to create a remote PSSession to the Office 365 Compliance Center, which is done by using the following cmdlet:

```
$Session = New-PSSession `
    -ConfigurationName Microsoft.Exchange `
    -ConnectionUri https://ps.compliance.protection.outlook.com/
     powershell-liveid/ `
    -Credential $cred `
    -Authentication Basic `
```

This cmdlet will be the same for everyone, unless you have a tenant in Germany. For Office 365 Germany, change the ConnectionUri value to https://ps.compliance. protection.outlook.de/powershell-liveid/.

We then have to import the session into our current PowerShell session in order to be able to manage the Office 365 Compliance Center; this is done by using the Import-PSSession cmdlet as seen here:

```
Import-PSSession $Session
```

This will import a temporary PowerShell module into our PowerShell session that contains all the latest Office 365 Security & Compliance Center cmdlets. The module name can be seen in the Name field, as shown in Figure 6-1. The name of this temporary module will be different every time you connect to the Office 365 Compliance Center.

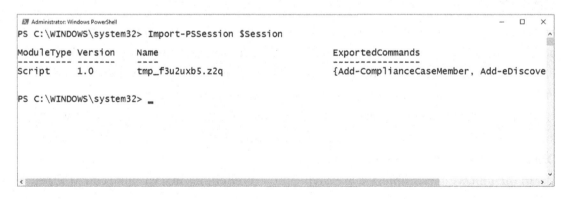

Figure 6-1. *Import-PSSession*

You are now connected to the Office 365 Compliance & Security Center. To view all the available cmdlets that you can use, run the `Get-Command -Module <Module Name>` cmdlet as seen in Figure 6-2.

```
Administrator: Windows PowerShell                                                    —    □    ×

PS C:\WINDOWS\system32> Get-Command -Module tmp_f3u2uxb5.z2q

CommandType     Name                                             Version    Source
-----------     ----                                             -------    ------
Function        Add-ComplianceCaseMember                         1.0        tmp_f3u2uxb5.z2q
Function        Add-eDiscoveryCaseAdmin                          1.0        tmp_f3u2uxb5.z2q
Function        Add-RoleGroupMember                              1.0        tmp_f3u2uxb5.z2q
Function        Enable-ComplianceTagStorage                      1.0        tmp_f3u2uxb5.z2q
Function        Get-ActivityAlert                                1.0        tmp_f3u2uxb5.z2q
Function        Get-AdminAuditLogConfig                          1.0        tmp_f3u2uxb5.z2q
Function        Get-AuditConfig                                  1.0        tmp_f3u2uxb5.z2q
Function        Get-AuditConfigurationPolicy                     1.0        tmp_f3u2uxb5.z2q
Function        Get-AuditConfigurationRule                       1.0        tmp_f3u2uxb5.z2q
Function        Get-CaseHoldPolicy                               1.0        tmp_f3u2uxb5.z2q
Function        Get-CaseHoldRule                                 1.0        tmp_f3u2uxb5.z2q
Function.       Get-ComplianceCase                               1.0        tmp_f3u2uxb5.z2q
Function        Get-ComplianceCaseMember                         1.0        tmp_f3u2uxb5.z2q
Function        Get-ComplianceSearch                             1.0        tmp_f3u2uxb5.z2q
Function        Get-ComplianceSearchAction                       1.0        tmp_f3u2uxb5.z2q
Function        Get-ComplianceSecurityFilter                     1.0        tmp_f3u2uxb5.z2q
Function        Get-ComplianceTag                                1.0        tmp_f3u2uxb5.z2q
Function        Get-ComplianceTagStorage                         1.0        tmp_f3u2uxb5.z2q
Function        Get-DataRetentionReport                          1.0        tmp_f3u2uxb5.z2q
Function        Get-DeviceComplianceDetailsReport                1.0        tmp_f3u2uxb5.z2q
Function        Get-DeviceComplianceDetailsReportFilter          1.0        tmp_f3u2uxb5.z2q
Function        Get-DeviceCompliancePolicyInventory              1.0        tmp_f3u2uxb5.z2q
Function        Get-DeviceComplianceReportDate                   1.0        tmp_f3u2uxb5.z2q
Function        Get-DeviceComplianceSummaryReport                1.0        tmp_f3u2uxb5.z2q
```

Figure 6-2. *The available cmdlets*

Let's take a look at the ones you will likely use most.

Office 365 Security & Compliance Center cmdlets

The Office 365 Security & Compliance Center PowerShell module allows you to create content searches, manage data-loss prevention policies, create eDiscovery case-hold policies and rules, as well as manage retention policies. Let's take a look at some of those. In Table 6-1 you can see some of the cmdlets for content search.

Table 6-1. *Content Search cmdlets*

Cmdlet	Description
Get-ComplianceSearch	Use the Get-ComplianceSearch cmdlet to view estimated compliance searches in Exchange Server 2016 and in the Office 365 Security & Compliance Center.
New-ComplianceSearch	Use the New-ComplianceSearch cmdlet to create compliance searches in Exchange Server 2016 and in the Office 365 Security & Compliance Center. You use this cmdlet to define the search criteria.
Start-ComplianceSearch	Use the Start-ComplianceSearch cmdlet to start stopped, completed, or not yet started compliance searches in Exchange Server 2016 and in the Office 365 Security & Compliance Center.
Get-ComplianceSearchAction	Use the Get-ComplianceSearchAction cmdlet to view information about compliance search actions in Exchange Server 2016 and in the Office 365 Security & Compliance Center.
Get-ComplianceSecurityFilter	Use the Get-ComplianceSecurityFilter cmdlet to view compliance security filters in the Security & Compliance Center. These filters allow specified users to search only a subset of mailboxes and SharePoint Online or OneDrive for Business sites in your Office 365 organization.

We also have cmdlets that allow us to manage data-loss prevention policies for our content. In Table 6-2 you can see some of those.

Table 6-2. *Data-loss Prevention (DLP) cmdlets*

Cmdlet	Description
Get-DlpCompliancePolicy	Use the `Get-DlpCompliancePolicy` to view data-loss prevention (DLP) policies in the Security & Compliance Center.
New-DlpCompliancePolicy	Use the `New-DlpCompliancePolicy` cmdlet to create data-loss prevention (DLP) policies in the Security & Compliance Center. DLP policies contain DLP rules that identify, monitor, and protect sensitive information.
Set-DlpComplianceRule	Use the `Set-DlpComplianceRule` to modify data-loss prevention (DLP) rules in the Security & Compliance Center. DLP rules define sensitive information to be protected and the actions to take on rule violations.
Get-DlpSensitiveInformationType	Use the `Get-DlpSensitiveInformationType` cmdlet to list the sensitive information types that are defined for your organization in the Security & Compliance Center. Sensitive information types are used by data-loss prevention (DLP) rules to check for sensitive information such as social security, passport, or credit card numbers.
Get-DlpSensitiveInformationType RulePackage	Use the `Get-DlpSensitiveInformation TypeConfig` cmdlet to view data-loss prevention (DLP) sensitive information–type rule packages in the Security & Compliance Center.

Another important category of cmdlets that you will use when managing the Office 365 Compliance Center is the Security and Permissions cmdlets. Table 6-3 covers the cmdlets used to assign different roles and groups for the Office 365 Compliance Center.

Table 6-3. *Office 365 Compliance Center Security and Permissions cmdlets*

Cmdlet	Description
Get-ManagementRole	Use the Get-ManagementRole cmdlet to view management roles that have been created in your organization.
Get-RoleGroup	Use the Get-RoleGroup cmdlet to retrieve a list of management role groups.
Set-RoleGroup	Use the Set-RoleGroup cmdlet to modify who can add or remove members to or from management role groups or change the name of the role group.
Add-RoleGroupMember	Use the Add-RoleGroupMember cmdlet to add members to a management role group.
Update-RoleGroupMember	Use the Update-RoleGroupMember cmdlet to modify the members of a management role group.

Now that we have looked at a few of the available cmdlets, let's take a look at how to use them.

Executing PowerShell cmdlets in the Office 365 Security & Compliance Center

Now that we are connected to the Office 365 Compliance Center, we can begin managing our security and policies using PowerShell. Let's start with the permissions.

Managing Permissions

To manage all the features and permissions of the Office 365 Security & Compliance Center, you need to be in the Organization Management role. By default, in Office 365, the Office 365 Global Administrators are assigned that role. If you are not an Office 365 Global Administrator, you might not be able to manage the Office 365 Security & Compliance Center until you get permission from your Global Administrator. At the time of writing this book, the Office 365 Compliance Center contains eight different roles, which you can see in Table 6-4.

Table 6-4. *Description of Roles in the Office 365 Compliance Center*

Role Group	Description
Compliance Administrator	Members can manage settings for device management, data-loss prevention, reports, and preservation.
eDiscovery Manager	Members can perform searches and place holds on mailboxes, SharePoint Online sites, and OneDrive for Business locations. Members can also create and manage eDiscovery cases, add and remove members to a case, and create and edit content searches associated with a case.
Organization Management	Members can control permissions for accessing features in the Security & Compliance Center and also manage settings for device management, data-loss prevention, reports, and preservation.
Reviewer	Members can only view the list of cases on the eDiscovery cases page in the Security & Compliance Center. They can't create, open, or manage an eDiscovery case. The primary purpose of this role group is to allow members to view and access case data in Advanced eDiscovery.
Security Administrator	Membership in this role group is synchronized across services and managed centrally. This role group is not manageable through the administrator portals. Members of this role group may include cross-service administrators as well as external partner groups and Microsoft Support. By default, this group may not be assigned any roles. However, it will be a member of the Security Administrators role group and will inherit the capabilities of that role group.

To assign a role to someone in the organization, you need to use the Add-RoleGroupMember cmdlet and specify the role as well as the member. For example, to add John Smith with the username john@office365powershell.ca to the Compliance Administrator group you would run the following cmdlet:

```
Add-RoleGroupMember -Identity "ComplianceAdministrator" -Member john
```

Tip   Being a member of the Organization Management does not automatically give you full control over the Office 365 Security & Compliance Center; you still need to add yourself to the other roles, such as eDiscovery Manager, to have access to everything. The Organization Management role allows you to give yourself those roles.

If we want to view the members of a certain group, we can run the Get-Role GroupMember cmdlet. For example, to view the members of the Compliance Administrators group, we would run the cmdlet seen in Figure 6-3.

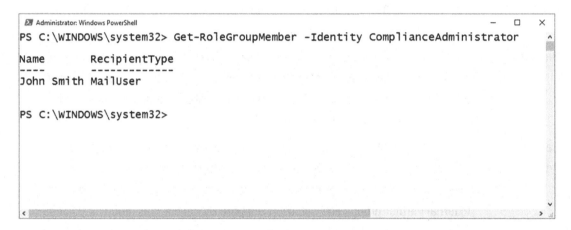

Figure 6-3. *Get-RoleGroupMember*

Now that we have looked at how to assign users into roles, let's learn how to start and view a compliance search from PowerShell.

Compliance Search

To start a new compliance search we need to use the New-ComplianceSearch cmdlet. This cmdlet has a lot of options on what to search and where to search for it. You can find some of the important parameters in Table 6-5.

Table 6-5. *New-ComplianceSearch Parameters*

Parameter	Description
Name	The Name parameter specifies the name of the compliance search. If the value contains spaces, enclose the value in quotation marks.
Case	The Case parameter specifies the name of an eDiscovery case that the new compliance search will be associated with. If the value contains spaces, enclose the value in quotation marks.
ContentMatchQuery	The ContentMatchQuery parameter specifies a content search filter. This parameter uses a text search string or a query that's formatted by using the Keyword Query Language (KQL).
ExchangeLocation	The ExchangeLocation parameter specifies the mailboxes to include. Valid values are: • A mailbox • A distribution group or mail-enabled security group (all mailboxes that are currently members of the group) • The value All for all mailboxes. You can only use this value by itself. To specify a mailbox or distribution group, you can use any value that uniquely identifies it. For example: • Name • Distinguished name (DN) • Email address • GUID
PublicFolderLocation	The PublicFolderLocation parameter specifies that you want to include all public folders in the search. You use the value All for this parameter.
SharePointLocation	The SharePointLocation parameter specifies the SharePoint Online sites to include. You identify the site by its URL value, or you can use the value All to include all sites.

To learn how to use the New-ComplianceSearch cmdlet, let's look at the following business case. Your company has been working on a top-secret project—a *PowerShell for Office 365* book—in collaboration with a partner called Apress. The information has been leaked, so you want to find all the items in both SharePoint documents and Exchange emails where the words "Apress" and "PowerShell" are included. With the previous requirements, the cmdlet we would need to run to create the compliance search would be:

```
New-ComplianceSearch `
     -Name "PowerShell Office 365 Book" `
     -SharePointLocation All `
     -ExchangeLocation All `
     -ContentMatchQuery "'Apress' AND 'PowerShell'"
```

We would then need to run the Start-ComplianceSearch cmdlet to start this search, as seen here:

```
Start-ComplianceSearch -Identity "PowerShell Office 365 Book"
```

While the compliance search is running, you can run the Get-ComplianceSearch cmdlet to see if the search is done, as seen in Figure 6-4. The status should be either "In Progress" or "Completed."

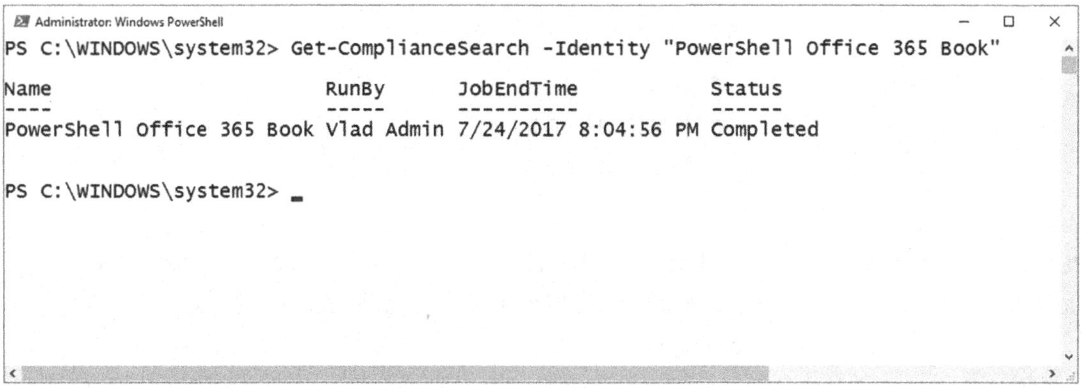

Figure 6-4. *Viewing the status of a compliance search*

Once the status is "Completed," you can view the results either directly from PowerShell or from the Office 365 Compliance Center. To view the results in PowerShell, you can use the New-ComplianceSearchAction cmdlet and specify the name of the compliance search, selecting only the results, as seen in this example:

```
New-ComplianceSearchAction -SearchName "PowerShell Office 365 Book"
-Preview | Select results |Format-Table -Wrap
```

Tip   To run the New-ComplianceSearchAction cmdlet with the -Preview switch, you need to have the eDiscovery Manager role. After granting yourself the role, it might take 24 hours for the cmdlet to work.

As seen in Figure 6-5, the Office 365 Compliance Center has found a document in SharePoint as well as an email in Exchange with those keywords.

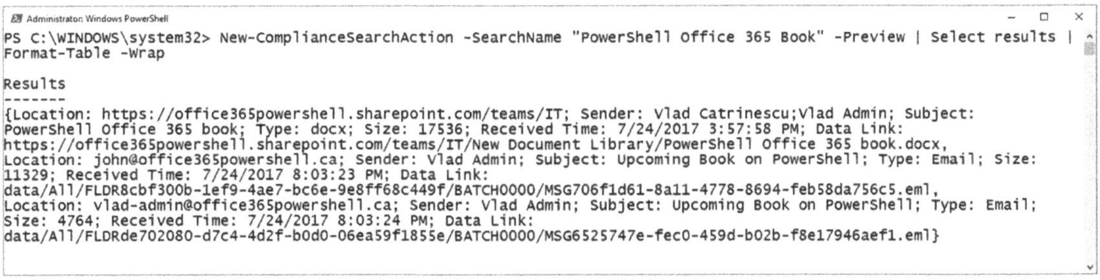

Figure 6-5. *Preview of a compliance search in PowerShell*

While it's pretty user friendly to create and start compliance searches in PowerShell, consuming them is not. Viewing the results from within the Office 365 Compliance Center allows us to better view their contents in a more user-friendly way, as seen in Figure 6-6.

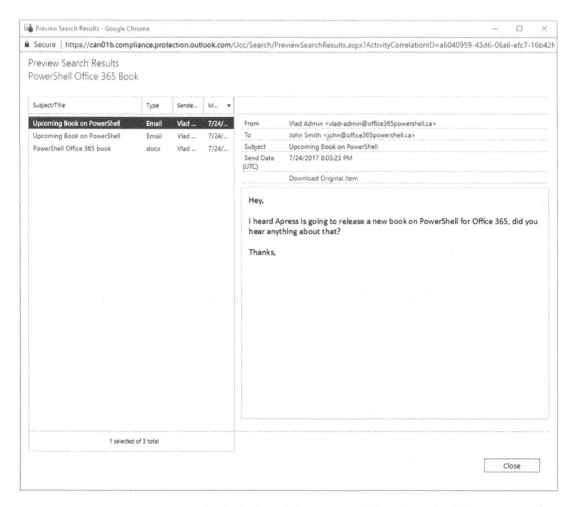

Figure 6-6. *Preview of a compliance search in the Office 365 Compliance Center*

Now that we have learned how to do a compliance search, we will learn how to search the Unified Audit Log.

Searching the Unified Audit Log

One of the benefits of Office 365 from a security and auditing point of view is the Unified Audit Log. The Unified Audit Log allows administrators and security managers to view the audit logs for all the services in Office 365 from a single location. While you can interact with the Unified Audit log from the Office 365 Admin Center, PowerShell can become useful in a variety of scenarios. To give an example, the Office 365 Unified Audit Log will only keep information for 90 days, and then that information is deleted. Multiple companies have regulations requiring them to keep this information for years, so they need to find a way to save this information into another system, such as an SQL database. Since PowerShell can interact with both Office 365 and Microsoft SQL Server, it is easy to create a script that will copy the information from the Unified Log into an SQL Server database.

The required cmdlets to interact with the Unified Audit Log are in the Exchange Online module, so the first thing I will do is connect to Exchange Online by using the following cmdlet:

```
$Session = New-PSSession -ConfigurationName Microsoft.Exchange
-ConnectionUri https://outlook.office365.com/powershell-liveid/ -Credential
$UserCredential -Authentication Basic -AllowRedirection
```

```
Import-PSSession $Session
```

The cmdlet we will use to perform searches is `Search-UnifiedAuditLog`, and we can view some of the most important parameters in Table 6-6.

Table 6-6. *Search-UnifiedAuditLog Parameters*

Parameter	Description
StartDate	The StartDate parameter specifies the start date of the date range. Use the short date format that's defined in the **Regional Options** settings on the computer where you're running the command. For example, if the computer is configured to use the short date format *mm/dd/yyyy*, enter **09/01/2015** to specify September 1, 2015. You can enter the date only, or you can enter the date and time of day. If you enter the date and time of day, enclose the value in quotation marks ("); for example, **"09/01/2015 5:00 PM"**. If you don't include a timestamp in the value for this parameter, the default timestamp is 12:00 AM (midnight) on the specified date.
EndDate	The EndDate parameter specifies the end date of the date range. Use the same formatting rules as for the StartDate parameter.
IPAddresses	The IPAddresses parameter filters the log entries by the specified IP addresses. You specify multiple IP addresses separated by commas.
Operations	The Operations parameter filters the log entries by operation. The available values for this parameter depend on the RecordType value. For a list of the available values for this parameter, see "Search the Audit Log in the Office 365 Security & Compliance Center" at https://support.office.com/en-us/article/Search-the-audit-log-in-the-Office-365-Security-Compliance-Center-0d4d0f35-390b-4518-800e-0c7ec95e946c?ui=en-US&rs=en-US&ad=US#PickTab=Activities

(*continued*)

Table 6-6. (*continued*)

Parameter	Description
RecordType	The RecordType parameter filters the log entries by record type. Valid values are: • AzureActiveDirectory • AzureActiveDirectoryAccountLogon • AzureActiveDirectoryStsLogon • ComplianceDLPExchange • ComplianceDLPSharePoint • CRM • DataCenterSecurityCmdlet • Discovery • ExchangeAdmin • ExchangeAggregatedOperation • ExchangeItem • ExchangeItemGroup • MicrosoftTeams • MicrosoftTeamsAddOns • MicrosoftTeamsSettingsOperation • OneDrive • PowerBIAudit • SecurityComplianceCenterEOPCmdlet • SharePoint • SharePointFileOperation • SharePointSharingOperation • SkypeForBusinessCmdlets • SkypeForBusinessPSTNUsage • SkypeForBusinessUsersBlocked • Sway • ThreatIntelligence • Yammer
ResultSize	The ResultSize parameter specifies the maximum number of results to return. The default value is 100, maximum is 5,000.

(*continued*)

Table 6-6. (*continued*)

Parameter	Description
SiteIds	The SiteIds parameter filters the log entries by site ID. You can specify multiple values separated by commas.
UserIds	The UserIds parameter filters the log entries by the ID of the user who performed the action.

Tip   To view all the parameters of the `Search-UnifiedAuditLog` cmdlet, navigate to the cmdlet page on TechNet: `https://technet.microsoft.com/en-us/library/ mt238501(v=exchg.160).aspx`

Now that we know the parameters, let's see how we can use them. If I wanted to view all the logs between October 1, 2017 and October 12, 2017, I would run the following cmdlet:

```
Search-UnifiedAuditLog -StartDate 10/1/2017 -EndDate 10/12/2017
```

The result shown in Figure 6-7 will return all the entries and their properties, with most of the details' being found in the `AuditData` parameter. You can optimize your scripts to return the information that you need from that parameter.

Figure 6-7. *Search-UnifiedAuditLog Filtered by date*

If I wanted to do a search that was more specific, I could, for example, search for what actions the user `vlad-admin@office365PowerShell.ca` did in SharePoint with the following cmdlet:

```
Search-UnifiedAuditLog -StartDate 10/1/2017 -EndDate 10/12/2017 -RecordType
SharePoint -UserIds vlad-admin@office365powershell.ca
```

I could also use the `ObjectId` parameter to discover what happened to a certain SharePoint document, for example. In the following cmdlet, I am searching on all activities between October 1 and October 12, 2017 on the `AUSTRALIA.docx` document:

```
Search-UnifiedAuditLog -StartDate 10/1/2017 -EndDate 10/12/2017 -ObjectIDs
"https://office365powershell.sharepoint.com/teams/HR/Shared Documents/
AUSTRALIA.docx"
```

As you can see in Figure 6-8, the account `vlad-admin@office365powershell.ca` uploaded the file on October 11, and that is the only activity that happened on the document so far.

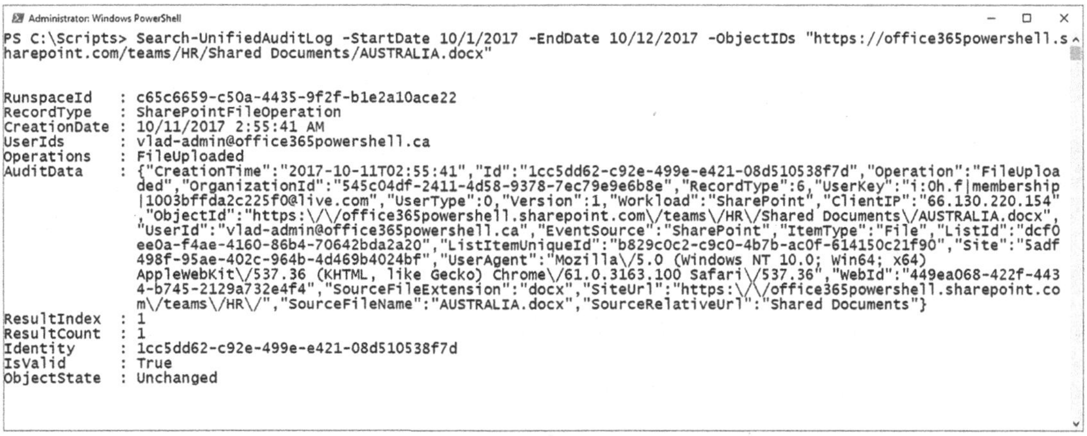

```
Administrator: Windows PowerShell
PS C:\Scripts> Search-UnifiedAuditLog -StartDate 10/1/2017 -EndDate 10/12/2017 -ObjectIDs "https://office365powershell.s
harepoint.com/teams/HR/Shared Documents/AUSTRALIA.docx"


RunspaceId    : c65c6659-c50a-4435-9f2f-b1e2a10ace22
RecordType    : SharePointFileOperation
CreationDate  : 10/11/2017 2:55:41 AM
UserIds       : vlad-admin@office365powershell.ca
Operations    : FileUploaded
AuditData     : {"CreationTime":"2017-10-11T02:55:41","Id":"1cc5dd62-c92e-499e-e421-08d510538f7d","Operation":"FileUploa
                ded","OrganizationId":"545c04df-2411-4d58-9378-7ec79e9e6b8e","RecordType":6,"UserKey":"i:0h.f|membership
                |1003bffda2c225f0@live.com","UserType":0,"Version":1,"Workload":"SharePoint","ClientIP":"66.130.220.154"
                ,"ObjectId":"https:\/\/office365powershell.sharepoint.com\/teams\/HR\/Shared Documents\/AUSTRALIA.docx",
                "UserId":"vlad-admin@office365powershell.ca","EventSource":"SharePoint","ItemType":"File","ListId":"dcf0
                ee0a-f4ae-4160-86b4-70642bda2a20","ListItemUniqueId":"b829c0c2-c9c0-4b7b-ac0f-614150c21f90","Site":"5adf
                498f-95ae-402c-964b-4d469b4024bf","UserAgent":"Mozilla\/5.0 (Windows NT 10.0; Win64; x64)
                AppleWebKit\/537.36 (KHTML, like Gecko) Chrome\/61.0.3163.100 Safari\/537.36","WebId":"449ea068-422f-443
                4-b745-2129a732e4f4","SourceFileExtension":"docx","SiteUrl":"https:\/\/office365powershell.sharepoint.co
                m\/teams\/HR\/","SourceFileName":"AUSTRALIA.docx","SourceRelativeUrl":"Shared Documents"}
ResultIndex   : 1
ResultCount   : 1
Identity      : 1cc5dd62-c92e-499e-e421-08d510538f7d
IsValid       : True
ObjectState   : Unchanged
```

***Figure 6-8.** Searching the Unified Audit Log for activities on a certain document*

As you can see, the Unified Audit Log is really a powerful tool for security administrators to be able to view auditing logs across all Office 365 services. By using PowerShell, you can get those results and export or transfer them to another system that will store them for longer than the 90 days they are stored in Office 365.

Conclusion

In this module, we have learned how to manage the Office 365 Compliance Center by using PowerShell. We first looked at the requirements and how to connect to the Compliance Center, and we then looked at the available cmdlets.

We also learned the different administrative roles that we can use to grant permissions to our users as well as how to assign them via PowerShell. Lastly, we looked at how to create, start, and view the results of a compliance search by using PowerShell.

In the next chapter, we will learn how to manage Office 365 Groups using PowerShell.

CHAPTER 7

Managing Office 365 Groups

Office 365 Groups connect Office 365 services in a single place, increasing user adoption and collaboration in the enterprise. While they have been very popular among users, they can be a challenge from a governance standpoint for most Office 365 administrators.

In this chapter, we will learn what modules are needed to manage Office 365 Groups, as well as how to do basic operations on them. We will then learn how to create advanced rules for who can create Office 365 Groups, naming conventions, and more.

PowerShell Modules to Manage Office 365 Groups

Since Office 365 Groups span multiple services in Office 365, there are multiple modules from which we can manage them. There is no specific module for Office 365 Groups; the two modules that we will have to connect to are the Exchange Online module we learned about in Chapter 4 and the Azure Active Directory PowerShell for Graph module we used in Chapter 2.

Note In order to allow customers to test cmdlets faster and get more feedback, Microsoft publishes two versions of the Azure Active Directory PowerShell for Graph modules: *General Availability Release* and *Public Preview Release*. At the time of writing this book, some of the Office 365 Group cmdlets were only available in the *Public Preview Release* module, but I encourage you to verify if those are now in the General Availability module.

© Vlad Catrinescu 2018
V. Catrinescu, *Essential PowerShell for Office 365*, https://doi.org/10.1007/978-1-4842-3129-6_7

To install the Azure Active Directory PowerShell for Graph–Public Preview Release module from the PowerShell Gallery, you will first need to have the same prerequisites discussed in Chapter 2, and then run the following cmdlet:

```
Install-Module -Name AzureADPreview -AllowClobber
```

Once the `AzureADPreview` cmdlet is installed, run the following cmdlets to connect to both Azure Active Directory and Exchange Online:

```
$cred = Get-Credential

$Session = New-PSSession -ConfigurationName Microsoft.Exchange
-ConnectionUri https://outlook.office365.com/powershell-liveid/ -Credential
$cred -Authentication Basic -AllowRedirection

Import-PSSession $Session

Import-Module AzureADPreview
Connect-AzureAD -Credential $cred
```

Now that you have the Preview version of the Azure AD module and are connected to both Azure Active Directory and Exchange Online, you can start managing Office 365 Groups.

Basic Operations

Let's start by learning how to perform basic operations on Office 365 Groups, such as creating, updating, and deleting them! While one of the basic operations would be viewing Office 365 Groups, we will cover that more in detail in the "Office 365 Group Reporting" section later in this chapter.

Creating an Office 365 Group

To create a group, use the `New-UnifiedGroup` PowerShell cmdlet, part of the Exchange Online module. In Table 7-1, you can find some of the most important parameters of the `New-UnifiedGroup` cmdlet.

Table 7-1. *Parameters of the New-UnifiedGroup cmdlet*

Parameter	Description
Alias	The `Alias` parameter specifies the Exchange alias (also known as the mail nickname) for the Office 365 Group. This value identifies the recipient as a mail-enabled object and shouldn't be confused with multiple email addresses for the same recipient (also known as proxy addresses). A recipient can have only one `Alias` value.
AccessType	The `AccessType` parameter specifies the privacy type for the Office 365 Group. Valid values are: • `Public`—The group content and conversations are available to everyone, and anyone can join the group without approval from a group owner. This is the default value. • `Private`—The group content and conversations are only available to members of the group, and joining the group requires approval from a group owner. You can change the privacy type at any point in the lifecycle of the group.
AlwaysSubscribeMembers ToCalendarEvents	The `AlwaysSubscribeMembersToCalendarEvents` switch controls the default subscription settings of new members that are added to the Office 365 Group. If you use this switch without a value, all future members that are added to the group will have their subscriptions set to `ReplyAndEvents`. If you use this exact syntax: `-AlwaysSubscribeMembersToCalendarEvents:$false`, all future members that are added to the group will have their subscriptions set to `ReplyOnly`.
AutoSubscribeNewMembers	The `AutoSubscribeNewMembers` switch specifies whether to automatically subscribe new members added to the Office 365 Group to conversations and calendar events. You don't need to specify a value with this switch.

(continued)

Table 7-1. (*continued*)

Parameter	Description
DisplayName	The DisplayName parameter specifies the name of the Office 365 Group. The display name is visible in the Exchange Admin Center, address lists, and Outlook. For Office 365 Groups, the DisplayName value is used in the unique Name property. However, because the DisplayName value doesn't need to be unique, the DisplayName value is appended with an underscore character (_) and a short GUID value when it's used for the Name property.
HiddenGroupMembershipEnabled	The HiddenGroupMembershipEnabled switch specifies whether to hide the members of the Office 365 Group from users who aren't members of the group.
Language	The Language parameter specifies the language preference for the Office 365 Group.

Note   To view all the parameters of the New-UnifiedGroup cmdlet, navigate to the TechNet page of the cmdlet.

To create a public group with the name *Office 365 Support Community* with the email o365community@office365powershell.ca you would run the following cmdlet:

```
New-UnifiedGroup -DisplayName "Office 365 Support Community" -Alias
o365community -AccessType Public
```

The group should only take a few seconds to create, and you will see a confirmation on the screen similar to that shown in Figure 7-1:

Figure 7-1. *Creating a public group*

Since this is a public group, every user could find the group from their Outlook Online and join it, as seen in Figure 7-2.

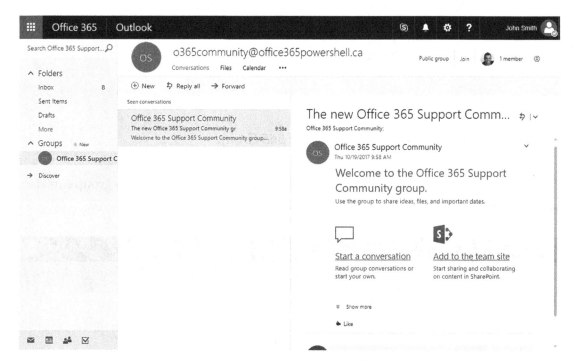

Figure 7-2. *Viewing an Office 365 public group in the browser*

Now, if you wanted to create a new *private* group called *2019 Reorganization* with an email address of 2019reorg@office365powershell.ca you would run the following cmdlet:

```
New-UnifiedGroup -DisplayName "2019 Reorganization" -Alias 2019reorg
-AccessType Private
```

Something that you will have to be aware of is that *private* means different things to different people, and some Office 365 administrators expect that once they create a private group, members that are not inside the group cannot find it. However, with Office 365 Groups, if a group is private and no additional configurations are made, every member of your organization can find the group, as seen in Figure 7-3.

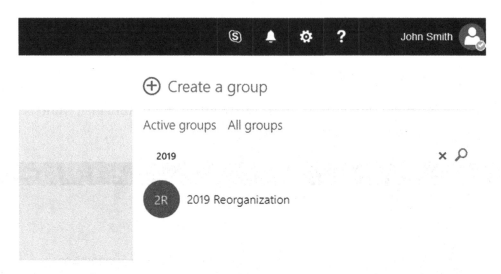

Figure 7-3. *Searching for a private Office 365 Group*

Furthermore, as seen in Figure 7-4, users who are not members of the group can also see who is in that group.

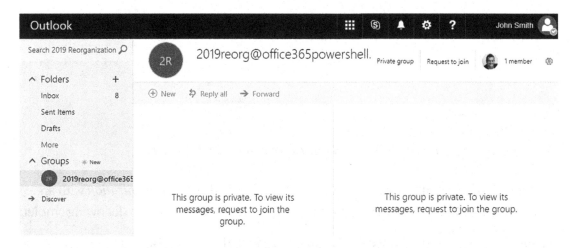

Figure 7-4. *Non-members can also view who the members are of a private Office 365 Group*

Luckily, with PowerShell you are able to both hide the group from the Discover tab as well as hide the member list if someone accidentally gets a direct link to the group. The bad news, however, is that hiding the membership of the group can only be done at group creation—not afterward. To create a new private group in which non-members cannot see the current members, you would need to specify the `-HiddenGroupMembershipEnabled` switch, as seen in the following example:

```
New-UnifiedGroup -DisplayName "Secret Reorganization" -Alias SecretReorg
-AccessType Private -HiddenGroupMembershipEnabled
```

The result, seen in Figure 7-5, is that while for now users can find the group, they do not see the members list at the top right or the "Request to join" button.

Figure 7-5. *Office 365 Group with hidden membership*

At this point, users can still find the group in the Discover tab of Outlook Online, so if you wanted to also hide it from there you would need to modify the group properties, since the required parameter is not available at group creation. Let's learn how to modify a group's properties after the group is created.

Updating Office 365 Groups

Once a group is created, to change its properties you need to use the `Set-UnifiedGroup` cmdlet. This cmdlet not only allows you to change some of the properties you specified when creating the group, such as the alias, email address, and display name, but also allows you to modify new properties that you cannot set directly when creating the group. Some of those new properties can be seen in Table 7-2.

Table 7-2. *Parameters of the Set-UnifiedGroup cmdlet*

Parameter	Description
CalendarMemberReadOnly	The CalendarMemberReadOnly switch specifies whether to set read-only calendar permissions for members of the group.
ConnectorsEnabled	ConnectorsEnabled specifies whether to enable the ability to use connectors for the Office 365 Group.
HiddenFromAddressListsEnabled	HiddenFromAddressListsEnabled specifies whether the Office 365 Group appears in the Global Address List (GAL) and other address lists in your organization.
MailTip	The MailTip parameter specifies the custom MailTip text for this recipient. The MailTip is shown to senders when they start drafting an email message to this recipient. If the value contains spaces, enclose the value in quotation marks (").
UnifiedGroupWelcomeMessageEnabled	The UnifiedGroupWelcomeMessageEnabled switch specifies whether to enable or disable sending system-generated welcome messages to users who are added as members to the Office 365 Group.

Note   To view all the parameters of the Set-UnifiedGroup cmdlet, navigate to the TechNet page of the cmdlet.

To continue what was started in the previous section, to hide an Office 365 Group from the Global Address List and from the Discover tab in Outlook Online, you would run the following cmdlet:

```
Set-UnifiedGroup -Identity SecretReorg -HiddenFromAddressListsEnabled:$true
```

Another very useful parameter to set for your groups is the `MailTip`. For example, my organization has an Office 365 Group for asking HR staff questions about policies. You might want to set up a MailTip reminding users not to share any private information in that group. This can be done using the following cmdlet:

```
Set-UnifiedGroup -Identity HRPublic -MailTip "This community is public to
all company, please do not share any private information"
```

Whenever someone sends a message to that group, the MailTip will be visible at the top of their Outlook or Outlook Online message, as seen in Figure 7-6.

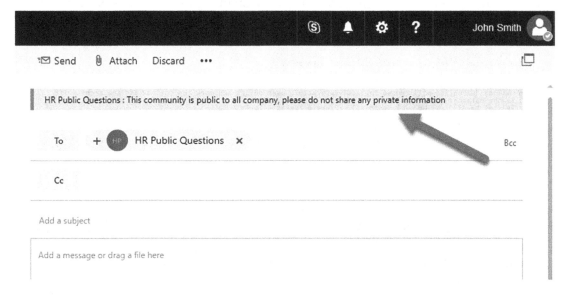

Figure 7-6. *Office 365 Group MailTip*

Now that we have learned how to modify the properties of an Office 365 Group, let's learn how to delete an Office 365 Group.

Deleting an Office 365 Group

Removing an Office 365 Group is done with the `Remove-UnifiedGroup` PowerShell cmdlet; you must specify the Office 365 Group you want to remove. You can use any of the values that uniquely identify the Office 365 Group, such as the following:

- Name
- Display name

- Alias

- Email address

- GUID

To remove the HRPublic group, you would run the following cmdlet:

```
Remove-UnifiedGroup -Identity HRPublic
```

By default, you will have to confirm that you want to delete the group, as well as any connected services inside that group, such as the group calendar, SharePoint site, Planner contents, and so on! This confirmation, seen in Figure 7-7, can be useful, but it can also be cumbersome when deleting multiple Office 365 Groups.

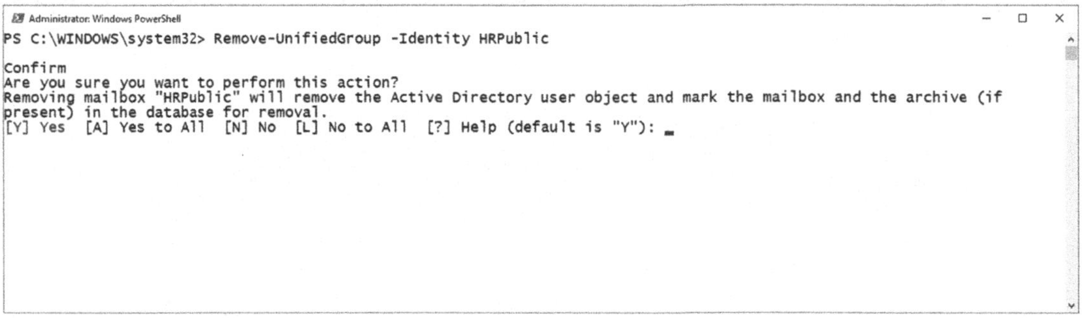

Figure 7-7. *Confirmation before deleting an Office 365 Group*

To skip the confirmation, you can use the -Confirm parameter as seen in the following example:

```
Remove-UnifiedGroup -Identity o365community -Confirm:$false
```

This will remove the Office 365 Group immediately, without requiring the person running the PowerShell cmdlet to reconfirm.

But what happens if you or a user deleted an Office 365 Group by mistake? Let's learn how to restore deleted groups.

Restoring a Deleted Office 365 Group

When an Office 365 Group is deleted, Microsoft keeps it for 30 days in a soft-deleted state, meaning you have 30 days to restore it if you need to. To view Office 365 Groups that have been deleted, use the Get-AzureADMSDeletedGroup, part of the AzureAD module. The result, seen in Figure 7-8, is the list of groups that are in a soft-deleted state.

```
Administrator: Windows PowerShell                                              —    □    ×
PS C:\WINDOWS\system32> Get-AzureADMSDeletedGroup

Id                                   DisplayName              Description
--                                   -----------              -----------
102c865c-af54-4cda-bb05-2c988b5a4fee Reorg 2018
34061a2b-dfcb-400e-bda4-3cca7656ded8 Private ReOrg
38a721a5-e95d-4b3c-9026-2c1a5d8751db Office 365 Support Community
50eb91e5-924a-4f19-8140-ed15cf756441 IgnitePrivate
78bb5639-2ea7-4eaa-b0f2-783611598f54 2018 Reorganization
a6daa502-24c6-4dfb-9dbe-502b96ac5e65 IgnitePrivate
a77e298f-fcaa-4805-9cb6-bc5644508813 Ignite Test              Ignite Test
bc416978-4df7-4d5e-80e2-c444b0394b06 IgnitePrivate
bddb3dcf-25c1-46ba-8878-d906c30db5a4 HR Public Questions
f0fa77fd-f0dd-4e5c-9fda-c3b73a755a2d PowerShell for Office 365 Book PowerShell for Office 365 Book


PS C:\WINDOWS\system32> _
```

Figure 7-8. *Office 365 Groups in a soft-deleted state*

Something that can also be useful is viewing the time the group was deleted, which is done by viewing the DeletedDateTime property, as seen here:

```
Get-AzureADMSDeletedGroup | Select Id, DisplayName, DeletedDateTime | Sort-
Object DeletedDateTime
```

By including the DeletedDate Time directly in the query, you can easily calculate when the group will be fully deleted, as seen in Figure 7-9.

```
Administrator: Windows PowerShell                                                                        —    □    ×
PS C:\WINDOWS\system32> Get-AzureADMSDeletedGroup | Select Id, DisplayName, DeletedDateTime | Sort-Object DeletedDateTim
e

Id                                   DisplayName              DeletedDateTime
--                                   -----------              ---------------
78bb5639-2ea7-4eaa-b0f2-783611598f54 2018 Reorganization      9/23/2017 7:58:08 PM
102c865c-af54-4cda-bb05-2c988b5a4fee Reorg 2018               9/23/2017 9:24:04 PM
a6daa502-24c6-4dfb-9dbe-502b96ac5e65 IgnitePrivate            9/23/2017 9:24:17 PM
a77e298f-fcaa-4805-9cb6-bc5644508813 Ignite Test              9/23/2017 9:24:44 PM
50eb91e5-924a-4f19-8140-ed15cf756441 IgnitePrivate            9/28/2017 12:01:05 PM
34061a2b-dfcb-400e-bda4-3cca7656ded8 Private ReOrg            9/28/2017 12:01:22 PM
bc416978-4df7-4d5e-80e2-c444b0394b06 IgnitePrivate            10/19/2017 7:17:38 PM
f0fa77fd-f0dd-4e5c-9fda-c3b73a755a2d PowerShell for Office 365 Book 10/19/2017 7:17:52 PM
bddb3dcf-25c1-46ba-8878-d906c30db5a4 HR Public Questions      10/19/2017 9:09:25 PM
38a721a5-e95d-4b3c-9026-2c1a5d8751db Office 365 Support Community 10/19/2017 9:10:08 PM

PS C:\WINDOWS\system32> _
```

Figure 7-9. *Viewing when an Office 365 Group was deleted*

Now that you can view the deleted groups, to restore a certain group you will have to use the Restore-AzureADMSDeletedDirectoryObject PowerShell cmdlet and give the ID of the group you want to restore. To restore the HR Public Questions group, you would run the following cmdlet:

```
$O365Group = Get-AzureADMSDeletedGroup | Where-Object {$_.DisplayName -eq
"HR Public Questions"}
Restore-AzureADMSDeletedDirectoryObject -Id $O365Group.Id
```

163

Note   It might take up to 24 hours for the contents of the group to be fully restored.

If you want to permanently delete a group without waiting for the 30-day soft-deleted period, you can force-delete it with the `Remove-AzureADMSDeletedDirector yObject` cmdlet, in which you must specify the ID of the Office 365 Group you want to permanently delete. For example, to permanently delete the Office 365 Support Community group, you would run the following cmdlet:

```
$0365Group = Get-AzureADMSDeletedGroup | Where-Object {$_.DisplayName -eq
"Office 365 Support Community"}

Remove-AzureADMSDeletedDirectoryObject –Id $0365Group.Id
```

You can verify if the group was successfully deleted by running the `Get-AzureADMSDeletedGroup` cmdlet. As you can see in Figure 7-10, both the group you have restored and the one you have permanently deleted are not in the list anymore.

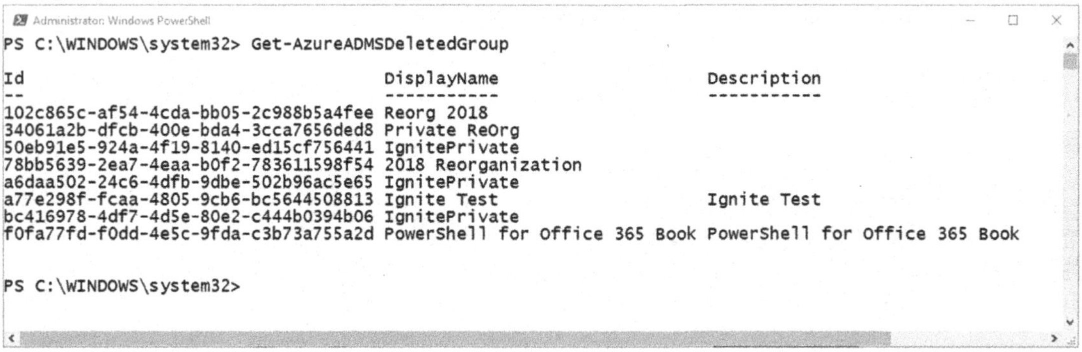

Figure 7-10. *List of deleted Office 365 Groups*

Now that you have learned how to create, update, and delete Office 365 Groups, let's look at how to manage users in an Office 365 Group.

Managing the Members of an Office 365 Group

Another very important aspect of managing Office 365 Groups is, of course, the users inside. With Office 365 Groups, membership information exists as a link between the group and the user accounts of its members. The three types of membership can be seen in Table 7-3. An Office 365 user can be present in one or more of these membership levels.

Table 7-3. *Office 365 Group Membership Levels*

Membership Level	Description
Owners	Group Owners are the administrators of the group. They can add or remove members, change the group name or description, and delete conversations inside the group.
Members	Group Members are users that will collaborate inside the Office 365 Group. They can create new conversations, add items inside the calendar (unless this setting is changed by an admin), and upload files to the group. They are also allowed to add new members in a public group. All Owners are also Members of the Office 365 Group, from a technical point of view.
Subscribers	A Subscriber is not a permission level, but simply a subset of the members who opted in to receive copies of the conversations and group calendar invites via email.

Managing the membership inside an Office 365 Group can be a little different than doing so in other applications you are currently managing. To add a user as an owner, you will first need to add that user as a member inside the group, and then you can add them as an owner. If you want completely remove the owner of a group, you will have to first remove them as an owner and then remove them as a member.

Viewing Office 365 Group Members

To view the current members of a group, you need to use the Get-UnifiedGroupLinks cmdlet, specifying the identity of the group and the type of membership level you want to view. For example, to view the members of the HR Public Questions group created earlier, you would run the following cmdlet:

```
Get-UnifiedGroupLinks -Identity "HR Public Questions" -LinkType Members
```

This cmdlet will the show the user alias of every user that is a member of the Office 365 Group, as seen in Figure 7-11.

Figure 7-11. *Members of an Office 365 Group*

You can also display multiple properties of the users directly from their profile. The following PowerShell cmdlet will return the owners of the HR Public Questions group as well as some properties about those users:

```
Get-UnifiedGroupLinks -Identity "HR Public Questions" -LinkType Owners |
Select DisplayName, WindowsLiveId, Department
```

You can view the results in Figure 7-12.

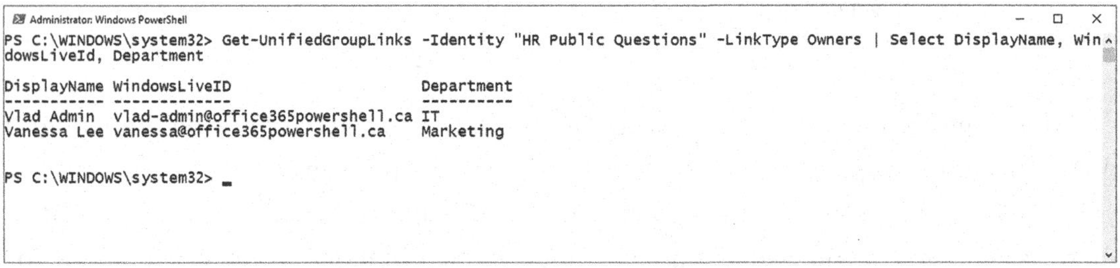

Figure 7-12. *Viewing the owners of an Office 365 Group as well as their properties*

Now that you know how to view members, let's take a look at how to add them.

Adding Users to an Office 365 Group

Adding users to an Office 365 Group is done with the `Add-UnifiedGroupLinks` cmdlet; you must specify the group you want to add users to, as well as the membership level you want to add them to. If you wanted to add Jeff and Vanessa as members to your group, you would run the following cmdlet:

```
Add-UnifiedGroupLinks -Identity "HRPublic" -LinkType Members -Links Jeff@
office365powershell.ca,vanessa@office365powershell.ca
```

If you wanted to add Vanessa as an owner afterward, you would run the following cmdlet:

```
Add-UnifiedGroupLinks -Identity "HRPublic" -LinkType Owners -Links vanessa@
office365powershell.ca
```

Remember that you cannot add someone with the owner or subscriber membership level until you add them as a member. If you try to, PowerShell will give you an error similar to that shown in Figure 7-13.

Figure 7-13. *Only members can be owners of a group*

Now that you have learned how to add users, let's learn how to remove users from an Office 365 Group.

Removing Users from an Office 365 Group

Removing users from an Office 365 Group is done with the `Remove-UnifiedGroupLinks` PowerShell cmdlet, in which you must specify the identity of the group from which you want to remove users, the users you want to remove, and what type of membership you want to remove them from. Remember that you cannot directly completely remove an owner from the group; you have to first remove them as an owner, and then as a member.

If you wanted to remove Vanessa as an owner of the group, you would run the following cmdlet:

```
Remove-UnifiedGroupLinks -Identity "HRPublic" -LinkType Owners -Links
vanessa@office365powershell.ca -Confirm:$False
```

At this point, Vanessa is still a member of this Office 365 Group and would still have contribute rights on the group. If you wanted to remove Vanessa from the group as a member as well, you would run the following cmdlet:

```
Remove-UnifiedGroupLinks -Identity "HRPublic" -LinkType Members -Links
vanessa@office365powershell.ca -Confirm:$False
```

As you have seen so far, doing basic operations on a group and managing its membership with PowerShell is pretty straightforward. But with Office 365 Groups' being so open by default, how do you avoid groups chaos inside your organization? Luckily, Microsoft has implemented multiple governance mechanisms that allow you to control and manage Office 365 Groups. Let's take a look at how you can implement an Office 365 Group governance inside your tenant.

Office 365 Group Governance

Implementing a governance in Office 365 can be a hard thing for the IT department. On one side, you want to make sure that your users stay secure, do not put sensitive information in the wrong place, and use Office 365 properly. On the other side, you do not want to block users from being able to create and collaborate by themselves without having to wait for IT for every small request they have. With Office 365 Groups and the AzureAD PowerShell module, Microsoft has set up a few control mechanisms that allow you to implement some controls, while still allowing your users to be productive and dynamic. Let's take a look at some of those settings.

Note   Most of the settings that we will cover in this section will require an Azure Active Directory Premium P1 license for every unique user that is a member of an Office 365 Group. Since Microsoft licensing changes often, make sure to check with your organization's licensing expert or partner to get the latest information.

Enforcing a Naming Policy and Blocked Words

First, we will cover enforcing a naming policy for a group, as well as setting a list of blocked words. For example, a user would not be able to create a group with sensitive words inside of the name.

A naming convention allows you to bring consistency to how your Office 365 Groups are named, as well as allows you to easily identify the owners of the group and its geographic location by pulling information directly from the creator's Azure AD user profile. To give you an example, a naming convention could be:

GRP_[Department]_[GroupName]_[CountryOrRegion]

If for example, Vlad Catrinescu is from Canada, in the marketing department, and wants to create a group with the name *SharePoint Campaign*, the final group name would be: *GRP_Marketing_SharePoint Campaign_Canada*.

The full list of user profile properties we can use is as follows:

- [Department]
- [Company]
- [Office]
- [StateOrProvince]
- [CountryOrRegion]
- [Title]

Tip   The total length of the prefixes and suffixes is restricted to 53 characters.

Blocked words allow you to prevent users from including certain words like *Payroll*, *CEO*, *CFO*, and so forth when creating Office 365 Groups. The entire Office 365 Group name will be checked for the blocked words. When working with blocked words you must be aware that there are no substring searches carried out when creating the group. For example, if your group-naming policy were GRP_[Department]_[GroupName]_[CountryOrRegion] and someone entered the name *Payroll*, the final name would be *GRP_Marketing_Payroll_Canada*.

Because the system does not search substrings, it would not block the group's creation even if *Payroll* were on your list of blocked words. However, if you set your naming policy with spaces, instead of underscores, as seen in GRP [Department] [GroupName] [CountryOrRegion], your final result would be *GRP Marketing Payroll Canada*, and the policy would apply; therefore, the user would not be able to create the group.

Some administrative roles, however, are exempt from these policies and will be able to create Office 365 Groups that contain blocked words or that do not follow the organization's naming policies. Those roles are the following:

- Global admin

- Partner Tier 1 Support

- Partner Tier 2 Support

- User account admin

- Directory writers

Now that you know what both policies do and how they work, let's see how to actually implement them. You will first have to create a new Active Directory Setting Object based on the Unified Group template. Microsoft offers several different settings templates in Azure Active Directory, which you can view by using the Get-AzureADDirectorySettingTemplate PowerShell cmdlet. While there are multiple templates, as you can see in Figure 7-14, for this task you will need to create a directory setting based on the Group.Unified template.

```
Administrator: Windows PowerShell                                                          –   □   ×
PS C:\WINDOWS\system32> Get-AzureADDirectorySettingTemplate

Id                                   DisplayName                         Description
--                                   -----------                         -----------
62375ab9-6b52-47ed-826b-58e47e0e304b Group.Unified                       ...
08d542b9-071f-4e16-94b0-74abb372e3d9 Group.Unified.Guest                 Settings for a specific Unified Group
4bc7f740-180e-4586-adb6-38b2e9024e6b Application                         ...
898f1161-d651-43d1-805c-3b0b388a9fc2 Custom Policy Settings              ...
5cf42378-d67d-4f36-ba46-e8b86229381d Password Rule Settings              ...
80661d51-be2f-4d46-9713-98a2fcaec5bc Prohibited Names Settings           ...
aad3907d-1d1a-448b-b3ef-7bf7f63db63b Prohibited Names Restricted Settings ...

PS C:\WINDOWS\system32> _
```

Figure 7-14. *Available AzureAD Directory Setting templates*

Note   The settings in the Group.Unified Azure Active Directory Object will apply to *all* the Office 365 Groups inside your tenant.

To create the new Azure AD Settings Object, run the following cmdlets:

```
$SettingTemplate = Get-AzureADDirectorySettingTemplate | where {$_.
DisplayName -eq 'Group.Unified'}

$NewAADSetting = $SettingTemplate.CreateDirectorySetting()

$NewAADSetting = New-AzureADDirectorySetting -DirectorySetting
$NewAADSetting
```

Then, run the following cmdlet to get your newly created Azure AD Directory Setting Object and save it in a new variable called $Setting:

```
$Setting = Get-AzureADDirectorySetting | where-object {$_.displayname -eq
'Group.Unified'}
```

If you want to see all the available options you can configure as part of this setting object, you can run the following cmdlet:

```
$Setting.Values
```

Right now your settings object, seen in Figure 7-15, will only have the default settings from the template.

Figure 7-15. *Default values of the new Azure Active Directory Setting Object*

To apply the naming convention policy, add your custom naming convention in the PrefixSuffixNamingRequirement property, as seen in the following example:

```
$Setting["PrefixSuffixNamingRequirement"] = "GRP [Department] [GroupName]
[CountryOrRegion]"
```

To apply certain blocked words, you would modify the `CustomBlockedWordsList` property with a comma-separated list of words you want to block, as seen in this example:

```
$Setting["CustomBlockedWordsList"]="CEO,Legal,Payroll"
```

Lastly, you can optionally enable the `EnableMSStandardBlockedWords` property, which blocks a list of inappropriate words that Microsoft manages that you wouldn't want in your group titles, as follows:

```
$Setting["EnableMSStandardBlockedWords"]="True"
```

To apply these updates to your Azure AD Directory Setting, run the `Set-AzureADDirectorySetting` cmdlet as seen here:

```
Set-AzureADDirectorySetting -Id $Setting.id -DirectorySetting $Setting
```

You can run the following cmdlets to verify that the settings have been updated:

```
$Setting = Get-AzureADDirectorySetting | where-object {$_.displayname -eq 'Group.Unified'}
$Setting.Values
```

As you can see in Figure 7-16, the settings have been successfully applied in your tenant.

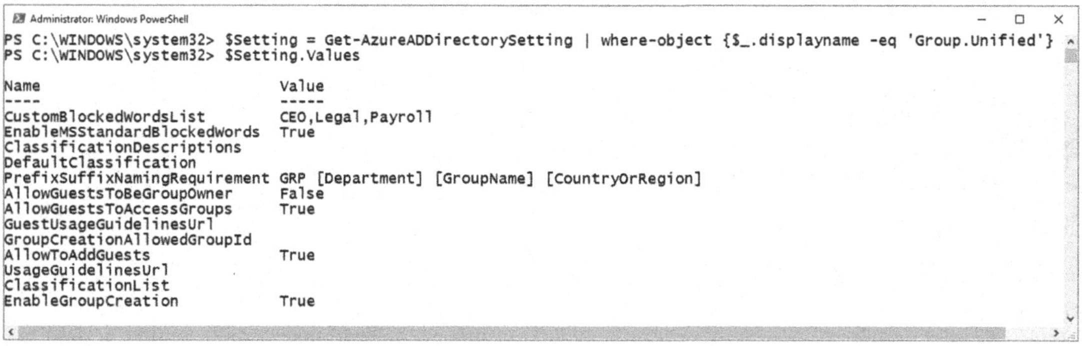

Figure 7-16. *Updated blocked-words and naming-convention settings*

Note   It can take a few hours for the settings to be applied in the user interface across all the Office 365 services.

To test that the policy has been successfully applied, you can navigate to each service that creates an Office 365 Group and test both the naming convention and the blocked words. Make sure to test using one of the accounts that is not part of the admin roles we previously talked about, as those policies do not apply to certain admin accounts. In Figure 7-17, you can see how the final group is shown in Outlook Online and the error message that is displayed when a user attempts to create a group with a blocked word.

Figure 7-17. *Naming policy and blocked words in Outlook Online*

Next up, in Figure 7-18 you can view how Planner is blocking a user from creating a group with a blocked word. Planner is compliant with the naming policy and will create the plan and the Office 365 Group with the correct policy; however, there is no preview of the final name of the Office 365 Group when creating it.

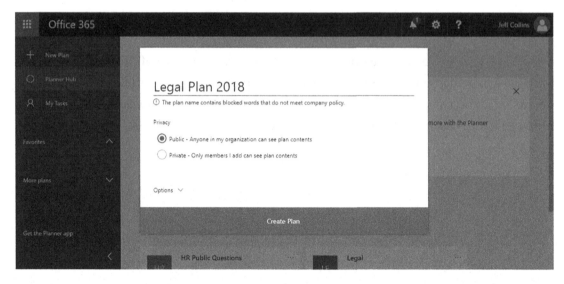

Figure 7-18. *Blocked words in Planner*

Microsoft Teams is also integrated with the policies in Office 365 Groups, and, as you can see in Figure 7-19, it's able to preview the name of the Office 365 Group as it's created.

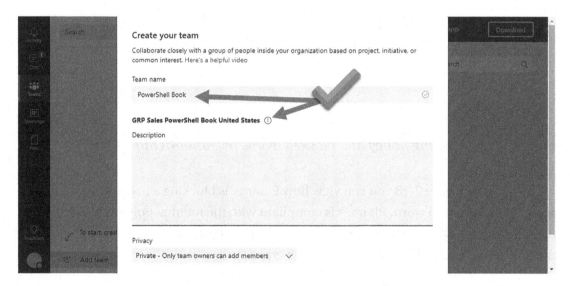

Figure 7-19. *Office 365 Groups naming policies in Microsoft Teams*

Microsoft Teams also supports blocked words and will tell the user right away if they attempted to create a team with a blocked word, as you can see in Figure 7-20.

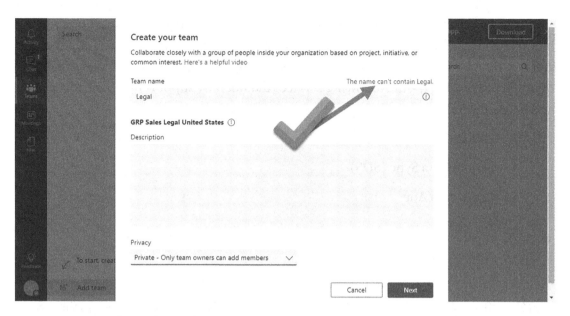

Figure 7-20. *Blocked words in Microsoft Teams*

The last example we will look at is Microsoft Stream. As you can see in Figure 7-21, Microsoft Stream supports both the naming policy preview and blocked words!

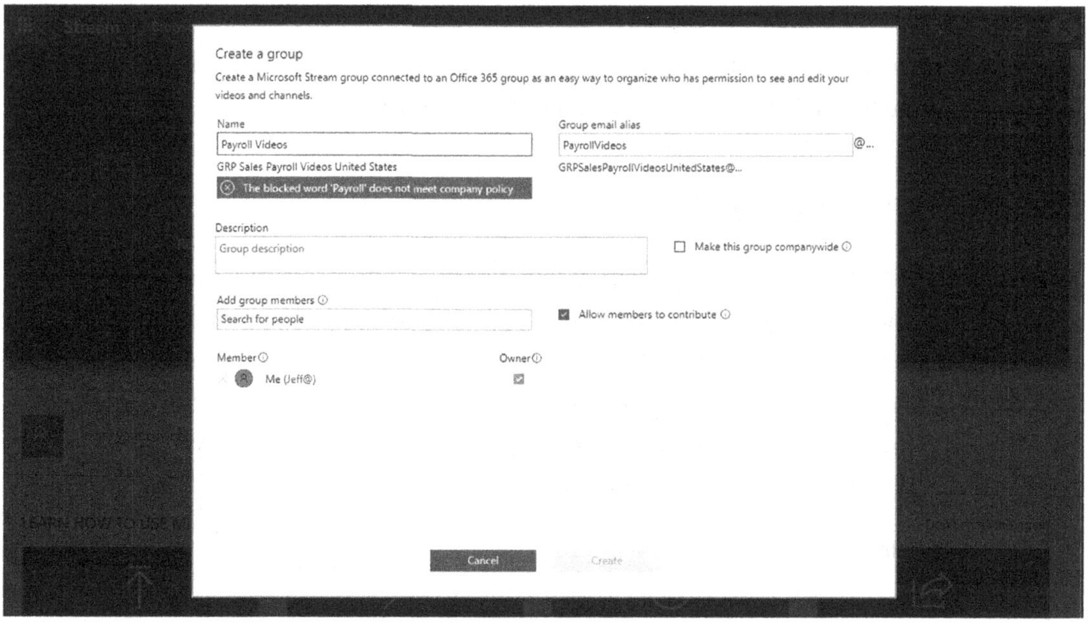

Figure 7-21. *Naming policy preview and blocked words in Microsoft Stream*

As you saw in the preceding examples, most Office 365 services support both the blocked words and the naming policies natively, so your users can see the group they are creating right away. At the time of writing this book—and it might have changed by the time you are reading it—the following services did not fully support naming conventions and blocked words:

- Dynamic CRM

- School Data Sync (SDS)

- Classroom App

- Power BI

- Azure Active Directory Portal

Note   To view the most up-to-date list of what services support naming policies and blocked words, visit the Office Support Page called "Office 365 Groups naming policy" at the following link: `https://support.office.com/en-us/article/Office-365-Groups-naming-policy-6ceca4d3-cad1-4532-9f0f-d469dfbbb552`.

Now that you have learned how to apply a naming policy and blocked words to your groups, it is time to see how to create classifications for them.

Group Classifications

Microsoft allows Office 365 administrators to set a list of classifications that users can apply to Office 365 Groups. At the time of writing this book, classifications are not doing anything technically; however, they are displayed at the top of every Office 365 Group. This allows users to know how sensitive the data in that Office 365 Group is and what security measures they need to take with the content inside that group. For example, you could set up the following classifications for your Office 365 Groups:

- Restricted

- Confidential

- Secret

- Top Secret

The choices that you present your users with in terms of classifications need to involve data sensitivity, as when selecting them, the question that Office 365 will ask your user is similar to "How sensitive is your data?" We will review what classifications look like in the user interface later in this section.

To implement the classification list, you will have to modify some properties of the Azure AD Directory Setting created earlier. First, get the Azure AD Directory Setting and save it into a variable called $Setting as seen here:

```
$Setting = Get-AzureADDirectorySetting | where-object {$_.displayname -eq 'Group.Unified'}
```

The first property you need to modify is the ClassificationList. This property accepts a comma-separated list of all the different classifications you want to make available. You can include spaces between the commas, such as *Top Secret*, but make sure to not include spaces between the classifications themselves. In the following cmdlet, I am setting the classification list previously discussed:

```
$Setting["ClassificationList"]="Restricted,Confidential,Secret,Top Secret"
```

You can then specify what default classification is proposed to your users by updating the DefaultClassification property. In the cmdlet below, I am setting the default to *Confidential*:

```
$Setting["DefaultClassification"]="Confidential"
```

Lastly, you can set the ClassificationDescriptions property, in which you can specify a description for each of the classifications in your list. These descriptions will help users make the right classification selection. This list needs to be in the format "Classification:Description,Classification:Description", where Classification matches one of the classifications in the ClassificationList property. In the example that follows, you can view a sample description for each classification level:

```
$Setting["ClassificationDescriptions"]="Restricted:Restricted material would cause undesirable effects if publicly available,Confidential:Confidential material would cause damage or be prejudicial to national security if publicly available,Secret:Secret material would cause serious damage to national security if it were publicly available,Top Secret:Top Secret is the highest level of classified information"
```

The last thing you have to do is apply the updates to your Azure AD Directory Setting by running the following cmdlet:

```
Set-AzureADDirectorySetting -Id $Setting.id -DirectorySetting $Setting
```

You are now ready to test if those settings have been successfully applied across Office 365.

Note   It can take a few hours for the settings to be applied in the user interface across all the Office 365 services.

When users create a new Office 365 Group from Outlook Online, they will be presented with a dropdown of the classification choices, as you can see in Figure 7-22.

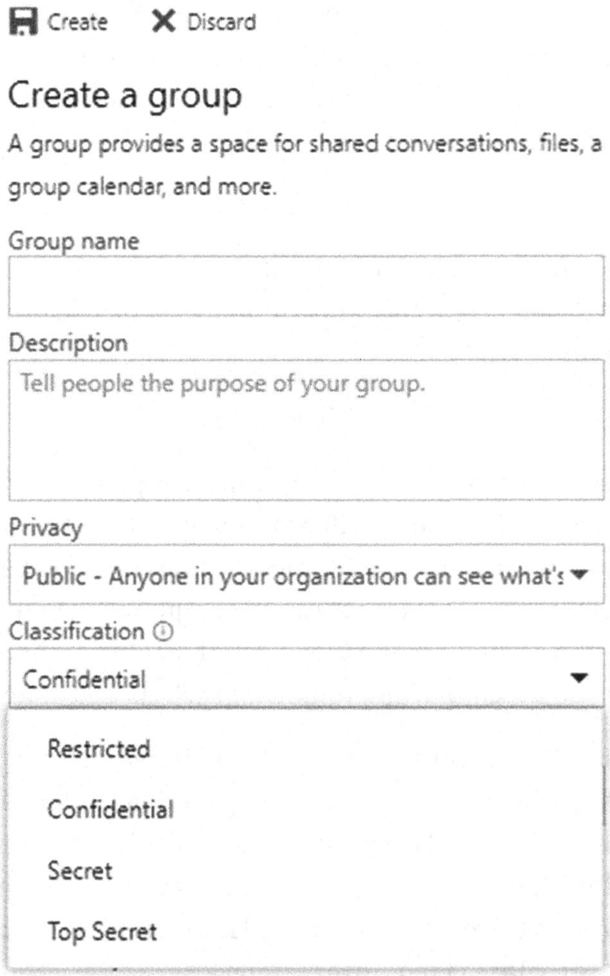

Figure 7-22. *Classification list in Outlook Online*

The classification list is also available in Stream, as you can see in Figure 7-23.

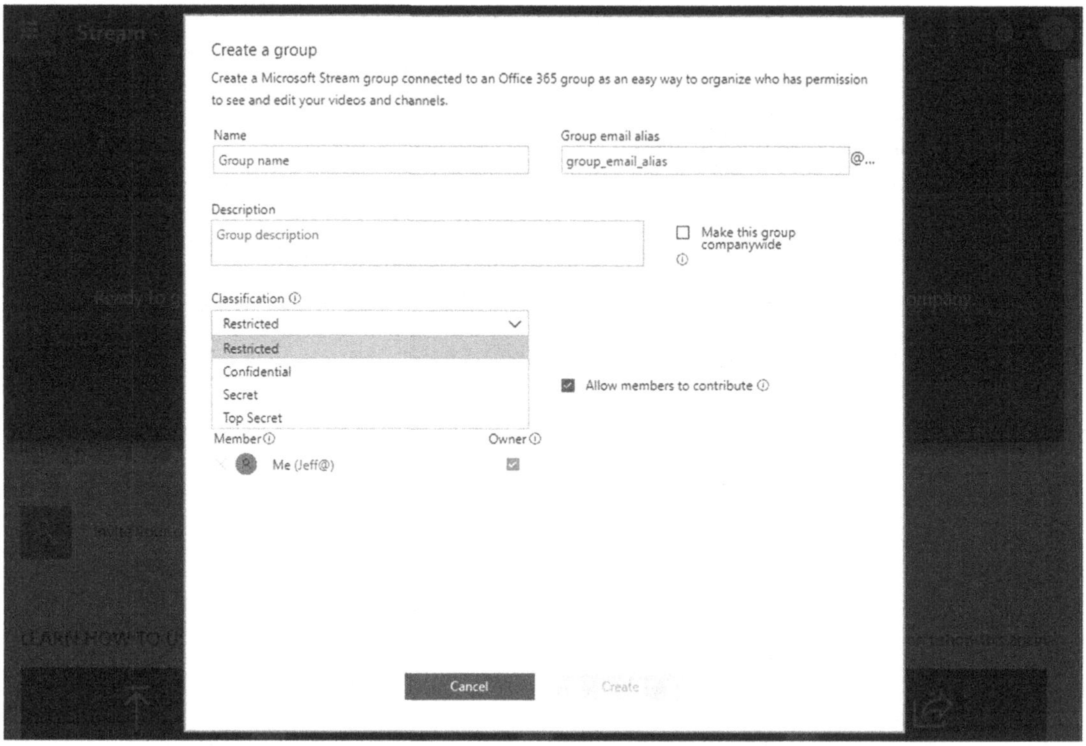

Figure 7-23. *Classification list in Microsoft Stream*

Lastly, classifications are also available in Microsoft Teams, as you can see in Figure 7-24; however, at the time of writing this book, the classification description did not show in Microsoft Teams.

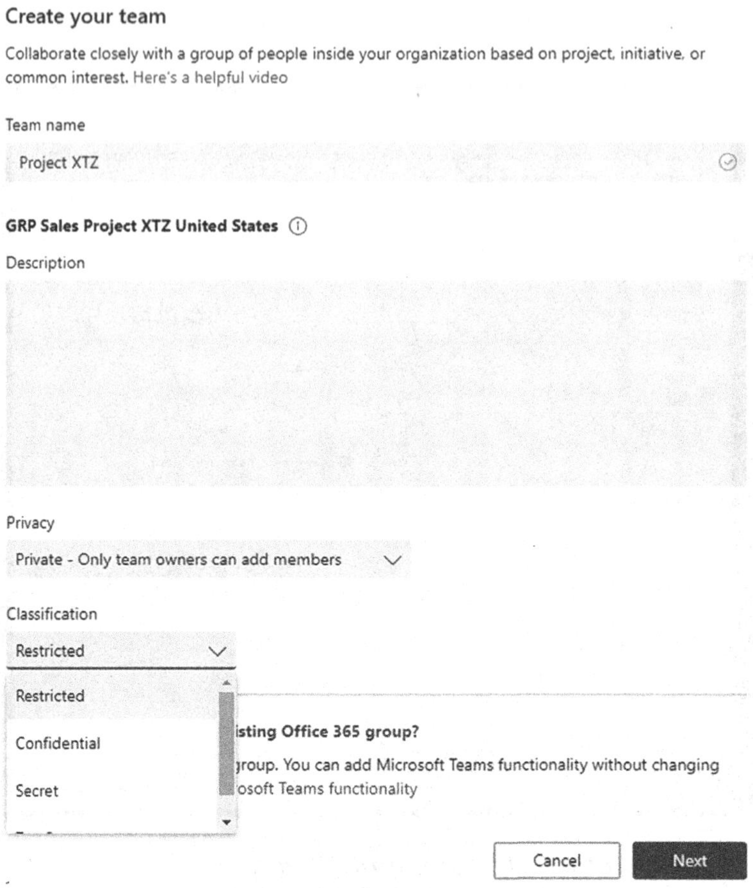

Create your team

Collaborate closely with a group of people inside your organization based on project, initiative, or common interest. Here's a helpful video

Team name

Project XTZ

GRP Sales Project XTZ United States ⓘ

Description

Privacy

Private - Only team owners can add members ⌄

Classification

Restricted ⌄

Restricted

Confidential

Secret

isting Office 365 group?

roup. You can add Microsoft Teams functionality without changing
osoft Teams functionality

Cancel   Next

Figure 7-24. *Classifications in Microsoft Teams*

After you have set up your groups classification list, you can use the Set-UnifiedGroup PowerShell cmdlet to apply classifications to existing groups. For example, if you wanted to add the Top Secret classification to the 2019 Reorganization group created earlier, you would run the following cmdlet:

```
Set-UnifiedGroup -Identity "2019reorg" -Classification "Top Secret"
```

You have now learned what classifications are and how to create a classification list with descriptions. Let's now look at the usage guidelines.

Usage Guidelines

With improved governance around your Office 365 Groups, an important step is to document what users can and cannot do. Office 365 allows you to set guidelines that are available to your users when an Office 365 Group is created or edited, as well as a separate set of guidelines for external users (guests). It is recommended that you host your internal guidelines on a site that all your employees have access to, such as the intranet, while hosting your guest guidelines on a public site that external users will be able to access.

To configure usage guidelines, you will have to modify some properties of the Azure AD Directory Setting you created earlier. First, get the Azure AD Directory Setting and save it into a variable called $Setting as seen here:

```
$Setting = Get-AzureADDirectorySetting | where-object {$_.displayname -eq
'Group.Unified'}
```

Then, set the UsageGuidelinesUrl property to the URL of your internal policies:

```
$Setting["UsageGuidelinesUrl"]="https://office365powershell.sharepoint.com/
SitePages/Office365GroupsPolicies.aspx"
```

Next up, set the guest policies by adding the URL to the GuestUsageGuidelinesUrl property as seen here:

```
$Setting["GuestUsageGuidelinesUrl"]="https://office365powershell.ca/
guestpolicy"
```

To apply the new properties to your Azure AD Directory Setting, you need to run the following cmdlet:

```
Set-AzureADDirectorySetting -Id $Setting.id -DirectorySetting $Setting
```

Note   It can take a few hours for the settings to be applied in the user interface across all the Office 365 services.

Once the usage guidelines are set up, a user creating a new group from Outlook Online will see a link to the internal usage guidelines, as you can see in Figure 7-25.

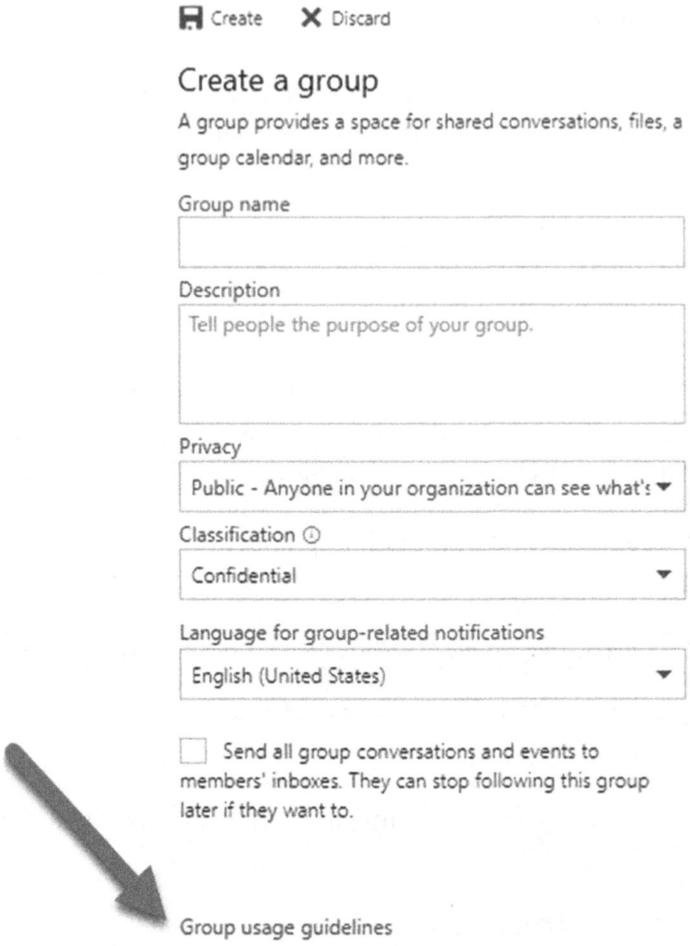

Figure 7-25. *Group usage guidelines when creating a new Office 365 Group*

When you invite an external user to an Office 365 Group, they will have a link to the guest usage guidelines at the bottom of their email, as you can see in Figure 7-26.

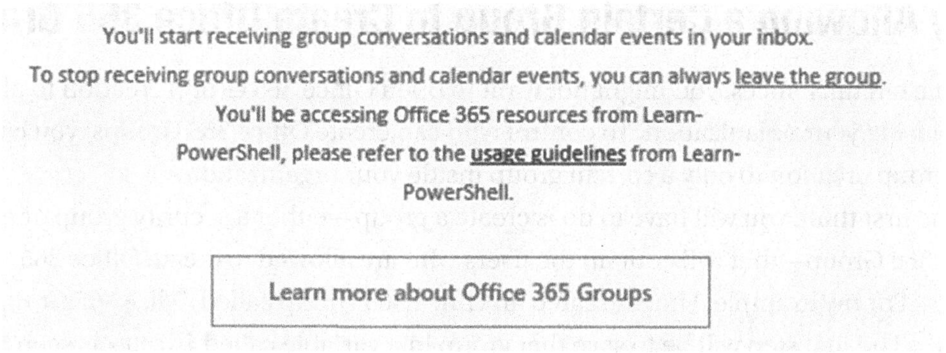

You'll start receiving group conversations and calendar events in your inbox.

To stop receiving group conversations and calendar events, you can always leave the group.

You'll be accessing Office 365 resources from Learn-
PowerShell, please refer to the usage guidelines from Learn-
PowerShell.

Learn more about Office 365 Groups

Figure 7-26. *Guest usage gidelines in the welcome email for Office 365 Groups guests*

When they click on the link, guests will first receive a message informing them that the guidelines are managed by your organization and not by Microsoft or Office 365, as you can see in Figure 7-27.

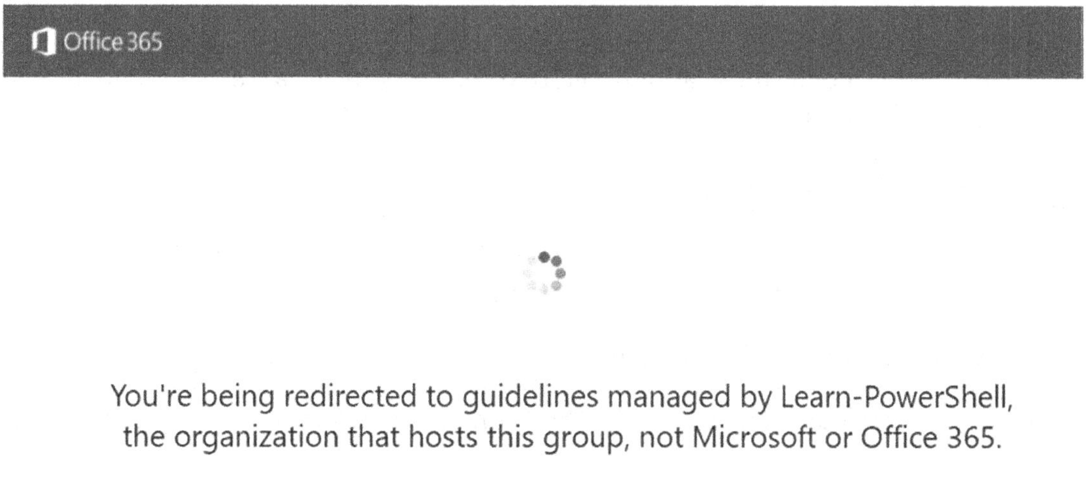

Office 365

You're being redirected to guidelines managed by Learn-PowerShell, the organization that hosts this group, not Microsoft or Office 365.

Figure 7-27. *Redirection notice for Office 365 guest guidelines*

You have now seen multiple ways to control how Office 365 users can create Office 365 Groups while following certain company policies, but what if you want to only allow a certain group of users to create groups?

Only Allowing a Certain Group to Create Office 365 Groups

In some circumstances, you might not want to open Office 365 Group creation to all the users inside your organization. To control who can create Office 365 Groups, you can limit group creation to only a certain group inside your organization.

The first thing you will have to do is create a group—either a security group or an Office 365 Group—that will contain the users who are allowed to create Office 365 Groups. For my example, I have created an Office 365 Group called *Office 365 Group Admins*. The first step will be to save that group in a variable called $Group as seen here:

```
$Group = Get-AzureADGroup -SearchString "Office 365 Group Admins"
```

Next up, I have to modify some properties of the Azure AD Directory Setting that was created earlier. I will first get the Azure AD Directory Setting and save it into a variable called $Setting as seen here:

```
$Setting = Get-AzureADDirectorySetting | where-object {$_.displayname -eq 'Group.Unified'}
```

I then need to modify the EnableGroupCreation property to False in order to disable Office 365 Group creation for all users:

```
$Setting["EnableGroupCreation"] = "False"
```

Afterward, I will add the ID of the group that will be allowed to create Office 365 Groups to the GroupCreationAllowedGroupId parameter:

```
$Setting["GroupCreationAllowedGroupId"] = $Group.ObjectId
```

Lastly, to apply the new properties to the Azure AD Directory Setting, I need to run the following cmdlet:

```
Set-AzureADDirectorySetting -Id $Setting.id -DirectorySetting $Setting
```

Note   It can take a few hours for the settings to be applied in the user interface across all the Office 365 services.

Once the setting is applied, users that are not in that group will not be able to see the "Create" button anymore in Outlook Online. Only the "Discover" button will be available, as seen in Figure 7-28.

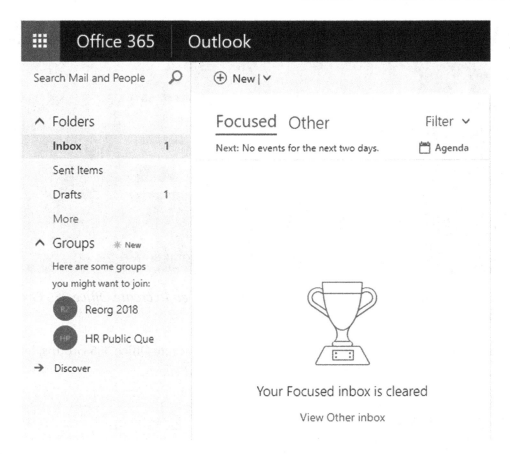

Figure 7-28. *Only the "Discover" button appears in Outlook Online*

Different Office 365 services will display different messages when Office 365 Group creation is disabled for that user. In Figure 7-29, you can see the message that users get when they try to create a new plan in Planner.

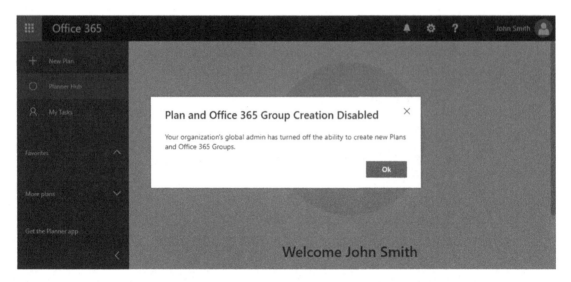

Figure 7-29. *User message when they are not allowed to create Office 365 Groups in Planner*

Now that you have learned how to control who can create Office 365 Groups, let's learn how manage policies for external users, also called *guests*.

Guest Policies

Guest policies allow you to customize whether external users can be added to your Office 365 Groups, and even allow you to block access for all existing users if required. There are three properties that you can set at the tenant level, which you can see in Table 7-4.

Table 7-4. *Tenant-wide Guest Policies*

Property	Description
AllowGuestsToBeGroupOwner	Indicates if guests can be added as owners of an Office 365 Group
AllowGuestsToAccessGroups	Indicates if guests are allowed to access Office 365 Groups. Setting this to `false` will also block guests that were already granted permission to access Office 365 Groups.
AllowToAddGuests	Indicates if you want to restrict the ability to add new guests to Office 365 Groups, but not restrict existing Office 365 guests to access groups they already have permission to.

If you want to completely restrict guest access tenant wide, you will have to modify the preceding properties of the Azure AD Directory Setting created earlier. You first get the Azure AD Directory Setting and save it into a variable called $Setting as seen here:

```
$Setting = Get-AzureADDirectorySetting | where-object {$_.displayname -eq
'Group.Unified'}
```

You then configure your settings to not allow guests to be group owners and to block everyone from adding external users or other guests to a group:

```
$Setting["AllowGuestsToBeGroupOwner"] = "False"
$Setting["AllowToAddGuests"] = "False"
```

To block existing as well as new guests in your Office 365 Groups, configure the following setting:

```
$Setting["AllowGuestsToAccessGroups"] = "False"
```

To apply the guest policies, you need to run the following cmdlet, which will update the Azure AD Directory Setting Object with the latest changes:

```
Set-AzureADDirectorySetting -Id $Setting.id -DirectorySetting $Setting
```

When anyone in your organization tries to invite a guest, they will get a message similar to that in Figure 7-30 and will not be able to add a guest—even if they are an Office 365 global administrator.

Save
Discard
OG
Office 365 Group ...
office365groupadmins@office3...
Private group
Before you can add guests as members of the group, you need to contact your administrator.
Enter the name of a person or a group
vlad@apress.com

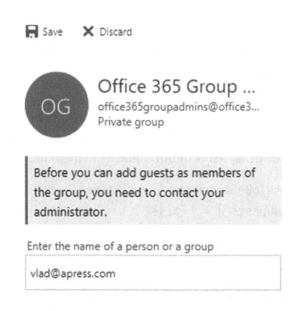

Figure 7-30. *Unable to add guests to an Office 365 Group*

What if you want to apply guest policies at the group level and not at the tenant level? For demo purposes, I have reverted the changes we just made that allowed guests tenant wide; we will block them for select groups instead. To only apply settings to certain groups, you need to create a setting based on the `Group.Unified.Guest` template. You can view all the available templates by running the `Get-AzureADDirectorySettingTemplate` cmdlet as seen in Figure 7-31.

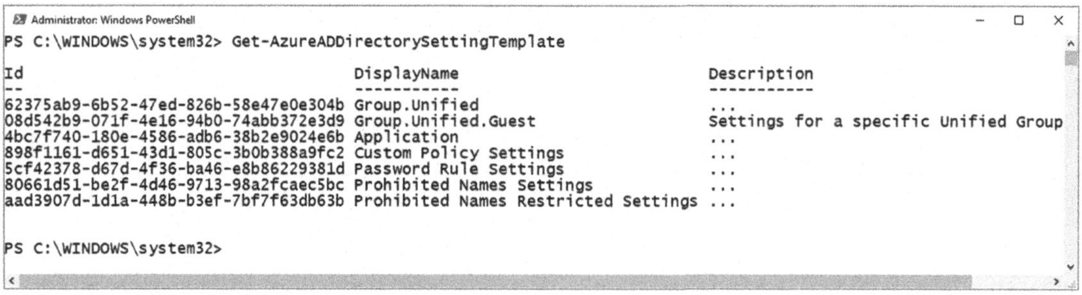

Administrator: Windows PowerShell
PS C:\WINDOWS\system32> Get-AzureADDirectorySettingTemplate
Id DisplayName Description
-- ----------- -----------
62375ab9-6b52-47ed-826b-58e47e0e304b Group.Unified ...
08d542b9-071f-4e16-94b0-74abb372e3d9 Group.Unified.Guest Settings for a specific Unified Group
4bc7f740-180e-4586-adb6-38b2e9024e6b Application ...
898f1161-d651-43d1-805c-3b0b388a9fc2 Custom Policy Settings ...
5cf42378-d67d-4f36-ba46-e8b86229381d Password Rule Settings ...
80661d51-be2f-4d46-9713-98a2fcaec5bc Prohibited Names Settings ...
aad3907d-1d1a-448b-b3ef-7bf7f63db63b Prohibited Names Restricted Settings ...
PS C:\WINDOWS\system32>

Figure 7-31. *Available Azure Active Directory Setting templates*

Now that you know the template you want to start from, you can run the following cmdlets to create a new directory setting:

```
$SettingTemplate = Get-AzureADDirectorySettingTemplate | where {$_.
DisplayName -eq 'Group.Unified.Guest'}
$NewSetting = $SettingTemplate.CreateDirectorySetting()
```

The Group.Unified.Guest directory setting only has one available property, which is AllowToAddGuests, as you can see in Figure 7-32.

```
Administrator: Windows PowerShell                                              —   □   ×
PS C:\WINDOWS\system32> $NewSetting.Values

Name             Value
----             -----
AllowToAddGuests True


PS C:\WINDOWS\system32>
```

Figure 7-32. *Available properties in the Group.Unified.Guest directory setting*

You then change the AllowToAddGuests property to False in order to block guest access in this setting:

```
$NewSetting["AllowToAddGuests"]=$False
```

To apply this setting to a group, save your Office 365 Group Admins group in a variable called $Group and then apply the Azure AD Object Setting to the Office 365 Group as seen here:

```
$Group = Get-AzureADGroup -SearchString "Office 365 Group Admins"
New-AzureADObjectSetting -TargetType Groups -TargetObjectId $Group.ObjectId
-DirectorySetting $NewSetting
```

Note   It can take a few hours for the settings to be applied in the user interface across all the Office 365 services.

To test that it worked, navigate to a group that does not have this group-level setting applied, and you should be able to add an external guest, as seen in Figure 7-33.

Figure 7-33. *Adding an external user to an Office 365 Group*

However, when you try to do the same thing in the Office 365 Group you have applied these new settings to, you will get an error similar to that in Figure 7-34.

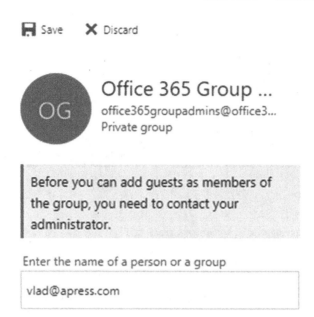

Figure 7-34. *Not allowed to add external users to this specific Office 365 Group*

You have now learned all the settings that allow you to control Office 365 Groups in your organization as far as who can create Office 365 Groups, what naming policy they should use, and so on. Next up, you will learn how to create reports on Office 365 Groups.

Office 365 Group Reporting

Once users start collaborating in Office 365 Groups that have your governance policies, you still want to keep an eye on what is happening inside your tenant. You can use the Get-UnifiedGroup cmdlet to view all the groups inside your organization, as well as their properties. When running the cmdlet, the basic properties returned are the Name, Alias, ServerName, and AccessType, which you can see in Figure 7-35.

```
Administrator: Windows PowerShell                                                    —    □    ×
PS C:\WINDOWS\system32> Get-UnifiedGroup

Name                      Alias                  ServerName         AccessType
----                      -----                  ----------         ----------
reorg2018_4826c469eb      reorg2018              yqbpr0101mb1442    Private
2019 Reorganization_6a... 2019reorg              yqbpr0101mb1442    Private
Secret Reorganization_... secretreorg            yqbpr0101mb1442    Private
HR Public Questions_ac... HRPublic               yqbpr0101mb1442    Public
Global O365 Administra... globaladmins           yqbpr0101mb1442    Private
GRPSalesOffice365Migra... GRPSalesOffice365...   yqxpr01mb0023      Public
GRPSalesStreamGroupUni... GRPSalesStreamGro...   yqbpr0101mb2130    Private
office365groupadmins_f... office365groupadmins   yqbpr0101mb2130    Private
GRPSalesProjectXTZUnit... GRPSalesProjectXT...   yqxpr01mb0293      Public


PS C:\WINDOWS\system32> _
```

Figure 7-35. *Running the Get-UnifiedGroup cmdlet*

You can also select any properties of the group; for example, the following cmdlet returns the display name, the date the Office 365 Group was created, the date it was last changed, and the classification of the group, as in Figure 7-36.

```
Administrator: Windows PowerShell                                                           —   □   ×
PS C:\WINDOWS\system32> Get-UnifiedGroup | Select-Object -Property DisplayName, WhenCreated, WhenChanged, Classification
| Format-Table

DisplayName                                              WhenCreated             WhenChanged            Classification
-----------                                              -----------             -----------            --------------
Reorg 2018                                               9/28/2017 10:25:53 AM   10/21/2017 12:42:50 PM Top Secret
2019 Reorganization                                      10/19/2017 11:34:58 AM  10/21/2017 11:13:45 AM Top Secret
Secret Reorganization                                    10/19/2017 1:09:08 PM   10/21/2017 12:42:51 PM Secret
HR Public Questions                                      10/19/2017 4:01:01 PM   10/21/2017 12:42:51 PM Confidential
Global O365 Administrators                               10/20/2017 6:09:24 PM   10/21/2017 12:42:53 PM Top Secret
GRP Sales Office 365 Migration Project United States     10/21/2017 12:41:30 AM  10/21/2017 12:42:53 PM Confidential
GRP Sales Stream Group United States                     10/21/2017 12:43:04 AM  10/21/2017 12:42:54 PM Secret
Office 365 Group Admins                                  10/21/2017 10:39:10 AM  10/21/2017 12:42:55 PM Restricted
GRP Sales Project XTZ United States                      10/21/2017 11:56:33 AM  10/21/2017 12:02:53 PM Restricted


PS C:\WINDOWS\system32>
```

Figure 7-36. *Viewing properties of our Office 365 Groups*

You can also use all the different cmdlets you have learned in this chapter to create scripts that are a bit more advanced. For example, the small script that follows will output all the groups in the Office 365 tenant, as well as the number of owners, members, and Subscribers in each group. You can view the results in Figure 7-37.

```
Administrator: Windows PowerShell                                                    —  □  ×
PS C:\WINDOWS\system32> Get-UnifiedGroup |
>>     select Id,Alias, AccessType, `
>>     @{Expression={([array](Get-UnifiedGroupLinks -Identity $_.Id -LinkType Members)).Count }; `
>>     Label='Members'},`
>>     @{Expression={([array](Get-UnifiedGroupLinks -Identity $_.Id -LinkType Owners)).Count }; `
>>     Label='Owners'},`
>>     @{Expression={([array](Get-UnifiedGroupLinks -Identity $_.Id -LinkType Subscribers)).Count }; `
>>     Label='Subscribers'} |
>>     Format-Table Alias,Members,Owners,Subscribers -AutoSize

Alias                                             Members Owners Subscribers
-----                                             ------- ------ -----------
reorg2018                                              3      1           0
2019reorg                                              1      1           0
secretreorg                                            1      1           0
HRPublic                                               2      1           0
globaladmins                                           1      1           0
GRPSalesOffice365MigrationProject990UnitedStates       2      1           2
GRPSalesStreamGroupUnitedStates                        1      2           0
office365groupadmins                                   2      1           2
GRPSalesProjectXTZUnitedStates                         1      1           1


PS C:\WINDOWS\system32>
```

Figure 7-37. *Script showing the number and type of members inside each Office 365 Group*

Tip Remember you can download the soft copy of these scripts in the GitHub repository of the book! You can find the link to the repository on the book's page on Apress.com.

```
Get-UnifiedGroup |
    select Id,Alias, AccessType, `
    @{Expression={([array](Get-UnifiedGroupLinks -Identity $_.Id -LinkType
    Members)).Count }; `
    Label='Members'}, `
    @{Expression={([array](Get-UnifiedGroupLinks -Identity $_.Id -LinkType
    Owners)).Count }; `
    Label='Owners'}, `
    @{Expression={([array](Get-UnifiedGroupLinks -Identity $_.Id -LinkType
    Subscribers)).Count }; `
    Label='Subscribers'} |
    Format-Table Alias,Members,Owners,Subscribers -AutoSize
```

As you can see, you can create some really awesome reports by using PowerShell for Office 365 Groups.

Conclusion

Office 365 Groups are one of the key collaboration tools in Office 365, and users love their integration with multiple Office 365 services. However, there are not that many management settings available for groups in the Office 365 Admin Center, and this is where PowerShell can save the day. In this chapter, we have reviewed everything you can do to manage Office 365 Groups with PowerShell, starting from basic operations such as creating, updating, and deleting an Office 365 Group all the way to tenant-wide governance settings that shape the way your organization will benefit from Office 365 Groups.

At this point in the book, you have learned how to manage all the services in Office 365, starting from your users and licenses in Azure Active Directory to other services such as SharePoint Online, Exchange Online, Skype for Business Online, the Security & Compliance Center, and Office 365 Groups, which spans many of the services previously named. In our next and final chapter, we will take what we learned in the first seven chapters of this book to the next level by automating scenarios across multiple Office 365 services.

CHAPTER 8

Automating Tasks with PowerShell

We are now in the final chapter of the book, and by now you should be able to manage every Office 365 service with PowerShell individually. In this chapter, you will take what you have learned to the next level by creating scripts that interact with multiple Office 365 services and solve real business problems.

Connecting to Multiple Office 365 Services

Connecting to multiple Office 365 services is done by combining everything you have learned in previous chapters. You will first have to create your credential object by running the Get-Credential cmdlet, as seen here:

```
$cred = Get-Credential
```

Next up, import all the modules you have worked with in this book—the AzureAD module to manage users and licenses, the SharePoint Online module for SharePoint Online, and finally the Skype Online Connector module to manage Skype for Business Online:

```
Import-Module AzureAD
Import-Module Microsoft.Online.SharePoint.PowerShell
Import-Module SkypeOnlineConnector
```

Afterwards, create the remote sessions required to connect to Skype for Business Online, Exchange Online, and the Office 365 Compliance Center:

```
$S4B = New-CsOnlineSession -Credential $cred
```

© Vlad Catrinescu 2018
V. Catrinescu, *Essential PowerShell for Office 365*, https://doi.org/10.1007/978-1-4842-3129-6_8

```
$Exchange = New-PSSession -ConfigurationName Microsoft.Exchange
-ConnectionUri "https://outlook.office365.com/powershell-liveid/"
-Credential $cred -Authentication "Basic" -AllowRedirection

$ComplianceCenter = New-PSSession -ConfigurationName Microsoft.Exchange
-ConnectionUri https://ps.compliance.protection.outlook.com/powershell-
liveid/ -Credential $cred -Authentication Basic -AllowRedirection
```

You then must import those sessions into your local PowerShell session with the following cmdlets:

```
Import-PSSession $S4B
Import-PSSession $Exchange
Import-PSSession $ComplianceCenter
```

And lastly, connect to Azure Active Directory as well as SharePoint Online with their module-specific cmdlets, as seen here:

```
Connect-AzureAD -Credential $cred
Connect-SPOService -Url https://office365powershell-admin.sharepoint.
com  -credential $cred
```

You are now connected to Azure Active Directory, SharePoint Online, Exchange Online, and Skype for Business Online as well as to the Office 365 Compliance Center, and you can use PowerShell cmdlets that work with all the services in a single window. Something that you have used throughout the book is the Get-Credential cmdlet to get the credentials of the user you want to connect to Office 365 with. But if you want to run a script at 2 a.m., you don't really want to be there to give the credentials. Let's take a look at what you can do to securely store your credentials and use them in your scripts.

Saving Credentials to Securely Use with PowerShell

There are multiple ways to securely store your credentials on the computer, but let's take a look at one of the ones I use most often, which is saving the credential object as an XML file on the computer. You will first run the Get-Credential cmdlet to get the credentials, and afterward you will use the Export-Clixml cmdlet to save the credential object into an XML file. The full cmdlet can be seen here:

```
Get-Credential | Export-Clixml C:\Scripts\pscred.xml
```

A pop-up similar to Figure 8-1 will appear, in which you will have to enter the username and password of the user you want to connect to Office 365 with.

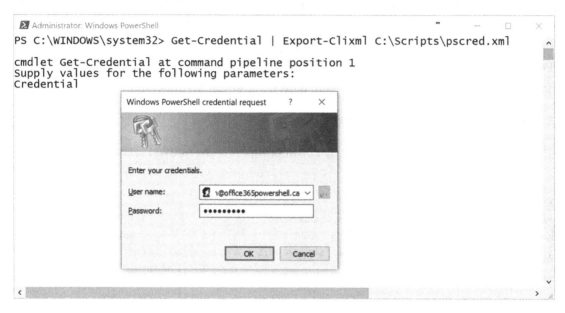

Figure 8-1. *Getting the credentials of a user before saving them to an XML file*

The XML file will include an export of the System.Management.Automation. PSCredential object, with the password encrypted, as seen in Figure 8-2.

```
 2   <Obj RefId="0">
 3     <TN RefId="0">
 4       <T>System.Management.Automation.PSCredential</T>
 5       <T>System.Object</T>
 6     </TN>
 7     <ToString>System.Management.Automation.PSCredential</ToString>
 8     <Props>
 9       <S N="UserName">vlad-admin@office365powershell.ca</S>
10       <SS N="Password">
         01000000d08c9ddf0115d1118c7a00c04fc297eb010000006f1089c9c0125b4b96f58ef47498f8
         020000000000020000000000010660000000100002000000092499ed497257345c9445532aca3fede
         dae47c8bd9f7c108d776b717287f486f000000000e8000000002000020000006a95668963e54b
         9d9d816dd180974fb7aed268dc691cc6207779c40a5bcb7fbc20000000603c22ddc51d01f710ed
         f3ff261a0e1e7dbb06d931f1b9471612577827ceaf7640000000d617d1accacb08241b68480e2c
         391b0072fa8f0dcc1e8bfcbdaed5490362c507cb48de29e0b0b8143909eb25fe8b6dc765d6a6e0
         a869727f020215a6c7389568</SS>
11     </Props>
12   </Obj>
13 </Objs>
```

Figure 8-2. *Credential object saved in an XML file*

The password is encrypted by using the native Windows Data Protection API (DAPI) functionality, and it can only be decrypted by the user who encrypted it and on this specific machine. It cannot be decrypted by another user on the same machine, or by the same user on a different machine. To use this XML file in your future scripts, you simply have to use the Import-Clixml cmdlet. In Figure 8-3, I am starting with a brand-new PowerShell window with an empty $cred variable, as seen on the first line. I then use the Import-Clixml cmdlet to import the file with my credential object in the $cred variable:

```
$cred = Import-CliXML C:\Scripts\pass.xml
```

Lastly, I test that this is working by connecting to Azure Active Directory.

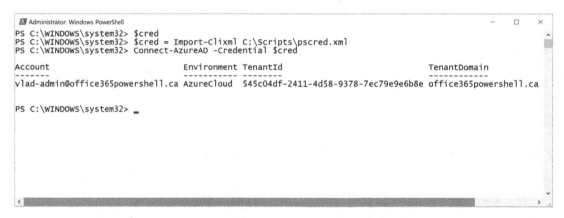

Figure 8-3. *Testing the XML file with my credential information*

Now that we have viewed some basic tricks, let's take a look at some automation scenarios!

Creating Users in Azure AD Using SharePoint as an Input

Let's start with our first scenario, which is automating the creation of users in Azure Active Directory and using a SharePoint list as an input. Throughout the examples in this chapter, you will see that when automating tasks in Office 365 where non-IT department personnel need to provide the input, I prefer to use SharePoint lists because of how easy they are to use for business users and how easy they are to secure from an IT perspective. I will first create a SharePoint list with the columns seen in Table 8-1 and with the name *New Users*.

Table 8-1. *Input List Columns*

Column Name	Type	Notes
Employee ID	Single Line of Text	Renamed the default `Title` column from the list. Internal name for this column will remain `Title`.
First Name	Single Line of Text	
Last Name	Single Line of Text	
JobTitle	Single Line of Text	
Department	Choice	
Manager	People Picker	
OfficePhone	Single Line of Text	
MobilePhone	Single Line of Text	
City	Single Line of Text	
State	Single Line of Text	
Country	Choice	
Processed	Yes/No	This column will tell PowerShell whether this account has already been created or not. By default it will be at No, and we will change it to Yes from our PowerShell script.

You can also view a sample of the input in Figure 8-4. The whole form is broken up into two parts and shown side by side to make it easier to consume.

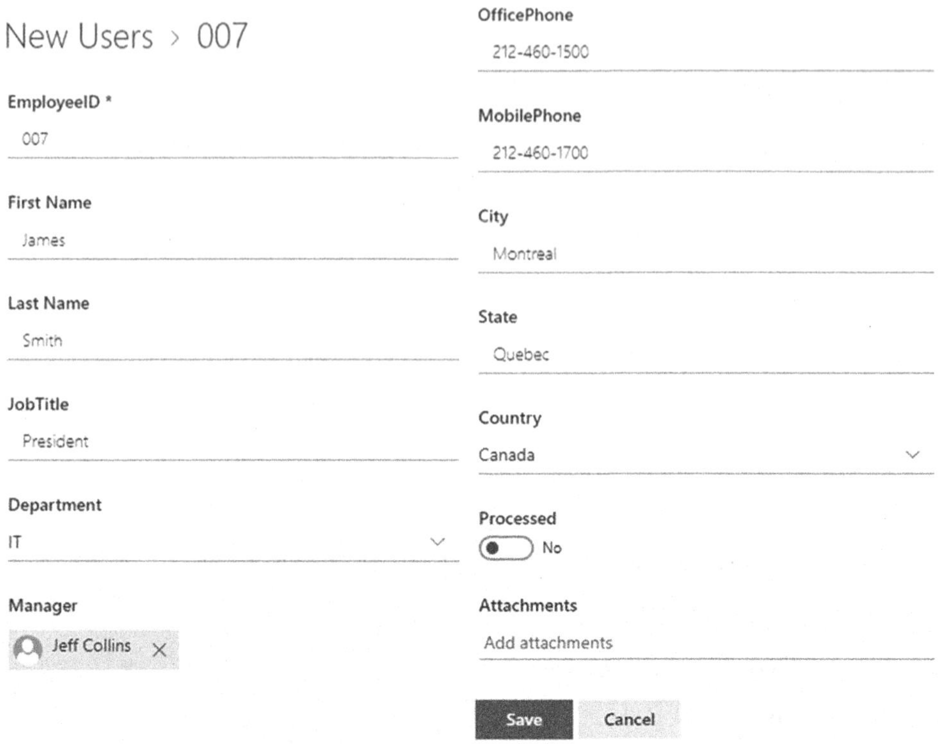

New Users > 007

EmployeeID *

007

First Name

James

Last Name

Smith

JobTitle

President

Department

IT

Manager

Jeff Collins ✕

OfficePhone

212-460-1500

MobilePhone

212-460-1700

City

Montreal

State

Quebec

Country

Canada

Processed

No

Attachments

Add attachments

Save   Cancel

Figure 8-4. *New User form*

Now that my list is ready, let's take a look at the PowerShell part. Since I have to read information from a SharePoint list, which is not possible using the PowerShell module provided by Microsoft, I will use the Office 365 Dev PnP PowerShell cmdlets, and since I will create users in Azure Active Directory I will also import the Azure Active Directory module:

```
Import-Module SharePointPnPPowerShellOnline
Import-Module AzureAD
```

I will then connect to both the site collection in which the list is located as well as Azure Active Directory:

```
$cred = Import-CliXML C:\Scripts\pass.xml
Connect-PnPOnline -Url https://office365powershell.sharepoint.
com  -credential $cred
Connect-AzureAD -Credential $cred
```

Next, I will use the Get-PnPListItem cmdlet to save the list in a variable:

```
$users = Get-PnPListItem -List 'New Users'
```

I will then start a `foreach` loop on each user, where the `Processed` column is at No, meaning all the users that haven't already been created with PowerShell. Next, I will save every column into a variable to make them easier to use later when I create the accounts.

In order to get the internal names (Key) of the fields, you can run the following cmdlet:

```
$users[0].FieldValues
```

This will show you all the fields of the first item in the list, as well as their values, allowing you to easily find out which is which, as seen in Figure 8-5:

```
PS C:\Scripts\Apress\Ch08> $users[0].FieldValues

Key                        Value
---                        -----
ContentTypeId              0x0100BC1E9BC63F665642A1B5C1ED0A41F7E6
Title                      007
_ModerationComments
File_x0020_Type
ComplianceAssetId
First_x0020_Name           James
Last_x0020_Name            Smith
JobTitle                   President
Department                 IT
Manager                    Microsoft.SharePoint.Client.FieldUserValue
OfficePhone                212-460-1500
MobilePhone                212-460-1700
City                       Montreal
State                      Quebec
Country                    Canada
Processed                  False
ID                         1
Modified                   11/22/2017 1:46:47 PM
Created                    10/30/2017 11:27:18 PM
Author                     Microsoft.SharePoint.Client.FieldUserValue
Editor                     Microsoft.SharePoint.Client.FieldUserValue
_HasCopyDestinations
_CopySource
owshiddenversion           14
```

Figure 8-5. *Finding out the internal names of our fields*

```
foreach ($user in $users|Where {$_.FieldValues.Processed -eq $false})
{
$EmployeeID = $user.FieldValues.Title
$FirstName = $user.FieldValues.First_x0020_Name
$LastName = $user.FieldValues.Last_x0020_Name
$JobTitle = $user.FieldValues.JobTitle
$Dept = $user.FieldValues.Department
$ManagerEmail = $user.FieldValues.Manager.Email
$OfficePhone = $user.FieldValues.OfficePhone
$Cell = $user.FieldValues.MobilePhone
$City = $user.FieldValues.City
```

```
$State = $user.FieldValues.State
$Country = $user.FieldValues.Country
$Email = "$FirstName.$LastName@office365powershell.ca"
```

When assigning a license to the user, I will need to provide the usage location of the user, which is the country, but as a two-letter country code. Since I do not want to ask my user, I will do a switch statement, as seen next, to set the $UsageLocation variable depending on the country of the user:

```
switch ($Country)
    {
        "Canada" {$UsageLocation = "CA"}
        "United States" {$UsageLocation = "US"}
        "Mexico" {$UsageLocation = "MX"}
        "France" {$UsageLocation = "FR"}
        default {throw "User Location not valid"}
    }
```

Now that I have all the information in variables, it's time to create the user. I will first create a new Password Profile object with the password that my company always uses for new users, which is Apress2017. I will also create my license objects with the E5 SKU ID:

```
$PasswordProfile = New-Object -TypeName Microsoft.Open.AzureAD.Model.
PasswordProfile

$PasswordProfile.Password = "Apress2017"

$PasswordProfile.ForceChangePasswordNextLogin = $true

$Sku = New-Object -TypeName Microsoft.Open.AzureAD.Model.AssignedLicense

$Sku.SkuId = "c7df2760-2c81-4ef7-b578-5b5392b571df"

$Licenses = New-Object -TypeName Microsoft.Open.AzureAD.Model.
AssignedLicenses

$Licenses.AddLicenses = $Sku
```

I will then use the New-AzureADUser cmdlet and give it all the parameters I saved earlier:

```
$NewUser = New-AzureADUser -GivenName $FirstName -Surname $LastName
-DisplayName "$FirstName $LastName" -UserPrincipalName $EMail -MailNickName
"$FirstName.$LastName" -AccountEnabled $true -PasswordProfile
$PasswordProfile -JobTitle $JobTitle -Department $Dept -UsageLocation
$UsageLocation -Country $Country -Mobile $Cell -TelephoneNumber
$OfficePhone -State $State -City $City
```

Next up, I will set the manager as well as the license for my new user:

```
$Manager = Get-AzureADUser -ObjectId $ManagerEmail
Set-AzureADUserManager -ObjectId $NewUser.ObjectId -RefObjectId $Manager.
ObjectId
Set-AzureADUserLicense -ObjectId $NewUser.ObjectId -AssignedLicenses
$Licenses
```

Once my user has been created, I want to notify the person who created the new account request that the user has been created. I will first save the information about the person who created the current item in two variables:

```
$RequesterDisplayName = $user.FieldValues.Author.LookupValue
$Requesteremail = $user.FieldValues.Author.email
```

I will then create the body of the email using HTML syntax, including variables that I previously created in the script, as well as in the subject of the email:

```
$body = "Hello $RequesterDisplayName , </br> The account for Employee
ID $EmployeeID has been created with the following details: </br>
<b>Username:</b> $Email </br> <b>Password:</b> Apress2017 </br> For any
questions, don't hesitate to open a Helpdesk Ticket."
```

```
$Subject = "Account Created for New Employee $EmployeeID"
```

I will then use the Send-MailMessage cmdlet to send the email to the person who requested the account:

```
Send-MailMessage -To $Requesteremail -from vlad-admin@office365powershell.
ca -Subject $Subject -Body $body -BodyAsHtml -smtpserver smtp.office365.com
-usessl -Credential $cred -Port 587
```

Lastly, I will change the value of the `Processed` column to `True` so that it marks that the account has been created and so it's not processed the next time the script runs. I will also close the `foreach` loop started earlier. The reason I create a variable on the `Set-PnPListItem` cmdlet is to avoid a bug in the Office Dev PnP cmdlets that would output an error of type *"The collection has not been initialized"*:

```
$updatedItem = Set-PnPListItem -List 'New Users' -Identity $user.id -Values
@{"Processed" = $true}
}
```

This is what the full script looks like. Note that I have moved the License and Password objects outside of the `foreach` loop so they do not get created again and again each time a user needs to be created!

```
Import-Module SharePointPnPPowerShellOnline
Import-Module AzureAD

$cred = Import-CliXML C:\Scripts\pass.xml
Connect-PnPOnline -Url https://office365powershell.sharepoint.com
-credential $cred
Connect-AzureAD -Credential $cred

$PasswordProfile = New-Object -TypeName Microsoft.Open.AzureAD.Model.
PasswordProfile

$PasswordProfile.Password = "Apress2017"

$PasswordProfile.ForceChangePasswordNextLogin = $true
$Sku = New-Object -TypeName Microsoft.Open.AzureAD.Model.AssignedLicense

$Sku.SkuId = "c7df2760-2c81-4ef7-b578-5b5392b571df"


$Licenses = New-Object -TypeName Microsoft.Open.AzureAD.Model.
AssignedLicenses

$Licenses.AddLicenses = $Sku

$users = Get-PnPListItem -List 'New Users'

foreach ($user in $users|Where {$_.FieldValues.Processed -eq $false})
{
```

```
$EmployeeID = $user.FieldValues.Title
$FirstName = $user.FieldValues.First_x0020_Name
$LastName = $user.FieldValues.Last_x0020_Name
$JobTitle = $user.FieldValues.JobTitle
$Dept = $user.FieldValues.Department
$ManagerEmail = $user.FieldValues.Manager.Email
$OfficePhone = $user.FieldValues.OfficePhone
$Cell = $user.FieldValues.MobilePhone
$City = $user.FieldValues.City
$State = $user.FieldValues.State
$Country = $user.FieldValues.Country
$Email = "$FirstName.$LastName@office365powershell.ca"
switch ($Country)
    {
        "Canada" {$UsageLocation = "CA"}
        "United States" {$UsageLocation = "US"}
        "Mexico" {$UsageLocation = "MX"}
        "France" {$UsageLocation = "FR"}
        default {throw "User Location not valid"}
    }

$NewUser = New-AzureADUser -GivenName $FirstName -Surname $LastName
-DisplayName "$FirstName $LastName" -UserPrincipalName $EMail -MailNickName
"$FirstName.$LastName" -AccountEnabled $true -PasswordProfile
$PasswordProfile -JobTitle $JobTitle -Department $Dept -UsageLocation
$UsageLocation -Country $Country -Mobile $Cell -TelephoneNumber
$OfficePhone -State $State -City $City

$Manager = Get-AzureADUser -ObjectId $ManagerEmail

Set-AzureADUserManager -ObjectId $NewUser.ObjectId -RefObjectId $Manager.
ObjectId

Set-AzureADUserLicense -ObjectId $NewUser.ObjectId -AssignedLicenses
$Licenses

$RequesterDisplayName = $user.FieldValues.Author.LookupValue

$Requesteremail = $user.FieldValues.Author.email
```

```
$body = "Hello $RequesterDisplayName , </br> The account for Employee
ID $EmployeeID has been created with the following details: </br>
<b>Username:</b> $Email </br> <b>Password:</b> Apress2017 </br> For any
questions, don't hesitate to open a Helpdesk Ticket."

$Subject = "Account Created for New Employee $EmployeeID"

Send-MailMessage -To $Requesteremail -from vlad-admin@office365powershell.
ca -Subject $Subject -Body $body -BodyAsHtml -smtpserver smtp.office365.com
-usessl -Credential $cred -Port 587

$updatedItem = Set-PnPListItem -List 'New Users' -Identity $user.id -Values
@{"Processed" = $true}
}
```

Now, let's test it out! I have logged in as Jeff and created the list entry seen in Figure 8-6.

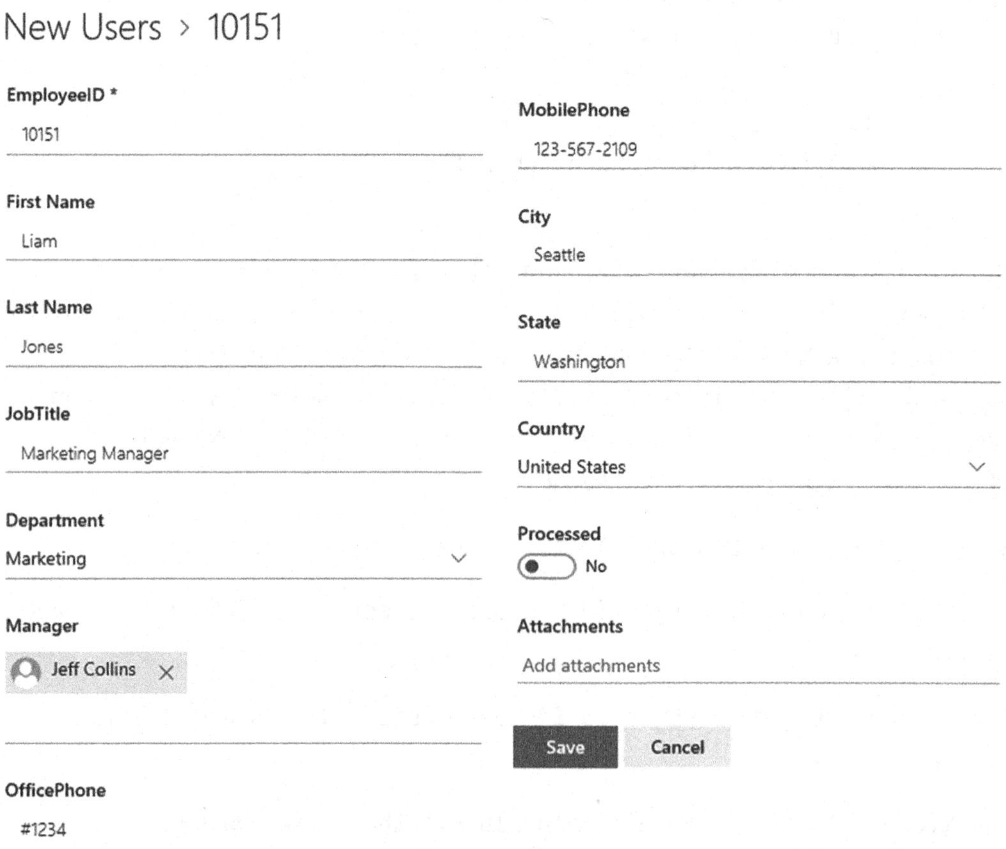

New Users > 10151

EmployeeID *
10151

First Name
Liam

Last Name
Jones

JobTitle
Marketing Manager

Department
Marketing

Manager
Jeff Collins ✕

OfficePhone
#1234

MobilePhone
123-567-2109

City
Seattle

State
Washington

Country
United States

Processed
No

Attachments
Add attachments

Save   Cancel

***Figure 8-6.** New User entry*

I will then run the full script that I have saved in a `.ps1` file. A few seconds later, I get the email to the Jeff Collins account with which I created the request stating that the account was created and everything seems good, as seen in Figure 8-7.

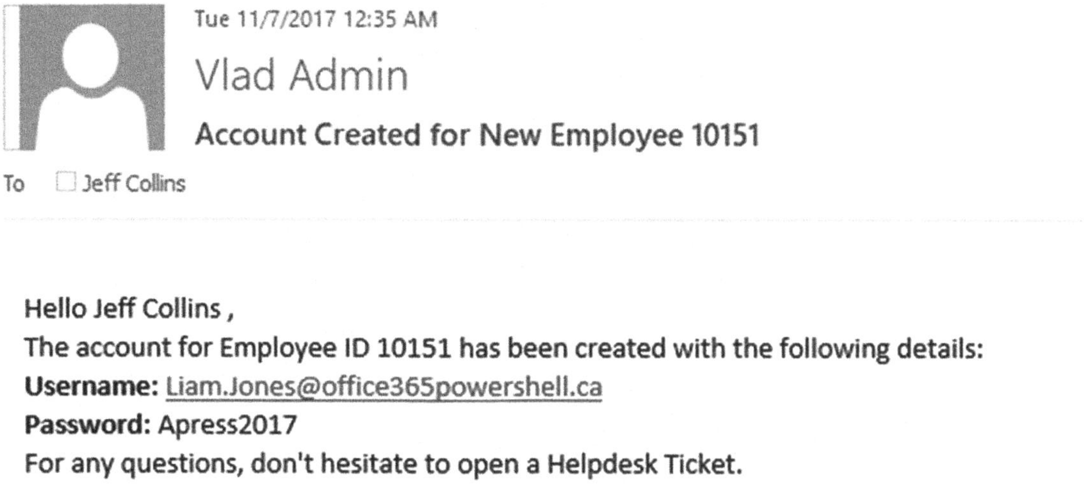

Tue 11/7/2017 12:35 AM

Vlad Admin

Account Created for New Employee 10151

To   ☐ Jeff Collins

Hello Jeff Collins ,
The account for Employee ID 10151 has been created with the following details:
Username: Liam.Jones@office365powershell.ca
Password: Apress2017
For any questions, don't hesitate to open a Helpdesk Ticket.

Figure 8-7. *Notification email from script*

As you can see in the Office 365 Admin Center, the user has been created, with the proper title and license, as seen in Figure 8-8.

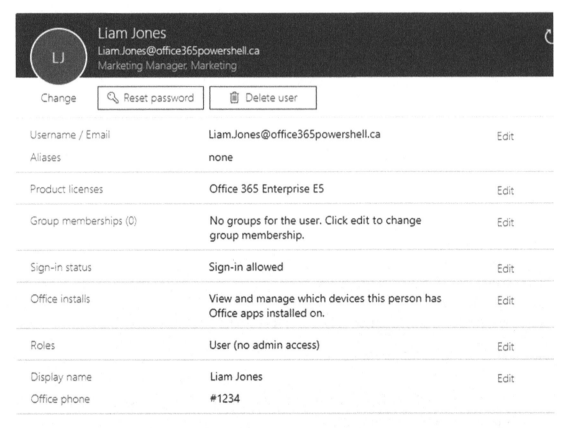

Figure 8-8. *Newly created user in the Office 365 Admin Center*

If we expand the properties, we can see that all the properties of the user have been updated, as seen in Figure 8-9.

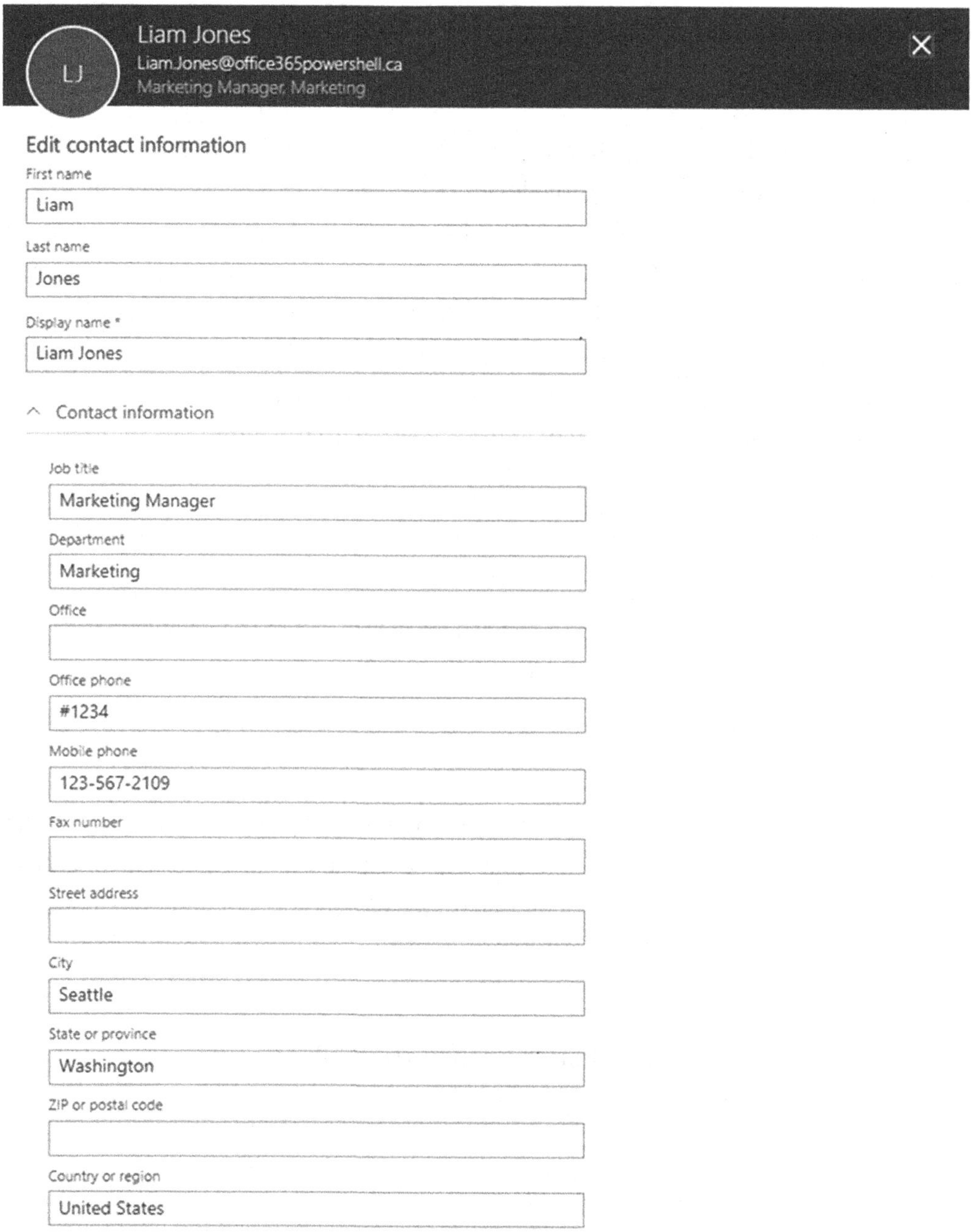

Liam Jones
LiamJones@office365powershell.ca
Marketing Manager, Marketing

Edit contact information

First name

Liam

Last name

Jones

Display name *

Liam Jones

∧   Contact information

Job title

Marketing Manager

Department

Marketing

Office

Office phone

#1234

Mobile phone

123-567-2109

Fax number

Street address

City

Seattle

State or province

Washington

ZIP or postal code

Country or region

United States

Figure 8-9.   *All properties of the newly created user*

We have successfully created a script that takes information from a SharePoint list and creates users in Azure Active Directory!

Add Users to an Distribution List Using SharePoint as an Input

This next scenario will work with SharePoint and Exchange Online. In many companies that I have worked for, there are multiple levels of support, and a lot of times the first level of support does not have any access to the Exchange Online Admin Center of a company. In this scenario, I will create a SharePoint list as an input form where help-desk personnel will be able to enter requests to add users to certain distribution lists. To make things more interesting, I will also create a PowerShell script that will keep a Choice column up to date with the existing distribution lists inside the organization. I will first create a SharePoint list with the columns seen in Table 8-2 and with the name *DL Request*.

Table 8-2. *DL Request List Columns*

Column Name	Type	Notes
Helpdesk Ticket ID	Single Line of Text	Renamed the default Title column from the list. Internal name for this column will remain Title.
User	People Picker	
Distribution List	Choice	
Processed	Yes/No	This column will tell PowerShell whether this item has already been processed or not. By default, it will be at No, and we will change it to Yes from our PowerShell script.

You can also view the form in SharePoint in Figure 8-10.

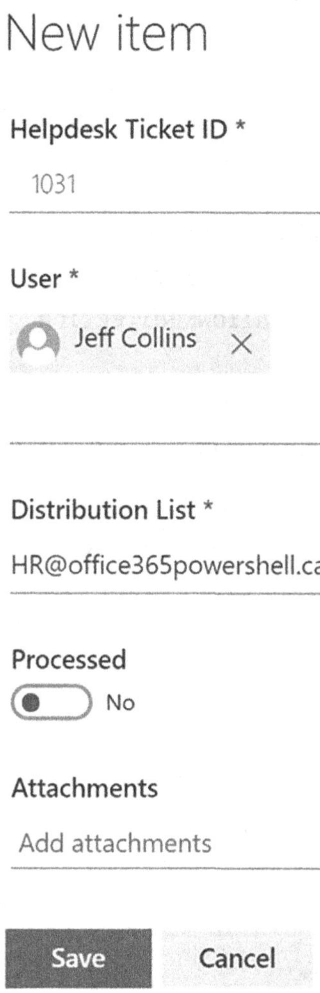

New item

Helpdesk Ticket ID *

1031

_____

User *

Jeff Collins   ✕

_____

Distribution List *

HR@office365powershell.ca   ⌄

_____

Processed

(●) No

Attachments

Add attachments

_____

[Save]   [Cancel]

Figure 8-10. *DL Request list form*

The first script I will create is the script that will make sure my `Distribution List` column is up to date. This script will connect to Exchange Online, get all the currently available distribution lists, and populate them in the column as available choices.

I will first get my credentials and import the SharePoint Online PnP module:

```
Import-Module SharePointPnPPowerShellOnline
$cred = Import-CliXML C:\Scripts\pass.xml
```

Next up, I will connect to the SharePoint Online site collection as well as Exchange Online:

```
Connect-PnPOnline -Url https://office365powershell.sharepoint.com
-Credentials $cred
```

```
$Exchange = New-PSSession -ConfigurationName Microsoft.Exchange
-ConnectionUri "https://outlook.office365.com/powershell-liveid/"
-Credential $cred -Authentication "Basic" -AllowRedirection
```

```
Import-PSSession $Exchange
```

I will now get the email address of all the distribution lists and save it in a variable as seen here:

```
$DistributionGroups = Get-DistributionGroup | Select  PrimarySmtpAddress
-ExpandProperty PrimarySmtpAddress
```

Next, I will find the ID of the Distribution List column by using the Get-PnPField cmdlet:

```
Get-PnPField -List "DL Request"
```

In Figure 8-11, you can see the ID of our column is b06268ba-4779-45f8-8b31-c2d33fd18f9f.

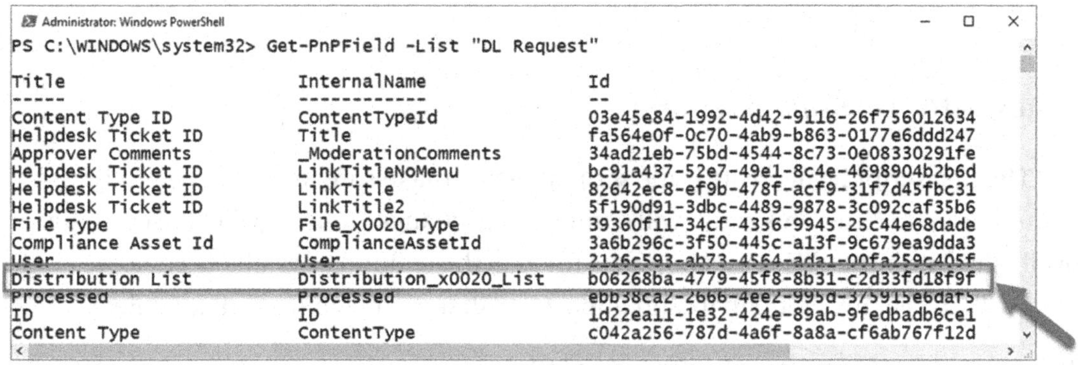

Figure 8-11. *Finding the ID of the DL Request distribution list*

Now what I know the ID, I can get the field and save it into a variable:

```
$DLField = Get-PnPField -List "DL Request" | Where {$_.ID -eq "b06268ba-
4779-45f8-8b31-c2d33fd18f9f"}
```

I can then update the `Choices` property of the column with the email addresses of the distribution groups that were previously saved in the `$DistributionGroups` variable:

```
$DLField.Choices = $DistributionGroups
$DLField.Update()
```

To apply the changes, I will run the following cmdlet:

```
Execute-PnPQuery
```

In Figure 8-12, you can see the final New Item form in the SharePoint Online list with the available choices in the Distribution List field.

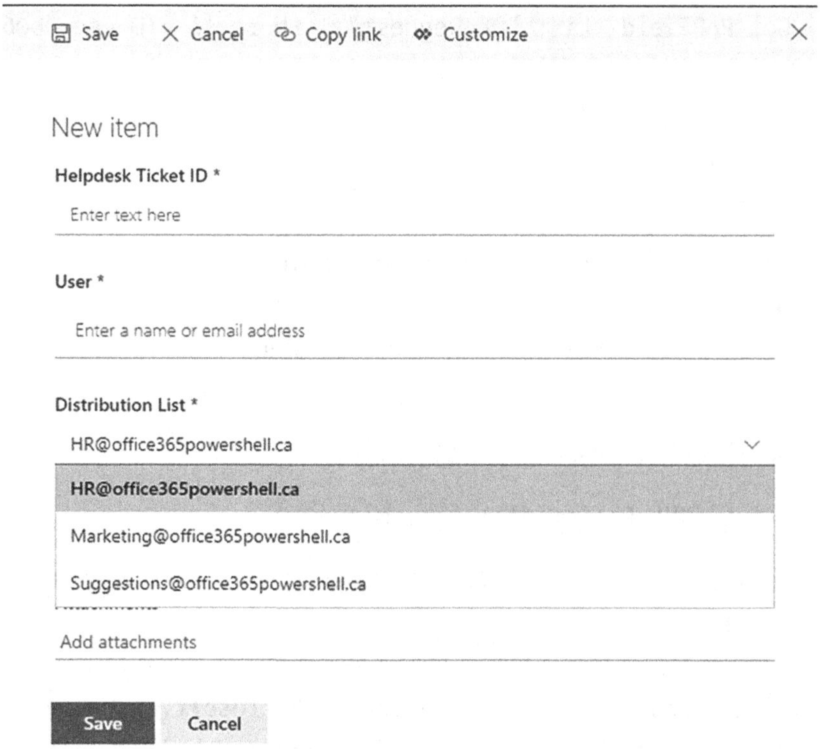

Figure 8-12. *Viewing the distribution lists as choices*

The script to update the Choice column with the list of distribution lists available in the Office 365 tenant is now complete; here is what it looks like when put together:

```
Import-Module SharePointPnPPowerShellOnline
$cred = Import-CliXML C:\Scripts\pass.xml
Connect-PnPOnline -Url https://office365powershell.sharepoint.com
-Credentials $cred

$Exchange = New-PSSession -ConfigurationName Microsoft.Exchange
-ConnectionUri "https://outlook.office365.com/powershell-liveid/"
-Credential $cred -Authentication "Basic" -AllowRedirection

Import-PSSession $Exchange

$DistributionGroups = Get-DistributionGroup | Select  PrimarySmtpAddress
-ExpandProperty PrimarySmtpAddress

$DLField = Get-PnPField -List "DL Request" | Where {$_.ID -eq "b06268ba-
4779-45f8-8b31-c2d33fd18f9f"}
$DLField.Choices = $DistributionGroups
$DLField.Update()
Execute-PnPQuery
```

Next up, I need to write the second script, which will take the information from the list and add the user to the chosen distribution list. I will first import the modules, get the credentials, and connect to both Exchange and SharePoint Online using the OfficeDev PnP cmdlets:

```
Import-Module SharePointPnPPowerShellOnline

$cred = Import-CliXML C:\Scripts\pass.xml

Connect-PnPOnline -Url https://office365powershell.sharepoint.com
-Credentials $cred

$Exchange = New-PSSession -ConfigurationName Microsoft.Exchange
-ConnectionUri "https://outlook.office365.com/powershell-liveid/"
-Credential $cred -Authentication "Basic" -AllowRedirection

Import-PSSession $Exchange
```

I will then get all the items in the *DL Request* list and start a `foreach` loop on all the items where the `Processed` field is set to `false`:

```
$NewDlMembers = Get-PnPListItem -List 'DL Request'
foreach ($Member in $NewDlMembers|Where {$_.FieldValues.Processed -eq
$false})
{
```

Next up, I will save the values of my three fields in variables so I can easily reuse them later:

```
$TicketNumber = $Member.FieldValues.Title
$DL = $Member.FieldValues.Distribution_x0020_List
$User = $Member.FieldValues.User.Email
```

I can now run the simple `Add-DistributionGroupMember` cmdlet to add the user to the required distribution list, as seen here:

```
Add-DistributionGroupMember -Identity $DL -Member $User
```

With the job done, I now need to notify the person who created the entry, telling them that the job is done and they can close the ticket. I will first get the information about the person who created the entry, and afterward I will send them an email letting them know the request has been completed. See here:

```
$RequesterDisplayName = $Member.FieldValues.Author.LookupValue
$Requesteremail = $Member.FieldValues.Author.email
```

```
$body = "Hello $RequesterDisplayName , </br> The account $User has been
added to the following Distribution List: $DL </br> You can now close
ticket number #$TicketNumber"
```

```
$Subject = "User added to requested DL for Helpdesk Ticket #$TicketNumber"
```

Lastly, I will use the `Send-MailMessage` cmdlet to send the email and the `Set-PnPListItem` cmdlet to change the value of the `Processed` field to `True`:

```
Send-MailMessage -To $Requesteremail -from vlad-admin@office365powershell.
ca -Subject $Subject -Body $body -BodyAsHtml -smtpserver smtp.office365.com
-usessl -Credential $cred -Port 587
```

```
Set-PnPListItem -List 'DL Request' -Identity $Member.id -Values @
{"Processed" = $true}
}
```

After running the script, the user in the SharePoint list will get added to the required distribution list and the person who created the request will get an email similar to that in Figure 8-13.

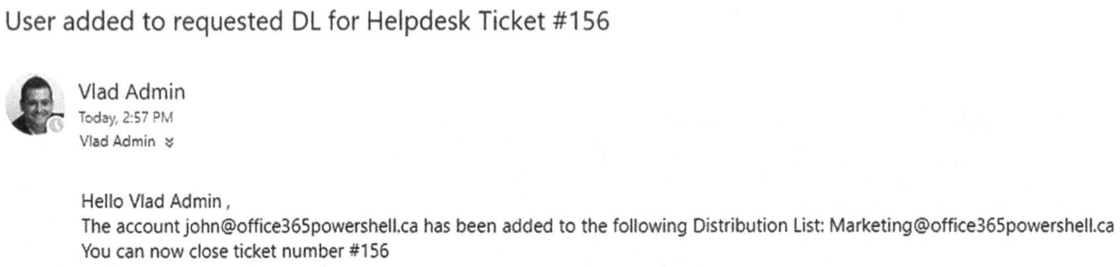

User added to requested DL for Helpdesk Ticket #156

Vlad Admin
Today, 2:57 PM
Vlad Admin ⌄

Hello Vlad Admin ,
The account john@office365powershell.ca has been added to the following Distribution List: Marketing@office365powershell.ca
You can now close ticket number #156

Figure 8-13. *Email notification after the script is completed*

Here is what the script looks like when put together:

```
Import-Module SharePointPnPPowerShellOnline

$cred = Import-CliXML C:\Scripts\pass.xml

Connect-PnPOnline -Url https://office365powershell.sharepoint.com
-Credentials $cred

$Exchange = New-PSSession -ConfigurationName Microsoft.Exchange
-ConnectionUri "https://outlook.office365.com/powershell-liveid/"
-Credential $cred -Authentication "Basic" -AllowRedirection

Import-PSSession $Exchange

$NewDlMembers = Get-PnPListItem -List 'DL Request'

foreach ($Member in $NewDlMembers|Where {$_.FieldValues.Processed -eq $false})
{
$TicketNumber = $Member.FieldValues.Title
$DL = $Member.FieldValues.Distribution_x0020_List
$User = $Member.FieldValues.User.Email
Add-DistributionGroupMember -Identity $DL -Member $User
```

```
$RequesterDisplayName = $Member.FieldValues.Author.LookupValue
$Requesteremail = $Member.FieldValues.Author.email

$body = "Hello $RequesterDisplayName, </br> The account $User has been
added to the following Distribution List: $DL </br> You can now close
ticket number #$TicketNumber"
$Subject = "User added to requested DL for Helpdesk Ticket #$TicketNumber"

Send-MailMessage -To $Requesteremail -from vlad-admin@office365powershell.
ca -Subject $Subject -Body $body -BodyAsHtml -smtpserver smtp.office365.com
-usessl -Credential $cred -Port 587


$updatedItem = Set-PnPListItem -List 'DL Request' -Identity $Member.id
-Values @{"Processed" = $true}
}
```

With this small automation scenario now done as well, let's take a look at a third one that provisions Office 365 Groups.

Office 365 Groups Provisioning

In the previous chapters, you learned how to work with Office 365 Groups using PowerShell, and you also learned how to use governance policies to block end-users from directly creating Office 365 Groups. In this automation scenario, you are going to create a SharePoint list in which users will enter requests for Office 365 Groups, as well as properties like classification, language, the members they would like to have inside to start with, and a few other settings. You will start by creating a SharePoint list where users will request Office 365 Groups. You can view the fields of the form in Table 8-3.

Table 8-3. *Office 365 Group Request List Columns*

Column Name	Type	Notes
Group Name	Single Line of Text	Renamed the default Title column from the list. Internal name for this column will remain Title.
Business Justification	Multiple lines of text	
Classification	Choice	This list of Classification matches the classifications created in the Office 365 Groups chapter.
Language	Choice	
Access Type	Choice	The available choices are Public or Private, which are out of the box, as well as Secret, which will be a private group with hidden membership and hidden from the Global Address List.
Members	Person or Group	List of users who will be added as members of the Office 365 Group
Owners	Person or Group	List of users who will be added as owners of the Office 365 Group
Processed	Yes/No	This column will tell PowerShell whether this item has already been processed or not. By default, it will be at No, and we will change it to Yes from our PowerShell script.

You can also view the SharePoint list form in Figure 8-14.

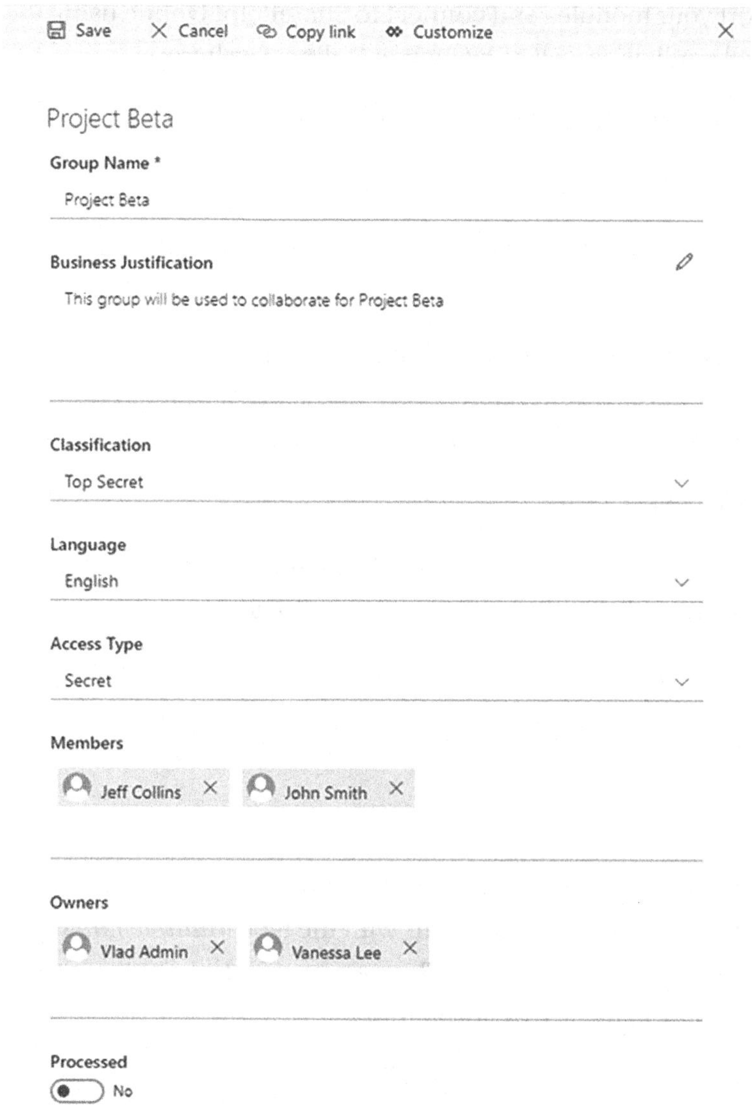

🖫 Save   ✕ Cancel   ⤬ Copy link   ⚙ Customize   ✕

Project Beta

Group Name *

Project Beta

Business Justification   ✎

This group will be used to collaborate for Project Beta

Classification

Top Secret   ⌄

Language

English   ⌄

Access Type

Secret   ⌄

Members

◯ Jeff Collins ✕   ◯ John Smith ✕

Owners

◯ Vlad Admin ✕   ◯ Vanessa Lee ✕

Processed

(●) No

Figure 8-14. *The Office 365 Group request form*

Tip   You could add an approval workflow using Microsoft Flow on the group creation and build your script to only create groups once they are approved.

First, import your modules and connect to SharePoint Online using the SharePoint PnP PowerShell cmdlets as well as Exchange Online. See here:

```
Import-Module SharePointPnPPowerShellOnline

$cred = Import-CliXML C:\Scripts\pass.xml

Connect-PnPOnline -Url https://office365powershell.sharepoint.com
-Credentials $cred

$Exchange = New-PSSession -ConfigurationName Microsoft.Exchange
-ConnectionUri "https://outlook.office365.com/powershell-liveid/"
-Credential $cred -Authentication "Basic" -AllowRedirection

Import-PSSession $Exchange
```

Then, get all the items in the Office 365 Group request list and start a foreach loop on all the items where the Processed column is at false:

```
$GroupRequests = Get-PnPListItem -List 'Office 365 Group Request'

foreach ($Group in $GroupRequests|Where {$_.FieldValues.Processed -eq
$false})
{
```

Next, save all the information from the columns into variables to make it easier to use later. Since SharePoint stores columns with the type *Multiple Lines of Text* in HTML format, use a -replace function on the *Business Justification* field value in order to return pure text without any of the HTML formatting:

```
$GroupTitle = $Group.FieldValues.Title
$Description = $Group.FieldValues.Business_x0020_Justification -replace
"<.*?>"
$Classification = $Group.FieldValues.Classification
$Language = $Group.FieldValues.Language
$AccessType = $Group.FieldValues.Access_x0020_Type
$Members = $Group.FieldValues.Members.Email
$Owners = $Group.FieldValues.Owners.Email
```

Next, create the GroupAlias variable by using the group title preceded by O365Group- and without any spaces:

```
$GroupAlias = "O365Group-$GroupTitle"  -replace '\s',''
```

The last variable you need to build is the language of the group. While in the SharePoint list the language was in a user-friendly name, you need to change it to a supported culture-code value from the Microsoft .NET Framework:

```
switch ($Language)
    {
        "English" {$LanguageCode = "en-US"}
        "French" {$LanguageCode = "fr-FR"}
        "Spanish" {$LanguageCode = "es-ES"}
        default {throw "Language not valid"}
    }
```

Now that you have everything you need saved in variables, start creating the Office 365 Groups. When creating the group, the big differentiator will be if they chose one of the out-of-the-box access types (Public or Private) or if they chose Secret, as that level does not actually exist, so you would need to manually configure some parameters such as the -HiddenGroupMembershipEnabled switch. Do an If statement on the AccessType variable first, and if it's Secret, create the group, specifying a Private access type using the -HiddenGroupMembershipEnabled switch and setting the -HiddenFromAddressListsEnabled property as well. Also, specify all the group properties, such as classification, languages, description, and display name.

```
If ($AccessType -eq "Secret"){

New-UnifiedGroup -DisplayName $GroupTitle -Alias $GroupAlias
-EmailAddresses "$GroupAlias@office365powershell.ca" -AccessType Private
-HiddenGroupMembershipEnabled -Classification $Classification -Language
$LanguageCode  -Notes $Description

Set-UnifiedGroup -Identity $GroupAlias -HiddenFromAddressListsEnabled $true
}
```

If it's not a secret Office 365 Group that you need to create, it means you need to create either a public or private one, so you will do an Else statement in which you will create an Office 365 Group using all the parameters you have saved from the user input and setting the -AccessType parameter to the $AccessType variable:

```
Else{
New-UnifiedGroup -DisplayName $GroupTitle -Alias $GroupAlias
-EmailAddresses "$GroupAlias@office365powershell.ca" -AccessType
$AccessType -Classification $Classification -Language $LanguageCode -Notes
$Description
}
```

What you need to do next is add the members and owners. Since in the SharePoint list those items are set at optional, you first need to make sure that some members have been entered, and, if yes, add those members to the group:

```
If ($Members)
{
Add-UnifiedGroupLinks -Identity $GroupAlias -LinkType "Members" -Links
$Members
}
```

Do the same thing for owners, and also make sure to first add them as members and them as owners in order to avoid any potential errors:

```
If ($Owners)
{
Add-UnifiedGroupLinks -Identity $GroupAlias -LinkType "Members" -Links
$Owners
Add-UnifiedGroupLinks -Identity $GroupAlias -LinkType "Owners" -Links
$Owners
}
```

Lastly, change the Processed column to Yes in order to mark this item as processed and then close the foreach loop you started at the beginning of the script. No email notification will be sent in this example as all the members that have been added to the group have already been notified. If needed in your specific scenario, you can add an email notification:

```
$updatedItem = Set-PnPListItem -List 'Office 365 Group Request' -Identity
$Group.id -Values @{"Processed" = $true}
}
```

To test it out, I have created a few entries in the list as seen in Figure 8-15. Some columns are not shown in order to make the text readable.

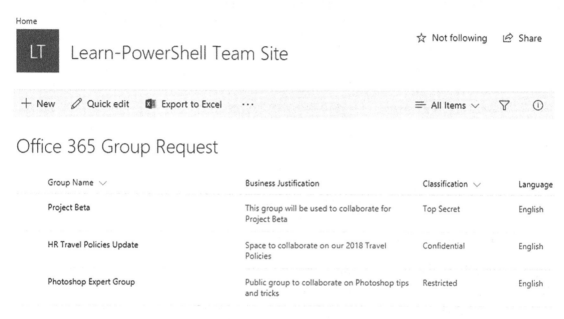

Home

LT   Learn-PowerShell Team Site   ☆ Not following   ☞ Share

➕ New   ✏ Quick edit   📊 Export to Excel   ⋯   ≡ All Items ∨   ▽   ⓘ

Office 365 Group Request

Group Name ∨	Business Justification	Classification ∨	Language
Project Beta	This group will be used to collaborate for Project Beta	Top Secret	English
HR Travel Policies Update	Space to collaborate on our 2018 Travel Policies	Confidential	English
Photoshop Expert Group	Public group to collaborate on Photoshop tips and tricks	Restricted	English

Figure 8-15. *Input for the Office 365 Group creation*

After the script has been run, the Office 365 Groups have been created, as seen in Figure 8-16, and members and owners have been added, even if you cannot see it in the figure.

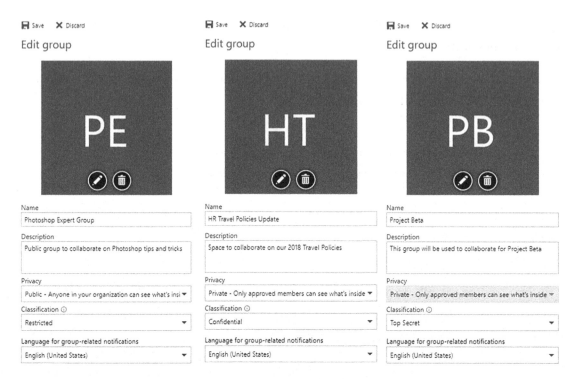

Figure 8-16. *Office 365 Groups created by script*

This is what the final script looks like when put together:

```
Import-Module SharePointPnPPowerShellOnline
$cred = Import-CliXML C:\Scripts\pass.xml
Connect-PnPOnline -Url https://office365powershell.sharepoint.com
-Credentials $cred
$Exchange = New-PSSession -ConfigurationName Microsoft.Exchange
-ConnectionUri "https://outlook.office365.com/powershell-liveid/"
-Credential $cred -Authentication "Basic" -AllowRedirection

Import-PSSession $Exchange

$GroupRequests = Get-PnPListItem -List 'Office 365 Group Request'
foreach ($Group in $GroupRequests|Where {$_.FieldValues.Processed -eq
$false})
{
$GroupTitle = $Group.FieldValues.Title
$Description = $Group.FieldValues.Business_x0020_Justification -replace
"<.*?>"
```

```
$Classification = $Group.FieldValues.Classification
$Language = $Group.FieldValues.Language
$AccessType = $Group.FieldValues.Access_x0020_Type
$Members = $Group.FieldValues.Members.Email
$Owners = $Group.FieldValues.Owners.Email

$GroupAlias = "O365Group-$GroupTitle"  -replace '\s',''
switch ($Language)
    {
        "English" {$LanguageCode = "en-US"}
        "French" {$LanguageCode = "fr-FR"}
        "Spanish" {$LanguageCode = "es-ES"}
        default {throw "Language not valid"}
    }

If ($AccessType -eq "Secret"){
New-UnifiedGroup -DisplayName $GroupTitle -Alias $GroupAlias
-EmailAddresses "$GroupAlias@office365powershell.ca" -AccessType Private
-HiddenGroupMembershipEnabled -Classification $Classification -Language
$LanguageCode  -Notes $Description

Set-UnifiedGroup -Identity $GroupAlias -HiddenFromAddressListsEnabled $true
    } Else
    {
New-UnifiedGroup -DisplayName $GroupTitle -Alias $GroupAlias
-EmailAddresses "$GroupAlias@office365powershell.ca" -AccessType
$AccessType -Classification $Classification -Language $LanguageCode -Notes
$Description
    }

If ($Members)
    {
Add-UnifiedGroupLinks -Identity $GroupAlias -LinkType "Members" -Links
$Members
    }
```

```
If ($Owners)
    {
Add-UnifiedGroupLinks -Identity $GroupAlias -LinkType "Members" -Links
$Owners
Add-UnifiedGroupLinks -Identity $GroupAlias -LinkType "Owners" -Links
$Owners
    }

$updatedItem = Set-PnPListItem -List 'Office 365 Group Request' -Identity
$Group.id -Values @{"Processed" = $true}
}
```

We have now looked at three real-life automation scenarios with PowerShell for Office 365. In the next section, we will look at a few tips and tricks on how we could optimize the scripts we did for better performance and user experience, tips that you could use in all of your PowerShell scripts!

Other Tips and Optimizations

Before finishing the book, let's look at a few final configurations or optimizations you can do with PowerShell for Office 365 that would make the automation scenarios in this chapter better.

Hiding Columns in SharePoint Online

One of the columns we used in all three of the previous scripts was the Processed column. This column worked really well; however, a problem happens when a user does not understand it and switches it to Yes when creating a new item. By using the Office 365 Dev PnP PowerShell cmdlets, we can hide certain columns in certain fields. Let's take the DL Request list, for example, for which you can see the New Item form in Figure 8-17.

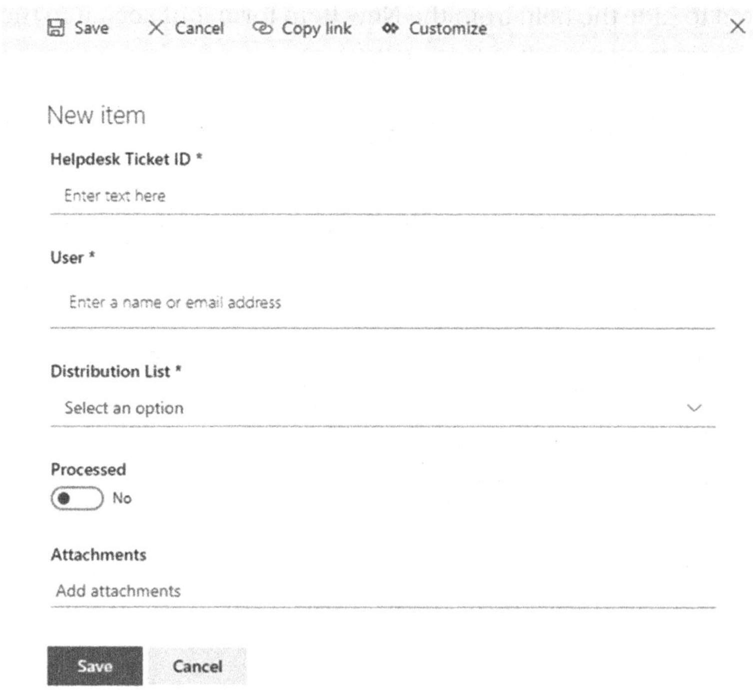

Figure 8-17. *The DL Request New Item form*

If we wanted to hide the Processed column in the New Item form, we would first import the Office 365 PnP PowerShell cmdlets and connect to our site collection:

```
Import-Module SharePointPnPPowerShellOnline
$cred = Import-CliXML C:\Scripts\pass.xml
Connect-PnPOnline -Url https://office365powershell.sharepoint.com
-Credentials $cred
```

We will then get the column and save it into a variable:

```
$ProcessedField = Get-PnPField -List "DL Request" | Where {$_.Title -eq
"Processed"}
```

Each field has three properties that will help us define where this field is shown, or not:

- SetShowInDisplayForm

- SetShowInEditForm

- SetShowInNewForm

If we wanted to hide the field from the New Item form, but keep it in the Display and Edit forms, we would run the following cmdlets:

```
$ProcessedField.SetShowInNewForm($false)
$ProcessedField.Update()
```

Lastly, we will run the following cmdlet to apply these changes to our site collection:

```
Execute-PnPQuery
```

The end result, seen in Figure 8-18, is that the Processed field is not seen when creating an item in that list:

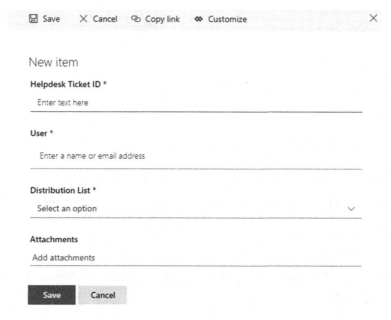

Figure 8-18. *Field hidden when creating an item*

However, the field is still visible when viewing the item or when editing it, as seen in Figure 8-19.

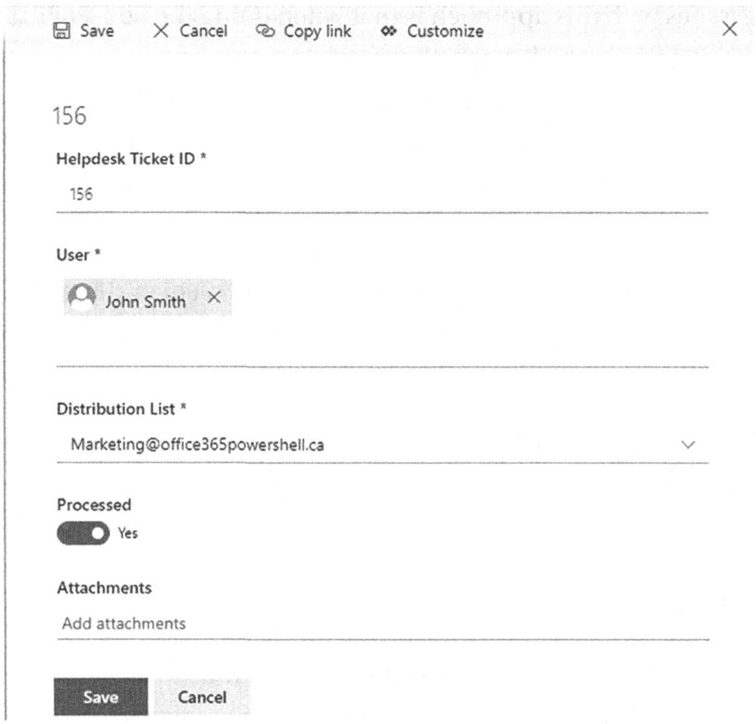

Figure 8-19. *Field visible in edit form*

Knowing how to change when a field is visible can allow you to customize the user experience and will only show the relevant columns when users create, edit, or view items!

Using CAML to Filter Items

In previous examples, we used code similar to the following to get items that had the Processed field set to No:

```
$NewDlMembers = Get-PnPListItem -List 'DL Request'
foreach ($Member in $NewDlMembers|Where {$_.FieldValues.Processed -eq
$false})
{ #code }
```

One of the issues with this approach is that when doing the `Get-PnPListItem` we will retrieve all the items in the list, which can take a long time and make our script less performant. With the Office 365 Dev PnP cmdlets, you can use Collaborative Application Markup Language (CAML) to filter the information that you get from SharePoint. For example, I could use the following cmdlet to only get the items where the field `Processed` is equal to `No`:

```
Get-PnPListItem -List "New Users" -Query "<View><Query><Where><Eq>
<FieldRef Name='Processed'/><Value Type='Boolean'>0</Value></Eq></Where>
</Query></View>"
```

Instead of returning all the items in the list in my PowerShell session, I would only get the pre-filtered ones, which would make my script faster!

Conclusion

In this chapter, we looked at PowerShell scripts that allow us to automate real-life scenarios that span multiple Office 365 services and can resolve real business needs.

As this is the final paragraph of the book, I would like to thank you for reading until the end, and I hope it was informative and will help you manage and automate your Office 365 tenant!

Index

A
Azure Active Directory, 6–8, 11

B
Blocked words
    Azure AD settings object, 173
    in Microsoft Stream, 177
    in Microsoft Teams, 176
    in Outlook Online, 175
    in Planner, 176
    update, 174

C
CAML, *see* Collaborative Application
    Markup Language (CAML)
Client-side object model (CSOM), 73
Collaborative Application Markup
    Language (CAML), 232
Connect-SPOService cmdlet, 52–53

D
Data-loss prevention (DLP) cmdlets, 141

E
Exchange online
    calendar and out of office, 100–104
    ConnectionUri, 86

contacts, 93, 95–96
distribution groups, 112–114
mailboxes, 96, 98–100
mailbox reporting, 116, 118
managing
    distribution group membership, 115
    organization settings, 109–111
MFA, 85
PowerShell, 86
SendAs and mailbox permissions, 104–108
users, 91–92

F
ForceChangePasswordNextLogin
    property, 19

G, H, I, J
Get-AzureADUserDirectReport cmdlet, 16
Get-AzureADUserManager cmdlet, 15
Get-CsOnlineUser cmdlet, 124
Get-RoleGroupMember cmdlet, 144
Guest policies
    add external guest, 191, 193
    block guests, 189
    Get-AzureADDirectorySetting
        Template cmdlet, 190–191
    Group.Unified.Guest directory
        setting, 191
    tenant level, 188–189

© Vlad Catrinescu 2018
V. Catrinescu, *Essential PowerShell for Office 365*, https://doi.org/10.1007/978-1-4842-3129-6

U, V, W, X, Y, Z

Get the eBook for only $5!

Why limit yourself?

With most of our titles available in both PDF and ePUB format, you can access your content wherever and however you wish—on your PC, phone, tablet, or reader.

Since you've purchased this print book, we are happy to offer you the eBook for just $5.

To learn more, go to http://www.apress.com/companion or contact support@apress.com.

Apress®

Printed in the United States
By Bookmasters